SUMMER

MARY HAPPY

19 & THE WORLD IS

YOUR OYSTER

SHUCK IT!

LOVE,

JAMES N' GABRIELLE.

SUBTITLES
on the foreignness of film

Ran
Akira Kurosawa

Prepare f

or battle!

If you want

- What are
- Lea

OKIEN
NIECZY

Clo

edited by ATOM EGOYAN and IAN BALFOUR

SUBTITLES
on the foreignness of film

an ALPHABET CITY MEDIA book
THE MIT PRESS Cambridge, Massachusetts London, England

Library of Congress Cataloging-in-Publication Data

Subtitles : on the foreignness of film / edited by Atom Egoyan and Ian Balfour.
     p. cm.
    Includes bibliographical references.
    ISBN 0-262-05078-1 (hc. : alk. paper)
    1. Motion pictures — Titling.   2. Foreign films.   I. Egoyan, Atom.   II. Balfour, Ian.
TR886.9.S83 2004
791.43 — dc22

                                            2004044813

10 9 8 7 6 5 4 3 2 1

Printed and bound in China by Hung Hing Off-Set Printing Co., Ltd.

INTRODUCTION
Atom Egyoyan and Ian Balfour

Images by Stefana McClure

Every film is a foreign film, foreign to some audience somewhere—and not simply in terms of language. The essays, interviews, and artworks in this collection take the figure of the subtitle as a point of departure in exploring the idea and the varieties of foreignness in film. Subtitles are only the most visible and charged markers of the way in which films engage, in direct and oblique fashion, pressing matters of difference, otherness, and translation. This collection is dedicated to unravelling what is at stake in such subtitled presentations and representations.

In the earliest phase of cinema there was no need for subtitles. Film was a silent medium and any written information—presented on cards between visual scenes—could be easily translated into any language and then physically cut into the print. Although the lips of silent film actors moved, the actors' exact choice of words was immaterial. Information and dramatic intention were conveyed by gesture, music, and precise textual information displayed on cards. Although these cards would often present dialogue in quotation marks ("I want to marry you" or "I'm going to kill you"), they often bore little relation to what the silent actor was actually saying. There was a lot of talking in silent films, but for all the words, at each screening only one language was legible: the written language of the target audience. There was little sense of a disjunction between the original language of the film's actors and the language on the cards.

The introduction of sound in the late twenties required new solutions to the problem of presenting dialogue to foreign audiences. The simplest solution—still practiced in some parts of the world—was to translate simultaneously the spoken text. This required the volume in scenes with dialogue to be turned down as a translator, sometimes speaking into an amplification system, presented his or her version of the text in the audience's native tongue. Often one and the same speaker presented the dialogue of numerous actors, rarely changing their emotional inflection of the text.

More commonly, dubbing is used to superimpose a second language over the original dialogue. In this process, professional actors are brought into a studio to record their translated lines. The words are then positioned sonically over the original dialogue. Music and sound effects are preserved from the sound track, and they are mixed with the replacement dialogue to achieve a sense of naturalness. If the performances are good, dubbing is a plausible way of making a film accessible to a foreign audience. In some countries, certain actors are consistently used to present a given star's lines. In Italy, for example, a certain dubbing actor will always be enlisted to dub Clint Eastwood's words. For Italians the movie star's iconic pronouncements ("Go ahead, make my day") will forever be associated with an Italian actor's voice.

The preferred technique for making foreign films accessible to a wider public is the subtitle. The subtitle was actually introduced as early as 1907, that is to say, still in the era of intertitles, but it did not really come into its own until the age of the talkies and their international distribution. The era of the modern subtitle was ushered in with the screening of *The Jazz Singer* in Paris in 1929, two years after its American release. Subtitles were quickly recognized by discriminating viewers as the most accurate way of preserving the director's and screenwriter's dramatic intentions. Technical or material

Ran: English subtitles to a film by Akira Kurosawa, 2003 wax transfer paper mounted on rag, 32" x 50"

constraints made subtitles, in the early days, labour-intensive and not all that cost-effective, though still only a fraction of the expense of dubbing. Over the course of its development, the process of subtitling has evolved from mechanical etching on the frame to chemical, laser, or optical burning. The technical advances have been uneven but relatively swift. In our time we have reached, at long last, a moment in which subtitles can now be programmed in the privacy of a filmmaker's home computer. Moreover, films can now easily be distributed with subtitles in multiple languages or even with multiple versions of subtitles in one language.

In this volume, subtitler Henri Béhar gives a vivid account of the profession, while others discuss the commercial, conceptual, and political dynamics of subtitling (Rich, Cazdyn, Sinha). At the same time, the idea of subtitles animates discussions of translation, otherness, representation, national identities, and the tasks of cultural interpretation. Thus the essays in *Subtitles* engage a wide range of ideas as to what constitutes the foreignness of film.

The interrelation of image and text, the movement from one to the other, is the subject of a number of projects. In Stephen Andrews's "Soundtrack" the artist makes sketches by hand—sonograms of a recording of his voice reading a poem. And Deborah Esch's "Archive of Devastation," a meditation on Derek Jarman's *Blue*, recounts how "no ninety minutes of cinema could deal with the eight years HIV takes to get its host... the reality would drive the audience out of the cinema. We don't lack images—just good ones."

What constitutes a "good image"? In taking still photographs on the set of *The Sweet Hereafter*, photographer Johnnie Eisen took some "accidental" shots of the characters staring into his lens—discards revealing stark portraits of the characters in Russell

La Grande Illusion: English subtitles to a film by Jean Renoir, 2002 graphite paper mounted on rag, 24" x 30"

Banks's novel. For these images Banks created "found" subtitles from his original text that could reflect on the emotional effect of the depictions. By taking these leftover images from the machinery of a film production (images that would otherwise never be used or seen), the writer is able to reclaim his authorial authority through a series of imaginary subtitles.

Sometimes a subtitle can provide access to spaces that would otherwise be indecipherable. Regarding a sequence from her film *Vendredi Soir* (*Friday Night*), Claire Denis describes a scene where her main character, from the distance of her car, is watching a couple inside a café. She sees them having a discussion, but can barely hear it. She's on the outside. The subtitles, on the other hand, present the dialogue with absolute clarity. When Claire Denis asked the subtitler if the text could be presented with missing letters or words—to reflect the viewer's experience of partial comprehension—she was told it would be impossible. The orthodoxy stated that "Either we have subtitles or we don't."

The iconic status of the subtitled screen in our time becomes strikingly visible in the art work of Stefana McClure. To make her drawings—each taking the title of one classic of Japanese or western cinema—she watches a film frame-by-frame and successively traces each subtitle on top of the others on a background of transfer paper. One is left with a monochrome screen whose only shapes are subtitles, or the blurry, faded indices of them. Often all we know is that there are—or once were—something like subtitles. But the subtitles remain as a kind of luminous fact, with the viewer facing the scene of translation and the difficulty of reading text and image together.

The presence of subtitles on a film screen might suggest that the only thing requiring translation is the words, as if images were somehow universally intelligible. Visual economies, however, can be conditioned by regional or national particularity or even by the singularity of an artist's vision. Thus Fredric Jameson addresses the virtues of thinking of Balkan film as a regional cinema with distinctive features that tend to solicit, from the outside, a rather narrow range of predictable and uncomprehending responses. Even more pointedly, Negar Mottahedeh analyzes the idiomatic visual economy of women in Kiarostami's films. She demonstrates in painstaking detail how the peculiar, government-ordained strictures on how women can be filmed—even observed—structures Kiarostami's own visual dynamics, as well as the extent to which he can render problematic those constraints even as he works within them.

Beyond—or distinct from—questions of national or regional cinematic difference and stylistically coded forms of otherness, contributors to *Subtitles* also asked how film itself might be considered foreign, that is to say, non-natural, in its formal qualities. Mary Ann Doane analyzes the peculiarities of how time has been represented from the early days of film onward. Film, she shows, presents us with modes of time that scarcely have equivalents in our ordinary perceptions: film defamiliarizes time. Or Jarman's *Blue* offers a singular experiment in form, with its single, abiding blue screen. Such films can transform our perceptions and conceptions of the real, starting with what is closest to home. The foreign, we might even say, begins at home—which gives a rather different spin to Dorothy's mantra in *The Wizard of Oz*: "There's no place like home." Salman Rushdie—so keenly attuned to the dialectics of exile and diaspora—rewrites Dorothy's dictum to read "There is no longer any such place as home."

Films conscious of a certain foreignness, according to Hamid Naficy, negotiate the terrain of the subtitle as more than simply a supplement to the "original" language of the film:

> Multilinguality, which necessitates extensive titling, turns the film frame into a calligraphic page, contributing to the film's overall accent. In traditional "foreign films," subtitles mediate between a spoken source language and a written target language on the screen. . . . However, there is no single or original source language for many accented films, which are made in the interstices and astride several cultures and languages. Subtitling is thus integral to both the making and the viewing of these films.

In such films—so increasingly common now as to be making inroads even in the still pervasively monolingual American market—the very status of the foreign is changing.

By the foreign, we by no means understand what usually counts as "exotica." Indeed, the vastly increased circulation of "world" film worldwide has had the salutary effect of making much of what once stood as exotic—in an old-fashioned *National Geographic* sort of way—a thing of the past. Globalization has left its prints on how cinema is made, circulated, and received. So when Brenda Longfellow takes up the pitfalls and possibilities of the contemporary anthropological gaze, she is describing one such shift. It's not as if globalization has resulted in a homogenized world cinema, with national, regional, and linguistic barriers fading to white or black: far from it. If Fredric Jameson can speak of a "geopolitical aesthetic," it is less to recognize the blending or levelling of differences than to suggest that, as of late, a world system is brought to bear in the production and reception of a vast array of films, however asymmetrically, across the globe. There surely is now a more highly articulated and integrated world system—thanks not least to the phenomenon of the international film festival—whereby cinema from Iran or Hong Kong takes its place alongside the now less hegemonic film production from European and American centres.

Even if at some levels and in some circles there is an unprecedented availability of

Swimming Pool:
English subtitles to a film
by François Ozon, 2004
blue transfer paper mounted
on rag, 7.5" × 9.75"

"foreign" films, Andrew Sarris has noted that the new generation of spectators "can't be bothered with the foreignness of foreign films." It's hard to overestimate this popular resistance to subtitles, the stakes of which are detailed, in institutional and commercial terms, in Ruby Rich's analysis of the monolingualism and xenophobia informing the American movie industry and American society more generally. This resistance has its tangled history, part of which is illuminated in John Mowitt's account of what, in the world of American institutions such as the Oscars, has counted, at different times, as a "foreign film."

These are clearly times when we need reflective, personalized—subtitled—images of how other people live their lives around the world. The popular Western media implies that news scenes of destroyed villages, of potential terrorists, and of subdued dicta-tors are all the visual proof required to distinguish between "us and them." But what we need are *subtitled* images—not an embedded journalist's commentary—that extend, rather than preclude, the possibility of relating to others.

We need to make sense of the foreign on our own terms. We have to define what is foreign to our individual experience, before we can hope to understand the roots of collective misunderstanding. Subtitles offer a way into worlds outside of ourselves. They are a unique and complex formal apparatus that allows the viewer an astounding degree of access and interaction. Subtitles embed us.

Hamid Naficy (2001)
An Accented Cinema: Exilic and Diasporic Filmmaking
Princeton: Princeton University Press

Salman Rushdie (2002)
Steps Across This Line: Collected Non-Fiction 1992–2002
New York: Knopf

A Short Film About Love:
English subtitles to a film by
Krzysztof Kieslowski, 2003
graphite paper mounted on
rag, 7.5" × 9.75"

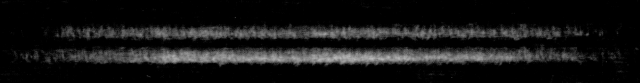

THE SWEET HEREAFTER
Russell Banks and Atom Egoyan

Photographs by Johnnie Eisen

THE SUBTITLES EXPERIENCE

Recently, I've had two formative subtitles experiences.

Months after I had seen an Iranian film projected in a cinema, I decided to watch it again on videotape. There was one scene near the middle of the film which I wanted to review, and I began to fast forward the tape. As I re-watched the film speeding through my machine, I became aware that I could read the subtitles and still follow the dramatic intention of the scenes in this accelerated form. In fact, the rigourous compositions and intricate dramaturgy now became a backdrop for the subtitles.

It occurred to me that one of the absolute governing principles of the cinephilic experience is the immutability of the viewers' physical relationship to the image that is projected. One sits in a theatre where a film unspools through a concentrated beam of light. There is nothing to change the fundamental and inevitable way in which the filmmaker's intentions are presented. There is no way to stop the film once it starts. It begins at a certain time whether one is present or not.

The experience of watching a video or a DVD, on the other hand, is based on the notion of personal familiarity, convenience, and what fits into one's daily life. As Susan Sontag points out in her essay "The Decay of Cinema," "The conditions of paying attention in a domestic space are radically disrespectful of film. To be kidnapped, you have to be in a movie theatre, seated in the dark among anonymous strangers. No amount of mourning will revive the vanished rituals—erotic, ruminative—of the darkened theatre."

My love of cinema is founded on subtitles. The sixties and seventies gave rise to a series of astonishing films that were made available to a general public through letters that appeared (or disappeared, if the screen image was white) at the bottom of the screen. They were my passport to an exotic world, and I loved the feeling of being surrounded in a foreign conversation to which I had access. It made me feel both exhilaratingly outside and inside at the same time.

It's quite possible that some of the films were enhanced by this effect. If I understood the Italian or the German, I might have found the dialogue unconvincing and pretentious. I was much more forgiving of words that were imposed on a screen that displayed a gorgeous black and white cinemascope scene, than if those same words had come out of a mouth whose language I understood. I fully trusted the filmmaker's intention to take me somewhere.

My second subtitles revelation occurred as I was reviewing my DVD of *The Sweet Hereafter* for a lecture, and accidentally pressed an incorrect button on the DVD menu. I found myself watching the film with English subtitles, designed for the hearing impaired. It was disorienting to see the images I had wrought from Russell Banks's book played back accompanied by words. The subtitles somehow seemed to trivialize the film's literary source. While I—the filmmaker—certainly wanted to instill a sense of trust in the viewer—to take them somewhere—the source book would have certainly taken them somewhere else.

This odd juxtaposition of the filmed image and the subtitled text seemed to present the central dilemma of this issue of *Alphabet City*. How do we effectively translate and present a point of view outside of our own experience? How do we find the words? How do we know that they're accurate? How do we address the inherent subjectivity of the aesthetic experience, whilst acknowledging its crucial role in providing objective information? How do we determine authority?

I wasn't raised in a town like the one depicted in Russell Banks's book. One of my most crucial responsibilities as a director is to cast the film—to find the gallery of actors that will inhabit the characters that the book presents. The actor chosen is, in a curious way, a personified subtitle to the script's intention, giving the viewer access to a range of subtle emotions and hidden sub-textual meanings.

I was inspired to review the publicity shots of the film, with the idea of inviting Russell Banks to react, years after the film was completed, to this gallery of faces. Johnnie Eisen—who has been the still photographer on almost all of my films—had taken hundreds of images. Most were very close in composition and tone to moments in the finished film. What I found most exciting, however, were the images that could never be used for publicity purposes. In this selection of photographs, the actors were looking directly into the lens—sometimes on purpose and often unintentionally—to form a series of extremely intimate and completely inadvertent portraits.

I then presented this selection to Russell Banks, and invited him to choose extracts from his novel to subtitle them. I was intrigued by the alchemy that might occur when the source writer is able to use his original words to respond to performances and images interpreted by others.

These are subtitles to an alternate version of the film.

—Atom Egoyan

She was well-liked, sober, hardworking.'

I myself understand him perfectly.[2]

Wendell didn't really give a damn about much.[3]

Risa, I knew, still had dreams.[4]

Mr. Stephens couldn't ever know the truth.[5]

...face darkly intelligent, eyes narrowed
with suspicion and intelligence.[6]

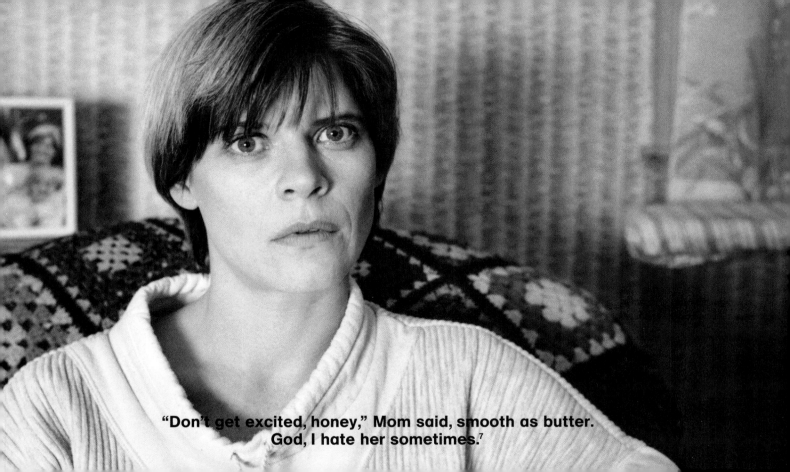

"Don't get excited, honey," Mom said, smooth as butter.
God, I hate her sometimes.[7]

I saw him as a thief,
just a sneaky little thief in the night.[8]

There was always something
noble about Billy Ansel.[9]

A beautiful, articulate fourteen-year-old girl
in a wheelchair. She was perfect.[10]

1. I damn sure did not want to go after Dolores Driscoll, and, for somewhat different reasons, neither did my clients. Never mind that her pockets weren't an inch deep; she was well-liked, sober, hardworking, from an old respected Sam Dent family, sole support of her crippled husband, and she'd been driving local kids to school safely for more than twenty years. Worse, the parents viewed her as having been victimized as much as they were themselves, and a jury would agree with them. "Poor Dolores," Risa had said. "She must have been destroyed by this" (Stephens 129).

2. Abbot was at one time an excellent carpenter, but in 1984 he had a stroke, and although he has recovered somewhat, he's still pretty much housebound and has trouble talking normally and according to some people is incomprehensible, yet I myself understand him perfectly. No doubt it's because I know that his mind is clear. The way Abbott has handled the consequences of his stroke is sufficient that he is a very courageous man, but he was always a logical person with a lively interest in the world around him, so I make an effort to bring him as much information about the world as I can. It's the least I can do (Driscoll 3).

3. I always liked Wendell, even though he was indeed, as Risa eventually discovered, lazy and pretty dumb and pessimistic. That's a hard combination for a wife to like, and frankly I never would have hired him to work for me, even if he had been one of the Vietnam vets who for a long time were the only people I hired at the garage. But Wendell made it relatively simple, by being good-looking and passive, for a man to call him a friend. (Some folks might regard him as low-key or easygoing, but I have to say passive.)

What it came down to was that in an important sense, Wendell didn't really give a damn about much. He liked sports—TV sports, that is; he was a little heavy in the gut to play any himself—and he was very fond of his son. Not like Risa was, of course, for she was much more intense about everything than he, but sufficiently fond to have his heart broken by the boy's death (Ansel 58).

4. There were no cars or trucks in sight as Risa brought her son across to the bus. He was Risa's and Wendell's only child and the frail object of all their attention. Wendell was a pleasantly withdrawn sort of man who seemed to have given up on life, but Risa, I knew, still had dreams. In warm weather, she'd be out there roofin the motel or repainting the signs, while Wendell stayed inside and watched baseball on TV (Driscoll 21).

5. Daddy would have concluded by now that I had lied, however, and he would try to tell that to Mr. Stephens. She lied, Mitch, she doesn't remember anything about the accident, she has no idea how fast Dolores was going. And Mr. Stephens would have to point out to him that, Sam, it doesn't mattter if she was lying or not, the lawsuit is dead, *everyone's* lawsuit is dead. Forget it. Tell the others to forget it. It's over. Right now, Sam, the thing you got to worry about is *why* she lied. A kid who'd do that to her own father is not normal, Sam.
But Daddy knew why I had lied. He knew who was normal and who wasn't. Mr. Stephens couldn't ever know the truth, but Daddy always would. He put my wheelchair into the trunk of the car and came around to the driver's side and got in and sat there for a minute with the key in his hand, looking at it as if he didn't quite understand its purpose. He said nothing for a long time (Burnell 216–7).

6. A few feet from the stove, sitting cross-legged on a huge overstuffed cushion like a Bedouin chieftain, was Wanda Otto, her face darkly intelligent, eyes narrowed with suspicion and intolerance. She was clearly ready to go to war. My kind of woman (Stephens 114).

7. Daddy was in the bathroom now, unscrewing the mirror.

"Well, sure, but he's got to arrange for the other side's lawyers to take a statement from you, a deposition, it's called, and then we all go to court, and you'll be asked to testify and so forth—"

"About what?" I hollered. "I don't even remember the accident! It's like I wasn't even there!"

"Don't get excited, honey," Mom said, smooth as butter. God I hate her sometimes (Burnell 172).

8. I looked at him, though. I looked right into him. I had changed since the accident, and not just in my body, and he knew it. His secret was mine now; I owned it. It used to be like I shared it with him, but no more. Before, everything had been fluid and changing and confused, with me not knowing for sure what had happened or who was to blame. But now I saw him as a thief, just a sneaky little thief in the night who had robbed his own daughter of what was supposed to be permanently hers— like he had robbed me of my soul or something, whatever it was that Jennie still had and I didn't (Burnell 179–80).

9. But it was more than sexy; there was always something noble about Billy Ansel. In high school, he was the boy other boys imitated and followed, quarterback and captain of the football team, president of his senior class, et cetera. After graduation, like a lot of boys from Sam Dent back then, he went into the service. The Marines. In Vietnam, he was field commissioned as a lieutenant, and when he came back to Sam Dent in the mid-seventies, he married his high school sweetheart, Lydia Storrow, and borrowed a lot of money from the bank and bought Creppitt's old Sunoco station, where he had worked summers, and turned it into a regular automotive repair shop, with three bays and all kinds of electronic troubleshooting equipment. Lydia, who had gone to Plattsburgh State and knew accounting, kept the books, and Billy ran the garage. The stone house up on Staples Mill they bought a few years laters, when the twins were born, and then renovated top to bottom, which it sorely needed. They were an ideal couple. An ideal family (Driscoll 27–8).

10. Fine by me. I had my agenda too. In spite of the injuries, Nicole Burnell looked good, and talked good, and she had suffered immeasurably and would for the rest of her life. A beautiful, articulate fourteen-year-old girl in a wheelchair. She was perfect. I could hardly wait to see the other side depose her (Stephens 103).

Russell Banks (1992)
The Sweet Hereafter
New York: HarperPerennial

Atom Egoyan (1997)
The Sweet Hereafter
Canada: Alliance Films

LITTLE LIFE LINES IN "DESPERANTO"
Patricia Rozema

In "Desperanto" I tried to make visible the experience of trying to access another culture when I can't speak the language. So I have my odd little Anglo character arriving in Montreal full of hope for contact and intimacy. But, tellingly, the room she gets has a view of a wall. All her experiences are various runnings into walls. Then I throw the poor thing into the worst social situation I could imagine, a situation that would make even the most articulate want to die and she does, for a moment. She pretends to fall asleep at a francophone party with Robert LePage rattling on happily beside her. In her dreams she finds subtitles, those imperfect little life lines that straddle, bore through and circumvent the walls.

She notices the subtitles explaining everything she didn't know before. Finding it difficult to read the subtitles at the bottom of the frame that are oriented towards the viewer, she squeezes in between us and the subtitles to better connect to the world on the other side. But it's hard to simultaneously read at the bottom of the frame and the expressions of the actors above, so she lifts them up. Then impulsively (she IS in a dream at a party after all) she slips one subtitle into her cleavage and another into her drink and drinks it. Finally she stands on the subtitles of a French song that sings "teach me, please teach me" and is taken away.

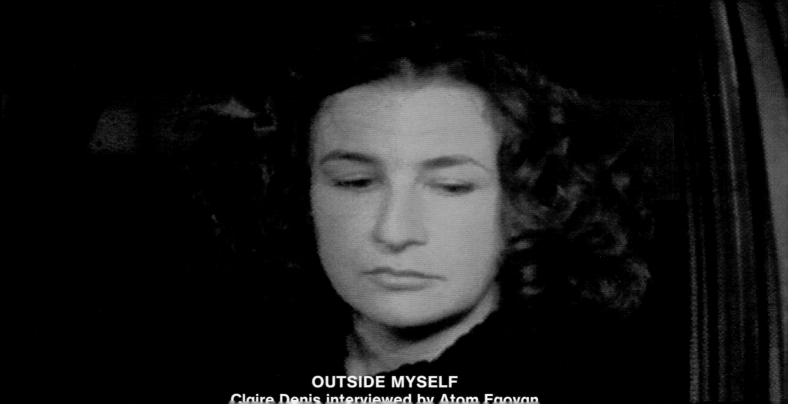

OUTSIDE MYSELF
Claire Denis interviewed by Atom Egoyan

Claire Denis: There is a verse by William Carlos Williams: "outside myself/there is a world." This verse turned me on because I think it's something that happens while making a film. Outside myself there is a world. In making the film, I experienced something like this.

Atom Egoyan: I want to talk about this idea of foreignness in film. Exactly this theme: outside yourself there is a world. The process of how we investigate that world, and how we show that world, is such an essential part of your cinema. You've spent so many years watching other people make films; you were on those sets; you were an AD [Assistant Director]. To what extent was how you represent a world formed by how you observed other people working?

With filmmakers like Jacques Rivette and Wim Wenders—though in completely opposite ways—with each of them I experienced that there is a moment on the set that you can grab and carry to the script. That the script is something that is there, but there is also a moment on the set, and it is the connection of those two moments that makes something. It's not freedom, but rather it is something that exists on the set that is somehow not exactly what you wrote. And I think Wim Wenders and Jacques Rivette have that. When I was their assistant I realized that this was more important for them than to have been boxed in by everything they had prepared. These are not accidents. There is a moment; and they were aware of that, and they were hoping for that. Ready for that. To be sure, they were also under pressure. But they were aware that there still is a fraction of time that is a moment you can grab.

And is that impulse the desire to capture something and to be able to fix it and preserve it? Because the moment that you're talking about is by nature ephemeral and the power of our medium is to fix something and make it concrete, make it last. If we didn't *know that it was going to last, would we still have the impulse to seek out the moment in that way?*

I'm not sure I understand.

This idea that you're talking about, this moment. We become very excited about how we can capture that moment and then show it and then project it. I am curious about the intersection between that impulse as something generous and something insidious. That there's something suspicious about that impulse as well. That we want that moment to do something that we are not capable of feeling at that moment.

I understand your question. And it's something that reminds me—and maybe this has something to do with film?—it reminds me of childhood and also adolescence. Those times when you still need to sit in your room in your loneliness. You feel things that you're not sure will belong to your life. I remember capturing moments and thinking that I hope my life will go towards them, moments which are maybe daydreams, maybe nothing at all.

But those things were exterior to you, things that you had to extend yourself toward. So were they foreign to your experience of the world?

Yes. And that's why being born outside of your world and being a foreigner—as I am, in a way, in France—made me aware of that desire to be inside, to not always to be outside. When we were shooting *Friday Night*, there is a scene where Valérie is in her car looking inside the café, watching the man drinking and speaking to the girl who is playing pinball. She's outside but she wants to be inside; and this is something that was, something that is in my life.

It is interesting that you bring this scene up, because this is exactly the scene that got me most excited. In that scene you can barely hear the dialogue in French. But last night

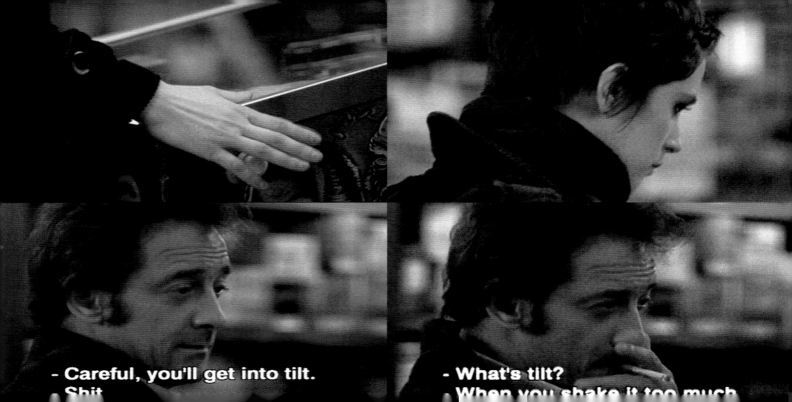

- Careful, you'll get into tilt.
- Shit.

- What's tilt?
- When you shake it too much.

as I watched the film, the subtitles made it absolutely clear what was being said.

I was actually against that. I asked the guy who did the subtitles if we could perhaps print them with one letter missing or one word missing—as artists, you know.... And he said that that doesn't exist in subtitles. Either we have subtitles or we don't have subtitles.

So why did we need to subtitle that scene?

I don't know. I was too weak to say.

I'm so glad you brought this up. I'd like to explore this more. This scene. It was a really powerful experience for me. Suddenly I had access—visually—to something that she was outside of. And it seemed to work metaphorically to underline the question of whether or not she is imagining a conversation she can't hear, but we suddenly have access to. It created a very strange chemistry. How do you negotiate in the translation of any intention this tension between being explicit and being hidden? Being mysterious? And when people expect to receive something, to what extent are you allowed to withhold? That would have been a perfect example, maybe, of a choice to not have subtitles at all.

Exactly. But it was the first time I worked with the guy who did the subtitles. Usually I work with another person. And probably I was afraid. I didn't trust myself enough to have it without subtitles. That's something I regret now.

That's not all it meant to me though. I don't know that anyone else was attending to it, but this was very fascinating to me. You made the decision during the mix to bury the sound and I'm sure in certain theatres you can't understand what is being talked about. And as you said, it's a very powerful moment in the film where she is outside and then she has an invitation to enter into this space. There are a number of moments in that film, and in your films generally, where there is that dynamic: there is somebody whose experience is outside, who wants to move towards something, who wants to create an identification.

Yes. In a way I think this movement is personal, part of my way of being alive. I always want to be inside and often I feel outside. And I think it's something that cinema can convey better than literature. Cinema has its own power. And for me that power has to do with exile. I know exile is a very powerful word. It means something very strong and very dramatic. But exile is sometimes in very tiny details. You can be exiled outside a café. This woman is in a car, seated beside a man. He is next to her for a long time and they have nothing to say. They are afraid of feeling that they might be attracted to each other. And it's only when she is outside and he's inside and he's smoking a cigarette, only when she can see him in the distance, that she feels she can make a choice: "I will make that step toward him. I was not able to make the step when he was seated next to me because he was so close I couldn't see him, in a way. I couldn't foresee myself next to him. But by seeing him in the distance, outside my world, means that I have to make that step." And I think this is the essence of what cinema has to do with exile. I'm sure of that. I don't know why, but it has struck me often. Maybe it's because the audience is also in this position. Outside the world of the film and yet so close. And yet you have to make the decision. A film that grabs you and holds you tight and never gives you the freedom to move toward—for me something is missing here. There must be, in a film, a certain distance, so that you have to step into it. And that's something—

That's something that you have to create. . . .

CULTURAL VENTRILOQUISM
Henri Béhar

It is World War I. The soldiers in the trenches are exhausted—dazed, confused, their faces covered with mud (courtesy of Max Factor). It is the last moment of calm before the climactic battle. Suddenly, a whirr. Faint at first, but growing stronger. One soldier takes a peek: "Tanks, tanks!" he shouts. At the bottom of the screen, the French subtitles blared: "*Merci, merci!*"

It happened in Paris to Sam Peckinpah's *Cross of Iron*; it is a subtitler's ultimate nightmare.

I am a subtitler, among other things. Since I was hired for Woody Allen's *Zelig* in 1983, I have subtitled more than one hundred French and English language films. Mostly from English into French, since, despite the enormous success of films such as *Life Is Beautiful* and *Il Postino* (Italian), *Diva* and *La Cage aux folles* (French), and all of Almodovar (Spanish), subtitled movies account for less than 1 percent of the total US domestic box office. From *Bull Durham* to *The Hours* and *Chicago* (including songs), *Good Will Hunting*, *Plenty*, *Shakespeare in Love*, *Menace II Society*, *The Apostle*, *American Buffalo*, *The Sweet Hereafter*, and *Boyz N the Hood*, it has been it has been my task to convey to the French, via subtitles, what it is that these English language films try to express, be they British, Irish, American, or Canadian.

Somehow, *Zelig* had set the tone: in hindsight, my specialty has been the literary and the linguistically idiosyncratic. I was born in Cairo, grew up in Paris, and have bounced back and forth between Europe and North America for longer than I can remember. I am a Jew. Although, intriguingly, an inordinate number of subtitlers worldwide are Jews, I don't know if Jewishness has anything to do with preparing you for this job, except that we have been expelled from so many countries that we speak a lot of languages. Perhaps it is in our genes that we learn languages quickly, or that each time we move, we have to—and actually want to—learn a culture from the ground up.

At home, we spoke French, English, Arabic, and Italian. My parents spoke Ladino when they didn't want "the kids to understand." (Needless to say, "the kids"—my brother and I—learned it really fast.) Later, as an adult, I also became relatively fluent in German and modern Spanish. At school we were taught to have *fun* with languages, and I still fondly remember the day our Latin and Ancient Greek teacher came in and said: "Today, we will speak only Latin in class." The feat is not speaking seventeen languages, but to enjoy playing within and between them. Subtitling is like playing 3-D Scrabble in two languages.

A large part of the basic process of subtitling is about as seductive as plumbing. The film, transferred onto a time-coded VHS video, goes through the *spotting* process. The dialogue (a printout of which is provided by the filmmakers) is broken down into sequences whose lengths determine how many words can be printed across the screen. Rules apply, some iron-clad: 1 character per 2 frames, less than 40 characters per line (spaces and punctuation included), no more than 2 lines per subtitle, and *never* go over a cut, unless absolutely forced to. The *spotter* is a true artist: spotting requires a strong sense of language and extreme sensitivity to the rhythm and flow of a film. With a bad spotting, the subtitler's difficulty increases ten-fold—with a good spotting, it's almost a breeze.

The lines are then translated, adapted to conform to spotting constraints, and reconciled with the time codes. The subtitles are synchronized with the dialogue and action, and tested in simulation (a trial run, so to speak). Refinements are made—the simulation is actually the last rewrite. Eventually, the final text is laser-etched on the print.

As Carrie Rickey, the *Philadelphia Inquirer* film critic, once put it: "Subtitling is a compli-cated tango during which [the subtitler] dances with the film until both are equal partners." You first watch the film a couple of times and make a few notes: In scene 12, "Get out of here!" is used not as "Leave this room at once!" but as "Are you kidding?" Then, setting the tape aside, you grab the dialogue list and start working on the text itself, trying to make sure you get it all right, checking out the puns and other *jeux de mots*, focusing on the translational problems. It is crucial that the dialogue list must be absolutely accurate.

This is not always the case.

Whoever transcribed the dialogue of Gus Van Sant's *Drugstore Cowboy* was probably partly deaf (at best) and definitely puritan; anything that had to do with the fuck word was transcribed as "inaudible." A sentence, therefore, might read: "(inaudible) you, you (inaudible) piece of (inaudible)! Where did you put the (inaudible) stash?" At some point, it begins to feel like a game.

More disturbing was the transcriber's deafness. One line read: "And God made a bet." Intriguing line, but it didn't make sense. Could it be poetry? After all, Beat Generation luminary William Burroughs is in the movie. Contacted by phone in Oregon, where he lives, Van Sant said he had "no idea what you are talking about. Give me the context." Matt Dillon, James Le Gros, and the two girls walk into a motel room. "Oh," said Van Sant, "the line is 'No hat on the bed!'" He was urged to correct the entire transcript at double-speed.

At the other end of the spectrum, you may get too many explanatory notes. "'Bro': short for 'brother'" is fine, but is "'Shit': vulgar expletive, used here to indicate surprise" really necessary?

Perfecting the dialogue list is the most labour-intensive stage of the process but also the most addictive and culturally enlightening. This is the stage where you go to the library—for Robert Duvall's *The Apostle*, I reread the Bible, in English *and* in French—or you pick up the phone and call your circle of expert friends. For *Rounders*, I contacted a Parisian gambler who insisted that he be barred from every casino in Europe (and some in Las Vegas): "If you were to play such and such a type of American poker game (with which the French are not familiar), what would the calls be?" For *Obsessed*, I called my doctor: "Given that the French for 'spinal tap' is *ponction lombaire*, would 'PL' be acceptable as an equivalent to 'ST,' which is commonly used in English?" (The answer was no.) For Forest Whitaker's gang-related film *Strapped*, I consulted a gang member from Los Angeles who had already helped me on Albert and Allen Hughes's *Menace II Society* and John Singleton's *Boyz N the Hood*. He took one look at the dialogue list and said: "This is Red Hook lingo"—leaving me utterly crushed at the prospect of having to deal with…what, Marseilles slang? Then I called a young hooligan from the Paris "zone": "How would *you* say this…*this week!*" Yes, slang changes that fast.

American slang has become another tongue of mine. In particular, black vernacular requires some astute handling on the part of the subtitler. In 1991, while preparing *Boyz N the Hood* for Cannes, I was shocked to hear blacks calling each other "nigger." Was it an epithet? A term of endearment? An epithet used as a term of endearment? Did we have an equivalent in French? Did I have the space to explain it? (Mercifully, I didn't.) By 1993 and *Menace II Society*, the word "nigger," when it was synonymous with "friend," got subtitled as *copain* or *mec*—"pal" or "guy"—or even "man" (in English). But by then, French slang had caught up.

It becomes even more intricate when you get into what could be termed the American equivalent of Cockney rhyming slang. At the end of *Boyz N the Hood*, Ice Cube decides to leave the neighbourhood. "Five thousand" he says, as he turns and walks into the sunset. *Cinq mille* didn't make sense and, pressed for time (and helped by the fact that the line was just muttered and the action was quite explicit), I decided, for the Cannes presentation, not to translate it. A few months later, by the time the film came out, I had learned that "Five thousand" stood for "Audi 5000," meaning "I'm outta here." And by then, I had added the missing subtitle: *Je me casse.*

Some references may never be fully translatable. In *Boyz*, Laurence Fishburne upbraids his son, Cuba Gooding, Jr., for hanging out in bad company by using a pejorative reference to African-American comics: "What are y'all, Amos and Andy? Are you Stepin and he's Fetchit?" Amos and Andy and Stepin Fetchit are not part of French culture and I needed a reference the French could understand. The subtitle reads, *Vous jouez a quoi, Laurel et Hardy? Il est Abbott, t'es Costello?* The racial element was lost. Ten years later, I haven't found a better alternative (Robinson and Friday?) but I am still working on it.

Because of the technical constraints, speed is the subtitler's enemy. From this point of view, David Mamet is a greater challenge than Shakespeare. Mamet's dialogue is extremely fast, and the overlapping dialogue and editing can drive you nuts. That, plus the staccato rhythms and Chicago slang, made subtitling *American Buffalo* one of my most difficult assignments. Add to that the inescapable fact that English is one-third more compact than French and you soon realize that subtitling is an exercise in frustration. Word-for-word transcriptions are out of the question; your job is not that of the literary translator, it is to give the *Cliffs Notes* to a movie. Or, as critic Carrie Rickey put it, "condensing sonnets into haikus."

Since minimalism is the watchword, everything counts. In Alain Cavalier's *Thérèse*, which I subtitled in English, the young nun who was to become Sainte Thérèse de Lisieux had an unfettered, juvenile passion for Christ, and her "beefs" with Jesus had the flavour of a lovers' quarrel. I decided (with Cavalier's consent) to keep all references to Christ in the lower case ("he" instead of "He," "thine" instead of "Thine," etc.). One American critic who saw the film in an advance preview thought the director was "showing disrespect and reduced the dialogue between Thérèse and Jesus to a lovers' tiff." Which, of course, was the whole point. When the eye and ear are not in sync, the filmgoer senses something is wrong, without knowing exactly what. In this case, the eye was able to alert the language-impaired ear to the point being made, and the lower case stayed.

Subtitling is a form of cultural ventriloquism, and the focus must remain on the puppet, not the puppeteer. Our task as subtitlers is to create subliminal subtitles so in sync with the mood and rhythm of the movie that the audience isn't even aware it is reading. We want *not* to be noticed. If a subtitle is inadequate, clumsy, or distracting, it makes everyone look bad, but first and foremost the actors and the filmmakers. It can impact the film's potential career.

During a trip to Bulgaria to (try and) select films for the Toronto International Film Festival, the late David Overbey was shown what he generously called "a Bulgarian western, sort of—actually, the epitome of the western cliché: you know, This-town-ain't-big-enough-for-the-both-of-us, good-guy-wears-white, bad-guy-wears-black, and ingénue-a-flowing-flowery-skirt." At one point, he recalled, Bad Guy barges into Ingenue's faux Wyoming *datcha*. As he grabs her and threatens her with a fate worse than death, she beats his powerful chest with her tiny little fists, uttering a torrent of protest. "Unless

this was a Monty Python-type movie—which it definitely wasn't," Overbey recalled, "no way what she said could be translated as 'Don't prank with me, you doddler!'"
In the end, the film never made the Festival circuit. But no one could blame the subtitler for that—could they?

Carrie Rickey (1999)
Not Lost in the Translation
The Philadelphia Inquirer March 3

THE BIRTH OF CINEMA
Kent U. Enns

For when there are many, each has his share of goodness and practical wisdom; and, when all meet together, the people may thus become something like a single person, who, as he has many feet, many hands, and many senses, may also have many qualities of character and intelligence. This is the reason why the many are also better judges of music and the writings of the poets: some appreciate one part, some another, and all together appreciate all. —Aristotle, *Politics*, III, 11

One late afternoon while having a drink in an unfamiliar town, I met a man who, reluctantly at first, agreed to speak with me. In time, he told me of a travelling performer who had once played in vaudeville houses and then later worked as a kind of masque or curtain-raiser to the main feature in those theatres that had started to show moving pictures. It was, the man said, before such flickerings came to seem more real than ourselves. In the later years especially, the audience was often hostile as it waited for an event that soon would diminish many of them. But even before cinema, the performer's act was always the same. He would stand at centre stage and say nothing. Sometimes a few gestures might be made, as if nervously. Other times only a grin. Or a blank. Inevitably, the hecklers started in first. Just one. Then another one or two. Sometimes many. With each word or shout the performer was as if struck by a blow. He winced. He cringed. At a terrible word he might fall to his knees and struggle upright again. Or not. It was only after collapsing that the performer would make pleadings with his eyes. A gesture. Tears.

On some evenings, the rain of blows did not relent. But on a good night different forces began to work from the audience. One member might call, "Get up! Please get up." As if there were no other path for the performer's slender dignity to take. Others begged the hecklers to stop. With each saving word the performer would rise slightly. On a great night he was the fleshly barometer of terrible agitations that rocked the theatre. A whole audience might seethe on itself as it witnessed the undulations of its own doings and undoings.

Often theatre operators had to drag him, spent and empty of tears, from the stage. On occasion, the performer might be led off, barely walking, from the proscenium. On the rarest of nights, the audience worked itself through to an eerie quiet. Some witnesses said it was like a calm that could at last accept the strange stage-bound cipher that had so moved them. Others said it was an exhaustion and there was no good in it. The man said on no matter what night he saw him, the performer seemed the best and the worst of his lowly trade.

With that, the old man finished his glass of beer and stood. I followed him into the streets of that crepuscular town and was soothed by the incandescing of its artificial lights.

SOUNDTRACK
Stephen Andrews and Anne Carson

Yes I admit a degree of unease about my

motives in making

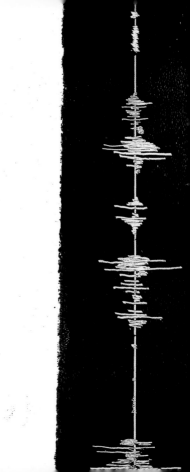

this documentary.

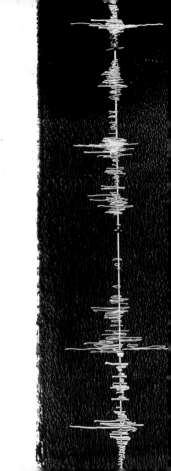

Mere prurience of a kind that is all too common nowadays

in public catastrophes. I was listening

TV MEN: Lazarus
DIRECTOR OF PHOTOGRAPHY: Voice-over

Yes I admit a degree of unease about my
motives in making
this documentary.
Mere prurience of a kind that is all too common nowadays
in public catastrophes. I was listening

to a peace negotiator for the Balkans talk
about his vocation
on the radio the other day.
"We drove down through this wasteland and I didn't know
much about the area but I was

Fascinated by the horrors of it. I had never
seen a thing like this
I videotaped it.
Then sent a 13-paged memo to the UN with my suggestions"
This person was a member

of the International Rescue Committee,
not a man of TV.
But you can see
how the pull is irresistible. The pull to handle horrors
and to have a theory of them.

But now I see my assistant producer waving her arms
at me to got
on with the script.
The name Lazarus is an abbreviated form of Hebrew 'El'azar,
meaning "God has helped"

I have long been interested in those that God has helped.
It seems often to be the case,
e.g. with saints or martyrs,
that God helps them to far more suffering than they would have
without God's help. But then you get

someone like Lazarus, a man of no
particular importance,
on whom God bestows
the ultimate benevolence, without explanation, then abandons
him again to his nonentity.

We are left wondering, Why Lazarus?
My theory is
God wants us to wonder this.
After all, if there were some quality that Lazarus possessed,
some criterion of excellence

by which he was chosen to be called
back
from death,
then we would all start competing to achieve this
But if
God's gift is simply random, well
for one thing
it makes a
more interesting TV show. God's choice can be seen emerging
from the dark side of reason

like a new planet. No use being historical
about this planet,
it is just an imitation.
As Lazarus is an imitation of Christ. As TV is an imitation of
Lazarus. As you and I are an imitation of

TV. Already you notice that
although I am merely
a director of photography,
I have grasped certain fundamental notions first advanced by Plato,
e.g. that our reality is just a TV set

inside a TV set inside a TV set, with nobody watching
but Socrates,
who changed
the channel in 399 B.C. But my bond with Lazarus goes deeper, indeed
nausea overtakes me when faced with

the prospect of something simply beginning all over again.
Each time I have to
raise my slate and say
"Take 12" or Take 13" and then "Take 14!"
I cannot restrain a shudder.

Repetition is horrible. Poor Lazarus cannot have known
he was an
imitation of Christ,
but who can doubt he realized, soon after being ripped out of his
warm little bed in the ground,

his own epoch of repetition just beginning.
Lazarus Take 2!
Poor drop.
As a bit of salt falls back down the funnel. Or maybe my pity
is misplaced. Some people think Lazarus lucky,

like Samuel Beckett who calls him "Happy Larry" or Rilke
who speaks of that moment in a game
when "the pure too-little flips over into the empty too-much"
Well I am now explaining why my documentary

focused entirely on the moment, the flip over moment.
Before and after
don't interest me.
You won't be seeing any clips from home videos of Lazarus
in short pants racing his sisters up a hill.

No footage of Mary and Martha side by side on the sofa
discussing how they manage
at home
with a dead one sitting down to dinner. No panel of experts
debating who was really the victim here.

Our sequence begins and ends with that moment of complete
innocence
and sport-when Lazarus licks the first drop of afterlife off the nipple
of his own old death.

I put tiny microphones all over the ground
to pick up
the magic
of the vermin in his ten fingers and I stand back to wait
for the miracle.

BORGES NIGHT AT THE MOVIES
Jorge Luis Borges

Translated from the Spanish by Calin-Andrei Mihailescu

During the thirties and forties, when he was letting himself be drawn into long chats with his friends on film topics, the eager theatre-goer Borges wrote a few short pieces on film. Sixteen short reviews remain (all published in the Buenos Aires magazine *Sur* between 1931 and 1945), together with a few notes, a prologue, and two synopses, written with Adolfo Bioy-Casares (for two movies by Hugo Santiago). Eduardo Cozarinsky has collected and edited them in *Borges en / y / sobre cine*; Waldman and Christ have translated them in *Borges in / and / on Film*. The three texts below are retranslated for *Subtitles*. Borges wrote on Eisenstein, von Sternberg, Chaplin, King Vidor, Ford, Hitchcock, Korda, Welles, Cukor, Dreyer, Mayo, Fleming, Wyler, and on such Argentinean directors as Mario Soffici and Luis Saslavsky; he wrote on others, also, less gently. His notations are short and to the point, displaying idiosyncrasies and turns of phrase not uncharacteristic of the style of his essays and fictions. Borges knew that subtitles volunteer a kind of proletarian resistance to the epidemic of foreignness, and that dubbing does little to fence off the sentimentalism of adaptation. As an unabashed man of letters, he vested his film interests mostly in plot developments; he went for the story and against its watering down that, according to his lifework, the novel thrives on (later he avowed that John Wayne embodied the hopes for a modern revival of the epic). Bring no popcorn: even before blindness came to him, Borges's movies were not quite on the screen—true movies never are.

—Calin-Andrei Mihailescu

FILM AND THEATRE[1]

Allardyce Nicoll, who teaches a course in the history of drama in Yale's halls of wisdom, recently published a large and weighty in-octavo on the "similarities and differences" between secular theatre and film. To bemoan the accomplished ignorance of this volume, whose bibliography includes 914 books and articles as well as more than 200 periodicals, from the Los Angeles *The Photodramatist* to the Charlottenburg *Das Publikum*, amounts to mere insolence. However, (t)his ignorance is not only incredible or improbable: it is also real. Professor Nicoll, a man well-versed in libraries, erudite in files and sovereign in catalogues, is almost illiterate when it comes to box offices. He has rarely gone to the cinema; more precisely, he started watching movies only a few years ago. About the silent era, about the period before 1929, he knows close to nothing; about the present one—awfully little. Thus we come to understand, without excusing or defending it, the omission of the works and names of Josef von Sternberg, Lubitsch, and King Vidor. As to his criterion, it suffices to transcribe this exemplary list of films which (according to him) justify the talkies as a genre: *The House of Rothschild*, *The Private Life of Henry VIII*, *Queen Christina*, *David Copperfield*, *The Story of Louis Pasteur*, *Little Women*, *Catherine the Great*, *Man of Aran*, *The Informer*. Of these nine redeeming films, two (*The Informer* and *Catherine the Great*) are good beyond doubt; one (*Man of Aran*) is a mere anthology of images; another (*The Private Life of Henry VIII*) is not insufferable; the remaining five justify—not to say, require—the burning down of the theatres which show them.... These two faults—awful taste and inadequate information—should be enough, according to good logic, to invalidate the book. Nevertheless, the facts are more complex: Allardyce Nicoll's premises are debatable, but the conclusions he usually draws from them are not. On the other hand, his application of the conclusions

1. Jorge Luis Borges (1936), Film and Theatre, *Sur* 26.

may seem not particularly sharp. I will offer an extreme example. On page 149, the author correctly ascertains that, "in order to secure economy, visual images are preferable to words if these visual images are sufficient to convey the impression desired. Fundamental to the cinema is that which is presented to the eye; this must ever take chief place. Words spoken occupy a secondary position."

He then applies his law to a certain Laurel and Hardy film [*Bonnie Scotland*, 1935]. Here is the plot: L. and H. come to take hold of a legacy in a Scottish village, which is a mirror and a paradigm of virtues most frigid. A duly Calvinistic and dried-up lawyer demands that they produce proof of their identity. Triumphantly, they take out some papers showing that they have been in prison, and they exultantly describe the dangers and mishaps of their escape and voyage as stowaways on a cattle boat. With a severity not unworthy of the lawyer, Professor Nicoll states that their tale represents nothing more than a "retrospective narrative," that "retrospective narratives" are by nature dramatic, rather than cinematic, and, *as a consequence*, the film should have begun in jail and shown the couple's escape, the chase after them, and their crossing of the Atlantic. Either I am entirely wrong or this objection is a true apotheosis of pedantry and formalism.

The mention of "retrospective narrative"—a literary device frequently found in the Homeric epics—brings us closer to an issue that the author discusses in the most interesting chapter of the book: the issue of cinematic time. Should artistic time correspond to real time? The answers are multiple. According to his own metaphor, Shakespeare put the accomplishments of many years into the turning of an hourglass; Joyce reverses the procedure and unfolds the one day of Leopold Bloom and Stephen Dedalus across the days and nights of his reader. More gratifying than the task of either shortening or lengthening a sequence is that of disarranging it, of jumbling up different times. In the realm of the novel, Faulkner and Joseph Conrad are those who have handled these reversals best; in film (which, as Allardyce Nicoll correctly notes, has unique means for producing such labyrinths and anachronisms), I recall only *The Power and the Glory* with Spencer Tracy. That movie, a man's life story, intentionally and movingly omits the chronological order. The first scene is that of his burial.

Another chapter approaches the interpolation of images which have metaphorical value. Chaplin shows a group of workers entering a factory; then a second pack, this time of sheep, entering a pen. "Ah, the human flock!" murmurs the enraptured audience, very satisfied to have recognized this cinematic avatar of a literary commonplace.[2] (Also, all feel they have attained the merit of an overarching maxim.)

2. *Modern Times* (1936).

AN OVERPOWERING FILM[3]

There are at least two plots in *Citizen Kane* (shown as *The Citizen* in the Republic of Argentina). The quasi-banal imbecility of the first, which aims to extort the applause of the very inattentive, can be formulated in this way: a vain millionaire accumulates statues, orchards, palaces, swimming pools, diamonds, vehicles, libraries, men and women; he discovers, like an earlier collector—whose observations are traditionally attributed to the Holy Ghost—that these miscellanies and plethoras are the vanity of vanities and all vanity. At the moment of his death, he desires one single object in the whole universe—a suitably meek sled that he has played with as a child!

The second plot is superior, vastly so. It links the memory of Kokeleth (Ecclesiastes) to that of another nihilist—Franz Kafka. The topic, both metaphysical and detectivistic, both psychological and allegorical, is the investigation of a man's secret soul by means of the works he has accomplished, of the words he has pronounced, and of the many destinies that he has destroyed. The procedure is the same as the one in Joseph Conrad's *Chance* (1914) and in the beautiful film *The Power and the Glory*: the rhapsody of scenes heterogeneous beyond any chronological order. Overwhelmingly, endlessly, Orson Welles shows fragments of the life of a man, Charles Foster Kane, and invites us to combine them to reconstruct him. The film abounds in forms of multiplicity and uncon-nectedness: the first scenes register the treasures amassed by Foster Kane; in one of the last scenes, a poor woman, luxurious and pained, plays with an enormous jigsaw puzzle on the floor of a palace that is also a museum. At the end, we understand that the fragments are not governed by a secret unity: the detested Charles Foster Kane is a simulacrum, a chaos of appearances. (A possible corollary, already foreseen by David Hume, by Ernst Mach, and by our own Macedonio Fernández: no one knows

3. Jorge Luis Borges (1941),
Un film abrumador, *Sur* 83.

who one is, no one is someone). In one of Chesterton's stories, "The Head of Caesar," I think, the hero observes that nothing is as frightening as a centreless labyrinth. This film is precisely this labyrinth.

We all know that a party, a palace, a great enterprise, a lunch for writers and journalists, a cordial atmosphere of frank and spontaneous camaraderie are essentially horrible; *Citizen Kane* is the first film which shows all of these with some awareness of their truth.

In general, the film's execution is worthy of its vast subject matter. There are shots of admirable depth, shots whose farthest planes (as in the Pre-Raphaelite paintings) are not less clear-cut and meticulous than the closest ones.

I venture to guess, however, that *Citizen Kane* will endure as certain films by Griffith or Pudovkin do—works whose historical value no one denies, but which no one goes to see again, either. It suffers from gigantism, pedantry, and tedium. It is not intelligent, it is genial, in the most nocturnal and most German sense of this word.

ON DUBBING[4]

The possibilities of the art of combination are not infinite, but they are usually frightening. The Greeks engendered the Chimera, a monster with a lion's head, with a dragon's head, and with a goat's head; the theologians of the second century—the Trinity, in which are inextricably entwined the Father, the Son, and the Holy Ghost; the Chinese zoologists—the *ti-yiang*, the supernatural, bright red bird outfitted with six feet and four wings, but with neither face nor eyes; the geometrists of the nineteenth century—the hypercube, a tetradimensional figure which contains an infinite number of cubes, and which is bounded by eight cubes and twenty-four squares. Hollywood has just enriched this vain terratological museum; by means of a malignant artifice called *dubbing*, they put forward monsters which combine the illustrious features of Greta Garbo with the voice of Aldonza Lorenzo. How can we fail to profess our admiration for this painful prodigy, for these ingenious phono-visual anomalies?

Those who defend dubbing will (conceivably) reason that the objections which can be brought against it can also be raised against any other kind of translation. This argument ignores, or evades, dubbing's main fault: the arbitrary insertion of another voice and of another language. Hepburn's or Garbo's voices are not accidental; rather, they are to the world one of its defining attributes. It is also fitting to remember that miming in English is different from Spanish.[5]

I have learned that they enjoy dubbing in the provinces. That is a mere argument from authority; as long as the syllogisms by such connoisseurs as Chilecito or Chivilcoy are not published, I, at least, shall not let myself be intimidated. I have also heard that those who have no English find dubbing delightful or tolerable. My knowledge of English is less perfect than my incomprehension of Russian; and yet I would not resign myself

4. Jorge Luis Borges (1945), Sobre el doblaje, *Sur* 128.
5. No few spectators ask themselves: Since there is usurpation of voices, why not of faces, too? When will the system reach its perfection? When will we see Juana González directly in the role of Greta Garbo in the role of Queen Christina of Sweden?

to seeing *Alexander Nevsky* again in a language other than the original, and I would watch it fervently for the ninth or tenth time if they were showing the original version, or one I would believe to be the original. This latter point is important: worse than dubbing, worse than the substitution that dubbing implies, it is the awareness of a substitution, of a deception.

There is no enthusiast of dubbing who would not wind up invoking predestination and determinism. They swear that this expedient is the fruit of an implacable evolution, and that soon we will have to choose between watching dubbed films and not watching films at all. The latter alternative is not so painful, given the worldwide decadence of cinema (barely tainted by such a solitary exception as *The Mask of Dimitrios*). Recent flops—I am thinking of Moscow's *A Nazi's Diary* or Hollywood's *The Story of Dr. Wassell*—prompt us to see this alternative as a sort of negative paradise. "Sight-seeing is the art of disappointment," Stevenson quipped; this definition fits cinema and also, with a sad frequency, that continuous and unavoidable exercise called life.

Jorge Luis Borges (1980)
Borges en / y / sobre cine
Eduardo Cozarinsky, ed.
Madrid: Fundamentos

——(1988)
Borges in / and / on Film
Gloria Waldman and Ronald Christ, trans.
New York: Lumen Books

Vladimir Braun (1942)
A Nazi's Diary (Voevoi Kinosbornik no. 9)
USSR: Mosfilm

George Cukor (1933)
Little Women
United States: RKO Radio Pictures Inc.

——(1935)
David Copperfield
United States: Metro-Goldwyn-Mayer (MGM)

Paul Czinner (1934)
Catherine the Great
United Kingdom: London Film Productions

Cecil B. De Mille (1944)
The Story of Dr. Wassell
United States: Paramount Pictures

William Dieterle (1935)
The Story of Louis Pasteur
United States: Warner Brothers

Sergei Eisenstein (1938)
Alexander Nevsky
USSR: Mosfilm

Robert & Frances Flaherty (1934)
Man of Aran
United Kingdom: Gainsborough Pictures

John Ford (1935)
The Informer
United States: RKO Radio Pictures Inc.

William K. Howard (1933)
The Power and the Glory
United States: Fox Film Corporation

Alexander Korda (1933)
The Private Life of Henry VIII
United Kingdom: London Film Productions

Rouben Mamoulian (1933)
Queen Christina
United States: Metro-Goldwyn-Mayer (MGM)

Jean Negulesco (1944)
The Mask of Dimitrios
United States: Warner Brothers

Alfred Werker (1934)
The House of Rothschild
United States: 20th Century Fox

WORD IMAGES
Raymond Bellour

Translated from the French by Sarah Nixon Gasyna

What does it mean, fundamentally, for Borges to be interested in cinema? It is not so much a matter of writing *about* it (Borges was for years a sort of amateur though vigilant film critic) or *for* it (he wrote screenplays with Bioy Casares—in particular, *Les Autres*, for Hugo Santiago), so much as being able to articulate a space that is shared by literature and film.

The visual metaphors that haunt Borges's writing are innumerable. They form a kind of abstract device that calls to mind the pomp with which the Baroque theatre organized a world inhabited by an omniscient gaze, which it plunged through dizzying metamorphoses. Borges constantly uses stand-ins and doubles, as an active principle. In doing so, he is reflecting the condition of a culture gripped by re-runs and repetition. He is also defining the nature of the writing act as linked to imagery, and specifically, to the image of one's self: *Borges and I*, "The other one," as he puts it. The writer, consequently, becomes a spectator, is someone who ceaselessly creates their own cinema, as much a prisoner of this mechanism as a real viewer of a film would be.

As it happens, at least on one occasion—in "The Mirror of Ink"—Borges expressed this question in such a way that makes it impossible for us to determine whether he was designating the act of writing, or that of producing and seeing images. It is as though this had become a spurious question in itself, or one and the same thing.

The controversial—and reported—account, a story of a story (often the case with Borges), posits a tyrant face-to-face with a sorcerer.[1] The former, Yākub the Afflicted, has just put to death the brother of the latter for having conspired against him, and the sorcerer only succeeds in obtaining clemency for himself by promising to make the tyrant behold "forms and appearances more marvellous than those of the *fanusi jihal*, the magic lantern."[2] He thus takes "a large sheet of Venetian paper, an inkhorn, a

1. First published in 1954, "The Mirror of Ink" recounts the alleged circumstances leading to the death, in 1842, of Yākub the Afflicted, "the cruelest of the governors of the Sudan," at the hand of the sorcerer Abderramen al-Masmudī (whose name, Borges suggests, "might be translated as 'The Servant of Mercy'"). Borges cites as his source the nineteenth-century explorer, translator, and author Sir Captain Richard Francis Burton. The attribution is a questionable one, however, and might in fact be the result of playful Borgesian misappropriation. As most translators of "The Mirror of Ink" have pointed out, dates, facts, and Burton's own account are not consistent with Borges's. [Trans.]
2. All excerpts from "The Mirror of Ink" are from Andrew Hurley's translation of Borges's *Collected Fictions*. [Trans.]

chafing-dish with live charcoal in it, a few coriander seeds, and an ounce of benzoin."
He cuts the paper into six strips, writes charms and invocations on the first five, and on
the last one inscribes these words from the Qu'rān: "We have removed from thee thy
veil, and thy sight is piercing." Next, he draws a magic square on Yākub's palm, and,
telling him to hold out his hand, pours into it "a circle of ink." The sorcerer asks him if
he can see his reflection in the circle. The tyrant confirms that he can, whereupon the
sorcerer instructs him not to raise his eyes. He then burns the ingredients and the invocations in the chafing-dish, and requests Yākub to "name the figure that he wishe[s] to
see." A horse, and then a herd of horses, come into view within the pool of ink.
One notes the effect of fusion that has been contrived between the words and images.
From the holy text that appeals (perhaps allegorically) to the power of the gaze, we
progress to a reflection of the self [*l'image de soi*], which becomes the first reality
proffered to the gaze. Next, through the fire that consumes the formulae (which ones,
we will never know) penned on the scrolls by the mage, the reflected self undergoes a
metamorphosis and turns into the image of that which the protagonist has designated
through his own words. The piece of paper and the words, written and uttered, are
redirected by the ink into the mechanism of writing; but the physical mirror, and the
square on which this device is inscribed, also function as a sort of screen on which
images accumulate and unfold as in the cinema. And so the sultan can demand to see
anything and everything, as he pleases, in his magic mirror:

> All the appearances of this world…all that dead men have seen, and all that living
> men see: the cities, the climes, and kingdoms into which this world is divided, the hidden
> treasures of its center, the ships that sail its seas, its instruments of war and music and
> surgery, its graceful women, its fixed stars and the planets, the colours taken up by the

> infidel to paint his abominable images, its minerals and plants with the secrets and
> virtues which they hold, the angels of silver whose nutriment is our praise and justification
> of the Lord, the passing-out of prizes in its schools, the statues of birds and kings that lie
> within the heart of its pyramids, the shadow thrown by the bull upon whose shoulders this
> world is upheld, and by the fish below the bull, the deserts of Allah the Merciful.

And so on, until the day the he commands the sorcerer "to show him the city men call Europe."

This wording is not without its significance. For, while Borges may be resorting to the accretion of cultural forms that is one of the tools of his fantastic relativism, it also suggests that the fate reserved for Yākub the Afflicted alludes, above all, to something that is particular to the Western imagination. And so it is that there materializes, on the biggest street of this legendary Europe, a Masked Man whose enigmatic figure is inserted, from this point on, into all the images produced for the tyrant by the sorcerer. Their forced collaboration proceeds at an accelerating rhythm until the day the tyrant wishes to see "a just and irrevocable punishment": a death. Yākub asks to be shown a condemned man, and when he sees that the man who has been brought forth is the one with the veiled face, he insists that the sorcerer unmask him before he is executed.

> [T]he horrified eyes of Yākub at last saw the visage—which was his own face. In fear and
> madness, he hid his eyes. I held in my firm right hand his trembling hand and commanded
> him to look upon the ceremony of his death. He was possessed by the mirror; he did not
> even try to turn his eyes aside, or to spill out the ink. When in the vision the sword fell
> upon the guilty neck, he moaned and cried out in a voice that inspired no pity in me, and
> fell to the floor, dead.

Let us add to this perfect image a few of the details furnished by the narrative. The executioner of the final death is the same one who killed the sorcerer's brother at the beginning, and is the same one who would have executed the sorcerer himself had he not escaped by his powers. And the method of execution is the same: by the sword. The veil that shrouds the face of the tyrant's double functions as a repetition of the veil that the Qu'rān verse at the beginning of the experiment stipulated be removed in order to activate the power of the gaze. The overall strategy is thus established under the seal of death, that scrupulous inversion of imaginative power. Those who surrender to this power, spellbound by the mirror, are destined to meet with a singular kind of death. They are bound to this imaginative force because it puts them at the mercy of their own image. Having recognized his reflection, the sultan ought to have repudiated it, to have died to himself, so that he could access other images, an infinity of images; but he ends up dying of his own hand because this reflection always returns under all the other images, as the index of an impossible, exhausting, gaze.

Borges's acumen in this story is to have adapted a legendary East in order to limn an invention conceived by the Western imagination. And by the same stroke, he dates this invention—to the very middle of the nineteenth century: "the fourteenth day of the moon of Barmajat in the year 1842." In this way, the mirror space, converted into a locus of projection, functions all the more naturally *at once as a screen and a blank page.* In order to elude death, the sorcerer offers up images that are more marvellous than those that the magic lantern can conjure. Beginning with Robertson's phantasmagoria at the end of the eighteenth century, the protracted invention of the cinema was effected through photography and many other technologies (the narrative revels in underlining how "the appearances within the mirror of ink, at first momentary or unmoving, became now more complex").

An entire century, during which was forged, in parallel, the idea of literature as experience and as a distinct destiny: the very force that Borges never stopped exploring and pushing to its limits. His own sleight of hand—and his innovation here as a writer—is to underscore, in a manner that is at once mythical, ludic, and historical, the emergence of a global mechanism within which words and images, literature and cinema, exchange their properties. This process is enacted from the same standpoint that placed the man before the mirror, troubled by his image—with a surfeit that imparts only a single desire: to live and die from it.

Jorge Louis Borges (1998)
Collected Fictions
Andrew Hurley, trans.
New York: Viking

EPISTOLARITY AND TEXTUALITY IN ACCENTED FILMS
Hamid Naficy

In the mid-1990s, while conducting research in Paris, I attended a private screening of Mohsen Makhmalbaf's *A Time to Love* (*Nowbat-e Asheqi*, 1991) at MK2 Productions, which was considering the film for distribution. Made by the best-known new director to emerge since the Iranian revolution of 1979, the film had been banned in the director's home country for its theme of love, in essence a *ménage à trois*. My friend Azadeh Kian and I were the only spectators in the comfortably appointed screening room. Perhaps partly to avoid the Iranian censors, Makhmalbaf had shot the film in Turkey with all of the dialogue in Turkish, a language I did not know beyond certain words. The film was subtitled, but in French, which at times passed too fast for my understanding, especially since I was trying to take notes. On these occasions, I would nudge Azadeh to translate for me. Reading the French subtitles, she would whisper the Persian translation into my ears. Trying to keep up with her translation and with the ongoing film and its subtitles, I was forced to take notes hurriedly in English and Persian, whichever served the moment best. Thus, watching this single film involved multiple acts of translation across four cultures and languages. This chain of linguistic and cultural signification pointed to the radical shift that has occurred in the globalization of cinema since my childhood. In those days, cinema screens were monopolized by the West, particularly by American films, and Third World people were more often consumers of these films than producers of narratives of their own. But now they are making and exhibiting films, not only in their own countries but also increasingly across national boundaries, finding receptive audiences in Western film festivals and commercial theatres and on television. This article deals with the films that postcolonial, Third World, and displaced native filmmakers have made in Europe and North America since the 1960s—the so-called postmodern era—with emphasis on a set of features that many of them share: the way diegesis overtakes mimesis by means of translations, titling, epistolarity, acousticity, and calligraphic textuality.

What occurred in the MK2 screening room involved not only watching and listening but also reading, translating, and writing. All of which are part of the spectatorial activities and competencies necessary for appreciating the works of these filmmakers, works I have termed "accented cinema" (Naficy 2001). This is by no means an established or cohesive cinema since it has been in a state of emergence in disparate and dispersed pockets of the globe. It is, nevertheless, an increasingly significant cinematic formation in terms of its output, which reaches into the thousands, its variety of forms and diversity of cultures, which are staggering, and its social impact, which extends far beyond exilic and diasporic communities to include the general public as well. If the dominant cinema is considered universal and without accent, the films that diasporic and exilic subjects make are accented. This accent emanates not so much from the accented speech of the diegetic characters—although that is part of it—as from the displacement of the filmmakers and their artisanal or collective production modes. Although many of their films are authorial and autobiographical, their authorship and autobiography need to be problematized as the filmmakers' relationship to their films and to the authoring agency within them is not solely one of parentage but also of performance. However, by putting the author back into authorship I counter a still-prevalent postmodernist (specifically poststructuralist) tendency, which either celebrates the death of the author or multiplies the authoring effect to the point of de-authoring the text. Accented filmmakers are not just textual structures or fictions within their films, but are also empirical subjects, situated in the interstices of cultures and film practices, existing outside and prior to their films. Their history matters.

Accented films are interstitial for they are created astride and in the interstices of social formations and cinematic practices. Consequently, accented films are simultaneously local and global and they resonate against the prevailing cinematic production practices, at the same time that they benefit from them. As such, the best of the accented films not only signify and signify upon the conditions of exile and diaspora—and deterritorialization in general—but also upon cinema itself. They signify and signify upon exile and diaspora by expressing, allegorizing, commenting upon, and critiquing the home and host societies and cultures as well as the deterritorialized conditions of the filmmakers. They signify and signify upon cinematic traditions by means of their artisanal and collective production modes, their aesthetics and politics of smallness and imperfection, and their narrative strategies that cross generic boundaries and undermine cinematic realism.

EPISTOLARITY
One of the most intriguing features of the accented films' narratives is their epistolarity, involving the use of the formal properties of letters and telephony to create and exchange meaning. Exile and epistolarity are constitutively linked because both are driven by distance, separation, absence, and loss, as well as the desire to bridge these multiple gaps. Whatever form the epistle takes, whether it is a letter, a note scribbled on a napkin, a telephone conversation, a video, or an email message, it becomes, in the words of Linda Kauffman, a "metonymic and a metaphoric displacement of desire" (38)—the desire to be with an other and to re-imagine an elsewhere and other times. Epistolarity is an ancient and rich genre of imaginative and critical literature and it involves the acts and events of sending and receiving, losing and finding, and writing and reading of

letters. It also involves the acts, events, and institutions that facilitate, hinder, inhibit, or prohibit such acts and events. Letters play a major role in the narrative of many classical fictional films to the point that they could be classified as epistolary films.[1]

Modern realist novels and classical Hollywood films are generally driven by an omniscient narrator and narrative system. Modern journalism, too, has encouraged "objective" reporting and omniscient narration. The authority of these types of narrators and narrative systems, however, has been challenged in various ways—by the stream of consciousness technique, free indirect style, and epistolary form. In traditional epistolary literature, the story is told by direct narration, that is, by means of letters written by one or more of the characters without the apparent intervention of the novelist. Through these letters, readers gain direct access to the characters' subjective viewpoints and emotional states and are affected by the intimacy, immediacy, and intensity of their interiority. Because it provides access to multiple viewpoints and voices, the epistolary form enhances the work's verisimilitude and psychological depth.

However, epistolary works are not only mimetic but also diegetic. They involve not only the direct discourse of the characters (usually in the first person) but also the indirect discourse of the novelist (usually in the third person). There is yet a third, free indirect discourse, which can initially appear to be in the indirect style, written by the author. However, upon scrutiny it becomes clear that this discourse is contaminated by the enunciative properties of the characters' speech. If early epistolary novels were largely written in direct and indirect styles, many modern and postmodern novels employ all three modes, especially free indirect style. African-American novels, particularly Alice Walker's *The Color Purple* and Zora Neale Hurston's *Their Eyes Were Watching God*, make very creative, intricate, and wonderful uses of free indirect style. One of the key

1. Among them are Frank Borzage's *A Farewell to Arms* (1933), William Wyler's *The Letter* (1940), Ernst Lubitsch's *The Shop Around the Corner* (1940), Henri-Georges Clouzot's *The Raven* (*Le Corbeau*, 1943), William Dieterle's *Love Letters* (1945), Max Ophuls's *Letter from an Unknown Woman* (1948), Jacques Tati's *Jour de Fête* (1948), and Joseph L. Mankiewicz's *A Letter to Three Wives* (1948).

contributions of this style is to force the dominant language (standard English, the language of indirect narration) to speak with a minoritarian voice (spoken black English, the language of direct speech). This free indirect voice is not a dual voice of both a character and a narrator, but a bivocal utterance that fuses both direct and indirect elements to express dramatically the double consciousness of a divided self (Gates 207–8). As such, free indirect discourse expresses well the bifurcated consciousness of exile and diaspora.

In film narratology, the direct style would include the characters' speech ("I am hungry") and point of view, or what Edward Branigan has called the character's "direct subjectivity" of "I am hungry." In the indirect style, a character's speech or thoughts are reported without quotation (125–6). The indirect style includes reflection of the characters and objects by means of mirror shots and eye-line matches and the projection of the character's mental processes, such as thinking, dreaming, fearing, desiring, and remembering, by means of expressive camera movements and editing (98–9). The free indirect style may include the interjection of the personal/direct discourse into the narratorial/indirect discourse. Point-of-view shots, cut-aways, perception shots, even certain shot-reverse-shot configurations may be considered cinematic instances of free indirect style. Reflection, projection, and introjection subjectivize the films and their characters and may create ambiguities about what is happening on the screen and who exactly the subjects are—i.e., the owners or the objects of the gaze, thought, voice, and the epistles. Such narrative ambiguity recreates and expresses the ambivalent subjectivity and hybridized identity of exilic and diasporic conditions.

The epistolary form is intensely dialogic. Address is not just a problem in epistolary films, but also a problematic of these films, as they inscribe several sets of dialogic relations: the relations between diegetic addressers and addressees who write and read each others' letters or who converse on the phone on-camera; the relations between diegetic addressers and some off-screen interlocutor whom they address with their epistles and whose epistles they receive; and the intertextual relation of the film text with itself, either addressing itself by means of self-reflexivity and self-referentiality or addressing its audience by means of direct address, captions, and titling. Accented films are replete with this latter form of address, which turns them into both epistolic and calligraphic texts.

The very fact of addressing someone in an epistle creates an illusion of presence that transforms the addressee from an absent figure into a presence, which hovers in the text's interstices. As "speech-for-another," the letter, in Terry Eagleton's words, is "over-hearing itself in the ears of the addressee" (52). The scene of the letter's reception is always already embedded in its scene of production (and vice-versa). In the classical realist cinema, letters function differently from film to film as they enter or exit the plot at different points. For example, they may set off the plot or end it; they may complicate or clarify the plot's trajectory or the characters' motivations and psychology; they may mislead, be mislaid, or be misdelivered.[2]

In the case of accented films, however, epistolarity appears to be less a function of plot formation and character motivation than an expression and inscription of exilic displacement, split subjectivity, and multifocalism. Freed from traditional linear, realist narration, these films tend to juxtapose direct, indirect, and free indirect discourses in novel and varied ways to produce a bewildering array of address forms. In the process, they raise fascinating questions about the identity of author, addresser, addressee, reader, recitor, and translator of the letters, and about their narratological functions

2. According to how they affect the plot and narration, classical Hollywood epistolaries may be divided into subcategories. There are, for example, films that feature undelivered letters (William Cameron's *Address Unknown*, 1944), misdelivered letters (Joseph Losey's *The Go-Between*, 1971), incriminating letters (Alfred Hichock's *Suspicion*, 1941), lost letters (Tay Garnnett's *Cause for Alarm*, 1951), indiscreet letters (Joseph L. Mankiewicz's *A Letter to Three Wives*, 1948), letters that bridge the years (Elia Kazan's *Sea of Grass*, 1947), or posthumous letters (Max Ophuls's *Letter from an Unknown Woman*, 1948).

and power relations. In accented epistolaries, letters are not written or delivered only to diegetic characters. In Chantal Akerman's *News From Home* (1977) and Mona Hatoum's *Measures of Distance* (1988), the addressee of the letters in each case is the filmmaker, who never visually appears in the film but whose voice reads her mother's letters on the audio track. Without access to extra-textual information, it would be impossible to ascertain from the films that the voices reading the letters belong to the respective directors, and not to their mothers or a third party. On the other hand, Akerman appears in her *Je, tu, il, elle* (1974) as a diegetic character who attempts to write letters to a lover who is not definitively identified, and it is her voice that reads the letters on the audio track. In *Lost, Lost, Lost* (1949–76), the voice of filmmaker Jonas Mekas addresses not only the diegetic characters (including himself), but also audience members. In Agnès Varda's *One Sings, the Other Doesn't* (*L'un chante, l'autre pas*, 1976), two women maintain their close friendship through a decade of separation by writing to each other and by reading each other's letters on-camera. In Fernando Solanas's epistolary film, *Tangos: Exile of Gardel* (1985), a fictitious Juan Uno sends letters and scraps of paper from Argentina to Juan Dos, his real-life double, in Parisian exile. In some accented epistolary films, the "voice-over" narration that contains the letters dominates the films' visuals to the point that they may be called "image-over" films.

In letter-films like Chris Marker's *Letter from Siberia* (*Lettre de Sibérie*, 1957), letters address the spectators. Jean-Luc Godard and Jean-Pierre Gorin, in *Letter to Jane: Investigation of a Still* (1972), do not actually deliver a letter to a diegetic character named Jane Fonda; rather, the film is their letter to the real-life actress Fonda, as a news photograph taken of her in North Vietnam instigated the letter-film. While in *Letter to Jane* the addressee is a real person who appears in the film, in Marker's *Sunless*

(*Sans Soleil*, 1987) the addressee is a fictional character who is absent from the film. The variety and complexity of the modes of address, as well as the juxtaposition of direct, indirect, and free indirect discourses in accented epistolaries, are staggering.

In addition, the epistles are not limited to written letters delivered, undelivered, or misdelivered by the postal system. Electronic epistolary media, such as telephones, answering machines, email, faxes, and audio and video cassettes, are widely employed, resulting in fragmented, multifocal, multivocal, and emotional narratives. Like Solanas in *Tangos: Exile of Gardel*, in *Calendar* (1993) Atom Egoyan tends to emphasize the magical and connective capabilities of the electronic epistolary media, although their disruptive capacities are also featured. His heavy use of these media prompted a *New York Times* reviewer to suggest a new title for *Calendar*: "Sex, Lies, Videotape, Film, Telephone, and Answering Machine" (Holden 18). Although video-within-film is an integral component of almost all of Egoyan's feature films, indeed, of his style, its use in this film—to document a trip to his ancestral homeland Armenia—turns the video into not only a narrative agent but also an exilic epistolary agent. This function of the video and the particular way in which the telephone and the answering machine are used to transmit multilingual conversations of desire and destruction across time and space, make *Calendar* Egoyan's most epistolary film.

ORALITY AND ACOUSTICITY

To speak of epistolary films as oral and acoustic texts is to acknowledge the central role of sound, voice, and language in them, and to differentiate them from oral literature. The differentiation is necessary because we cannot assign to them the status of some original orality—that which existed before writing. They are only secondarily oral, in that they partake of a kind of post-oral, post-written, post-print, post-Third World, postcolonial, and post-modern electronic orality and acousticity. This "postal" orality is driven by such factors as the filmmakers' national origins and current national status and by their films' multilingualism, their specific inscription of human speech and voice, and their epistolary structures and contents.

Although all of the accented filmmakers are post-literate, many of them have their origin in societies that maintain side-by-side with print and electronic literacy a residual oral culture that influences the stories they tell and the manner in which they tell them. Residual orality impacts their films' formal, stylistic, and thematic systems, giving them a different accent. This may be evidenced in privileging of oral culture themes and spoken formulas, as in Julie Dash's *Daughters of the Dust* (1991); in emphatically familial and collective relations, as in Mira Nair's *Mississippi Masala* (1992) and *The Perez Family* (1995), and in Gregory Nava's *El Norte* (1983), *My Family* (1995), and the *American Family* TV series (2002); in mixing real and magical elements, as in Charles Burnett's *To Sleep with Anger* (1990) and Nava's *El Norte*; in the intermixing of the past with the present, as in Euzhen Palcy's *Sugar Cane Alley* (*Rue cases nègres*, 1983); and in the presence of translators, storytellers, and griot figures, who retell ancient stories or resituate today's events in the context of ancient stories, as in Jean Rouch's *The Lion Hunters* (*La Chasse au lion à l'arc*, 1964) and Haile Gerima's *Harvest: 3000 Years* (1974). There is yet an emerging type of electronic orality, acousticity, and visuality, informed by the Internet, digitization, voice and music sampling techniques, and interactivity.

The accent comes about not just from these sources of residual orality or of new digital orality but also from the coexistence and intermixing of orality and literacy, of digital orality and digital visuality, of colonialism and postcolonialism, of nationalism and postnationalism, of communism and postcommunism, and of premodernism, modernism, and postmodernism. The accented style, therefore, is "postal," "copresent," and "intermixed."

The acousticity of accented epistolaries stems from the specific inscription of sound and voice in them. One of the characteristics of sound that distinguishes it from vision is that sound is perishable, evanescent, and unstable. Unlike vision that can be stabilized in its existence, sound exists only when it is dying or coming into being; it cannot be frozen in place like a still frame. Further, if sight is analytical, operating by isolating and distancing the seer from the seen, sound is immersive, functioning to incorporate and unify the sender of the sound with its recipient (Ong 71–4). While images may exist separately from their producing agency, no voice exists without the force that generates it, the breath (32). Thus there exists a unique relationship between voice, interiority, and identity, and it is perhaps because of this that voice and speech are always associated with potency and magical power.

All societies appear to associate speech and voice with proximity and presence. In film studies, too, speech and voice have been treated as the guarantors of "immediacy and presence in the system of absence that is cinema" (Affron 105). However, theories of sound in cinema that pose sound as counteracting the cinema's basic lack, place a "fetishistic value" on sound. Their overemphasis on synchronized sound turns diegetic speech into the "sound analogue of the shot/reverse shot formation" that sutures the viewer/listener to the "safe place of the story" (Silverman 45). However, the sound track, like the image track, involves mediations, translations, and representational practices that push the sound into the realm of ideology, as something that is produced, not as something that simply emanates.

In accented films, particularly the epistolaries, the high value ascribed to synchronous diegetic sound does not entirely hold, and their use of silence and sound misalignment can turn the best of them into counterhegemonic discourses on ideology and cinema. There are long periods of silence in Akerman's *Je, tu, il, elle* or just ambient sound in Elia Suleiman's "Homage by Assassination" (1991) and *Chronicle of a Disappearance* (*Segell ikhtifa*, 1996). There is no synchronized sound in some films, as in Marker's *Letter from Siberia* and the sparing use of it in others, as in Mekas's *Lost, Lost, Lost*. Voice-off, voice-over, and image-over narrations often cast doubt on the identity of the speaking subject, the addressee of the epistles, and the voice that is reading them, as in Mitra Tabrizian's *Journey of No Return* (1993) and Marker's *Sunless*. The misalignment of voice and person can be especially counterhegemonic in the representation of women because it goes against the classical film style, which insists on both synchronization and silencing of women. Trinh T. Minh-ha's *Surname Viêt Given Name Nam* is centrally concerned with Vietnamese women as speaking subjects, but they speak in a highly accented English that is out of sync. Although these women are subtitled, the subtitling is also deliberately out of sync, lagging behind or running ahead of the subjects' utterance. In addition, the subtitles do not exactly match what the women are saying.

Despite such counterhegemonic sound practices, there is a strong tendency in the accented films to preserve the native language as the marker of belonging and authenticity. Its interpellating authority, its bonding effect, its prison-house is desired, especially by filmmakers who wish to maintain an organic relationship both with their original culture and their communities of address. There is a particular insistence on language and a complex interplay between language and national identity. Linguistic nationalism is an attribute both of the accented films and of the Middle Eastern and Iranian ethnic television (Naficy 1988, 1993, 2001).

CALLIGRAPHIC TEXTUALITY

Multilinguality, a defining characteristic of accented film, necessitates extensive titling, which turns the film frame into a calligraphic page, contributing to the film's overall accent. In traditional "foreign films," subtitles mediate between a spoken source language and a written target text on the screen. In the US, dubbing and subtitling of foreign films has created a paradoxical situation with its own peculiar solution: distributors do not want to dub films into English because apparently American audiences do not appreciate the "lip-flapping" that results, and they do not want to subtitle foreign films because that automatically reduces the film's market. Hence, there exists a preference for remaking popular foreign films as English language films. However, there is no single original or source language for many accented films, as they are made in the interstices and astride several cultures and languages. Subtitling is thus integral to both the making and the viewing of these films. Out of necessity, subtitles must condense several lines of dialogue into brief textual snippets timed to the flow of the images. This requires a very skillful and economic translation of the original spoken words—one of several forms of translations that produces the accent. There are many occasions, however, when the subtitles are either too long to be read in time or one set of subtitles partially covers over another set in a different language. And there are the amusing and annoying experiences of having to read badly or incorrectly translated and spelled titles. These problems particularly plague the subtitling of many Third World and accented films, heightening their accentedness.

In some epistolary films, words are either superimposed over the images or the flow of images is interrupted to display intertitles. However, these titles are treated in the tradition of the best silent-era films, as essential to the narrative. In that era, intertitles commented on the action, attested to the accuracy of a setting, identified location, imparted information, explained difficult terms or abstract concepts (such as the passage of time), played on the viewers' emotions, and expressed the characters' feelings and thoughts (Dick 14–7). In addition, the punctuation, typeface, type size, and layout of the text on the screen were designed to suggest, symbolize, or emphasize. With the arrival of sound, the use of intertitles in narrative cinema dwindled, but letters, notes, newspaper headlines, signposts, street signs, highway signs, plaques, and other forms of written and graphic information continued to serve some of the functions of intertitles. However, alternative cinemas, including avant-garde and accented cinemas, have continued to experiment with on-screen titling as an expressive, narrative, and calligraphic component (see MacDonald).

Mekas's exilic diary films are filled with English language intertitles of various types, typefaces, layout, and lengths, which turn them into calligraphic letter-films of longing. These serve a number of specific functions. In *Lost, Lost, Lost*, for example, the intertitles identify, describe, and comment on people and places ("Gideon," "on 23rd St. pier DP's arrive in America," "Our life on 13th St. goes on"), journeys taken ("A trip to L.I. with Weinbergs"), passage of time ("Later same year," "The long winter"), various activities ("A picnic"), and events ("his first salary," "At the city hall, people gather to protest air raid tests"). Although the titles are usually informational, at times they are emotional, reiterating feelings already expressed by Mekas's own voice-over ("I walked, my heart crying from loneliness"), removing the possibility of narrative suspense.

Most of the intertitles are printed title-cards, but some are typewritten. Sometimes, intertitles and filmed images alternate in such a way as to create a visual rhythm. Other calligraphic and rhythmic uses of the intertitles occur during the celebrated "rabbit shit" haiku sequence, in which brief scenes are numbered from one to several dozen in ascending order. The printed and typed intertitles have a rough-edged, rough-draft quality (occasionally containing crossed-out words) that reinforces the small, artisanal, improvisational, and "imperfect" aesthetics of the films, emphasizing the notion that we are watching someone's diary in the making.

Trinh's *Surname Viêt Given Name Nam* uses superimposed titles and subtitles extensively, graphically, and critically. Their large numbers and varied contents and layout give this film a truly calligraphic accent. Throughout, subtitles consisting of the translation of the film's dialogue and voice-over and of Vietnamese poetry and proverbs are displayed, as is customary, in the lower third of the screen. However, on many occasions, what the diegetic women say in Vietnamese or in heavily accented English is superimposed in different layouts, as blocks of English text on various regions of the film frame, including over the characters' faces. These graphic titles, or what Trinh calls "visualized speech" (193), act as traditional subtitles by aiding spectator comprehension. However, they also serve other graphic, critical, and deconstructive functions. The film's deconstructive project begins with its title, which plays on, parodies, and critiques attempts at naming a heterogeneous country or nation such as Vietnam, and it ends with listing the various names of Vietnam.

To these text-based complexities must be added Trinh's filming style that in *Surname Viêt Given Name Nam*, like in her other films, violates many of the norms of cinematic realism as a critique of those norms. For example, in some sequences she places the subjects on the margins of the frame or decenters them by panning away from them. Close-up shots that would normally show the subjects full-face end up cutting off part of their faces. The film also subverts the accepted practices of lip-synching and title synchronization. Extra long or short duration titles draw attention to themselves and to the spectatorial readerly activities that are involved. Finally, on-camera actors speak the words of actual women recorded in off-camera documentary interviews. In these ways the boundary between documentary and fictional films is blurred and the authenticity and authority of the nonfictional is undermined. Self-reflexive ruminations of the women and of Trinh herself about the process of filmmaking further erodes the distinction of the film forms. The audio track is equally complex, consisting of songs, a mixture of real or reenacted first-person narration and interviews (in different Vietnamese dialects and in accented English), and multiple voices and voice-over narrations that compete for attention. Consequently, the film enacts both the problems and the problematic of linguistic, cinematic, and exilic translation and displacement. Indeed, it poses translation and displacement as theoretical problems for both diegetic characters and audiences.

These techniques comment upon cinema and reality, instead of just recording, reporting on, or representing reality. They denaturalize the classic cinema's realist style and posit female subjectivity and spectatorial activity as multiple and shifting. The spectators are forced to engage in several simultaneous activities of watching, listening, reading, translating, and problem solving. However, because these techniques do not necessarily support each other due to their asynchrony and critical juxtaposition, the spectatorial activities do not fuse into an easily coherent interpretation. While such an outcome is Trinh's stated aim of endowing each activity with "a certain degree of autonomy" (Trinh

207), it is also the source of the film's obscurantism. The film critiques the patriarchal suppression of women in socialist Vietnam and among Vietnamese exiles, but in its emphatic critique of Vietnam, it seems to reproduce Cold War conceptions.

If Virgil Grillo and Bruce Kawin are correct in their analysis, subtitles and intertitles encourage two different types of reading activities, depending on the side of the brain to which they appeal. According to them, subtitles tend to appeal to the right hemisphere, encouraging syntaxic reading, that is, experiencing the whole film—consisting of dialogue, images, and subtitles—more or less simultaneously. On the other hand, intertitles appeal to the left hemisphere, facilitating parataxic reading, that is, experiencing the whole film in an additive way, by combining the various elements consciously (27). If the former type of reading is more simultaneous and emotional, the latter is presumably more discrete and intellectual. The accented calligraphic epistolaries that contain both super-imposed titles and intertitles may thus involve both types of readings, accounting for their dissonant spectatorial experience.

However efficient subtitles are, they are unable to convey subtle differences in the characters' accented speech, which may imply important differences in power and other relations. Michel Khleifi's *Wedding in Galilee* (*Urs al-jalil*, 1987) is a case in point. The film is about the wedding of a Palestinian village chief's son, in an area that is occupied by Israel. The chief must obtain the Israeli military governor's permission for the elaborate traditional wedding. Although the two leaders converse in Arabic, each speaks a different form of it, denoting their profound power differences, as occupied and occupier. The village chief speaks in the colloquial Arabic that ordinary Arabs use while the governor uses the literary Arabic that is reserved for official and journalistic functions. The subtitles fail to render this linguistic power difference. This kind of loss in translation is also characteristic of accented cinema.

In *History and Memory* (1991) Rea Tajiri uses rolling or static titles that literally question the very images on which they are superimposed. The images consist of clips from Hollywood feature films and newsreels and from US government documentaries made to justify the internment of Japanese-Americans during the Second World War. In one sequence, a rolling intertitle on a black background, accompanied by a voice-over narration, describes how one day government agents removed Tajiri's family home from its foundations, never to return it, because the family (all of them American citizens) had been classified as "enemy aliens." This is followed by a clip from a documentary by the Office of War Information, in which a government official explains to the camera that the Japanese attack on Pearl Harbor has turned the United States' west coast into a "potential combat zone." He then reminds the audience that over one hundred thousand Japanese live in that zone, a third of whom are "aliens" and considered to be a potential danger if Japan were to invade the mainland. As he is speaking, the following captions are superimposed on his image, slowly, and line by line:

> Who
>
> Chose
>
> What story to tell?

Tajiri's on-screen question can be applied to *History and Memory* itself, and to the sequence about the loss of her family home. In that case, the question would bring under scrutiny not only the politics of the government's official story but also that of the filmmaker's own personal story—an effect perhaps unintended by the filmmaker. As in the case of *Surname Viêt Given Name Nam*, such critical juxtapositions and their intended and unintended dissonant effects are emblematic of the accented style.

Since in *History and Memory* titles are superimposed on sound film-clips, they compete with existing dialogue, voice-over narration, on-camera narration, and musical passages. This potentially produces an instance of Derridean double writing and reading, in which neither the audio nor visual text assumes primacy. However, the government and Hollywood films are clearly marked as suspicious source-texts that need to be commented upon by means of deconstructive titling.

There is a tradition in Islamic exegesis in which sacred or authoritative source texts are commented upon by learned scholars in explanatory texts. Historically, the texts were memorized and recited verbatim to preserve their sacredness and authority, while this was not necessary for the commentaries. To aid memorization, the texts were made extremely compact, their very density necessitating explanation. When it came to rendering this text/commentary form into writing, an ingenious method of imbricating the two emerged. On the page, the text is frequently interrupted by commentary that ranges from trivial observations to lengthy and important doctrinal elaboration. However, the two retain their separate identities as colour, typeface, and mode of address differentiate them (Messick 30–1). The resulting intertextual artifact is calligraphically very elaborate and its interpretation is equally complex, for it involves switching back and forth between the already familiar—because memorized—text and the larger commentary in which it is embedded. This Islamic form of exegesis appears to have some relevance for the analysis of the epistolary films that are calligraphically accented. Mekas's *Lost, Lost, Lost*, Hatoum's *Measures of Distance*, Suleiman's *Homage by Assassination*, Trinh's *Surname Viêt Given Name Nam*, Tajiri's *History and Memory*, Meena Nanji's *Voices of the Morning* (1992) are filmic examples of such intertextual calligraphic artifacts. Although their visuals generally act as the source text and their titles as secondary or explanatory texts, that is not always the case. Their calligraphic accent lies both in the way the titles comment upon or complement the visuals and in the way in which they and the visuals merge to form one unified text.

Brinkley Messick's study of Yemeni society demonstrates that when the procedures of providing official explanations for core texts are reiterated from childhood and are dispersed in all private and public domains, they can lead to the creation of a "calligraphic state." Likewise, the classical cinema's realist style, practiced for decades by mainstream directors who are widely sanctioned by the culture industries of the West, constructs what, following Messick, may be called the "cinematic state." The epistolary film's calligraphic strategies tend to subvert some of the tenets of that state. To that extent, they are part of "resistance cinema." Godard's deconstructive uses of graphic and calligraphic textuality since his landmark film *La Chinoise* (*The Chinese Girl*, 1967), are examples of strategies that subvert the cinematic state of dominant cinema.

Charles Affron (1982)
Cinema and Sentiment
Chicago: University of Chicago Press

Edward Branigan (1992)
Narrative Comprehension and Film
New York: Routledge

Bernard F. Dick (1990)
Anatomy of Film
New York: St. Martin's Press

Terry Eagleton (1992)
The Rape of Clarissa: Writing, Sexuality and Class Struggle in Samuel Richardson
Minneapolis: University of Minnesota Press

Henry Louis Gates, Jr. (1988)
The Signifying Monkey: A Theory of African-American Literary Criticism
New York: Oxford University Press

Virgil Grillo and Bruce Kawin (1981)
Reading at the Movies:
Subtitles, Silence, and the Structure of the Brain
Post Script: Essays in Film and the Humanities 1:1

Stephen Holden (1993)
Technology, a Tripod, a Romantic Triangle
The New York Times (October 16)

Linda S. Kauffman (1986)
Discourses of Desire:
Gender, Genre, and Epistolary Fictions
Ithaca: Cornell University Press

Scott MacDonald (1995)
Screen Writings:
Scripts and Texts by Independent Filmmakers
Berkeley: University of California Press

Brinkley Messick (1992)
The Calligraphic State:
Textual Domination and History in a Muslim Society
Los Angeles: University of California Press

Hamid Naficy (1988)
Narrowcasting and Diaspora:
Middle Eastern Television in Los Angeles
Living Color: Race and Television in the United States
Sasha Torres, ed.
Durham: Duke University Press

——(1993)
The Making of Exile Cultures:
Iranian Television in Los Angeles
Minneapolis: University of Minnesota Press

——(2001)
An Accented Cinema: Exilic and Diasporic Filmmaking
Princeton: Princeton University Press

Walter J. Ong (1982)
Orality and Literacy: The Technologizing of the Word
New York: Routledge

Kaja Silverman (1988)
The Acoustic Mirror:
The Female Voice in Psychoanalysis and Cinema
Bloomington: Indiana University Press

Trinh T. Minh-ha (1992)
Framer Framed
New York: Routledge

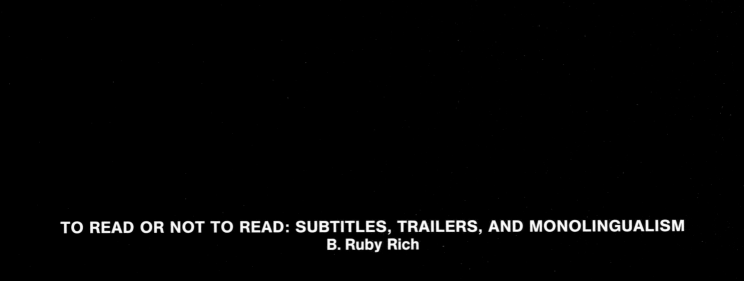

TO READ OR NOT TO READ: SUBTITLES, TRAILERS, AND MONOLINGUALISM
B. Ruby Rich

1. THE PRELUDE

In the fall of 2002, a year after the World Trade Center disaster and the US bombing of Afghanistan but many months prior to the US invasion of Iraq, I found myself eating dinner in a Paris brasserie with my partner Mary and her mother. It was a hard trip for her Michigan-born-and-bred mom, as she discovered with considerable chagrin that most Parisians hadn't bothered to learn English in order to accommodate American tourists.

On that autumn evening, however, my mother-in-law suddenly recognized the cadences of Dutch at a nearby table occupied by an exuberant group of students celebrating their Parisian holiday. After introducing herself and her own Dutch heritage, she questioned the young people with considerable interest on the origins of their language facility. They answered her while nonchalantly switching between English (for her), French (for the waiter), and Dutch (for each other and the serious flirting she was interrupting). They were art students, as it turned out, not linguists. "It's because of our cinema," a pair explained, "We see all our films with subtitles, not dubbed, and so we learn other languages easily."

Consider that serendipitous encounter, then, as the start of this essay, however much in advance of its arrival on the page.

2. THE RECENT PAST, WHEN FOREIGN WAS STILL FOREIGN

Subtitled films were the sign of hipness when I was coming of age. It was a time when art house cinemas were still flourishing, nurtured by college students and Americans who had gone abroad and wanted to keep their cosmopolitan status up-to-date. For a time, foreign films had been the route to sexiness, first when US films were hygienicized by puritanical production codes that dictated such now-ludicrous items as separate twin beds for married couples and, again, when censorship began to be abandoned elsewhere and soft-core movies that were the norm in Scandinavia were sensational taboos here. From Simone Signoret and Anna Magnani to the anonymous blondes of so many Swedish films, European cinema gave Americans a cinematic taste of forbidden fruit. Once the courts felled censorship laws in the US, however, homegrown product took over, porn cinemas proliferated, and the art houses that used to offer foreign films exclusively began to disappear.

Enter the National Endowment for the Arts and the New York State Council on the Arts, both of which provided start-up and ongoing funding for non-profit exhibition centres (like the Film Forum in New York City and the Pacific Film Archive in Berkeley) intended to take the place of the defunct art houses and keep non-commercial cinema alive. That early 1970s landscape of non-profit film centres dedicated to the exciting new cinema emerging worldwide (Fassbinder, Gutiérrez Alea, Godard, Pasolini, Oshima, Wenders, Jarman, Leduc, Solas, etc.) was the one I inhabited as a young professional first testing my chops in film curatorship.

Subtitled films from other countries were our stock in trade. It's what people couldn't find elsewhere. That, along with experimental films (Brakhage, Frampton) and redeemed Hollywood auteurs (King Vidor, Nicholas Ray), was what they came to see. I remember the calls that would pour in to the Film Center of the School of the Art Institute of Chicago every time we showed a French film. "What is the title of the book it's based on, please? I want to read it in French to prepare." The ladies with time on their hands were bent on improvement. Perhaps they were opera fans, for they treated movies as though they were librettos to be studied in advance. I still remember a colleague's delight when a Chabrol film allowed us to answer, "Patricia Highsmith, so you can just read it in English." When we showed the latest New Latin American Cinema offering, though, the crowd changed and every leftist and solidarity committee member in Chicago would pack the theatre. If it was an Eastern European movie, the huge immigrant communities long settled in Chicago (then boasting a Polish language daily newspaper) would show up. Audiences self-selected, the general foreign film audience was a myth, and we could have our pick of films that had no other option for exhibition.

I remember well the moment when I first noticed a change. The time was the mid 1970s. We had always secured Fassbinder and Herzog films from the Goethe House in New York City, but suddenly they were unavailable. The Goethe Institutes had been the cultural arm of the West German government, a network set up independent of the state apparatus in a reaction to the Nazi era and Goebbels's control of culture as an integral aspect of the Third Reich. Suddenly, though, the New German Cinema that had been nurtured in this way broke through to theatrical viability. The Goethe House lost the ability to show these films and so did we, but the filmmakers wanted the larger audiences that only a theatrical release could bring. There was another dilemma, too: only theatrical play dates could guarantee critical attention. Most newspapers refused to let their critics review films playing only one of two nights at museums or film centres. By the end of the 1970s, there was a niche audience establishing for art house films with subtitles. Films from France, West Germany, and the UK dominated the field, but in 1978, one of the biggest hits was a little film from Brazil: Bruno Barreto's *Dona Flor and Her Two Husbands*. Sonia Braga proved that sex and exoticism still sold, even with subtitles.

In the 1980s, the foreign film circuit properly became a business as the entire world of film exhibition was irrevocably altered by forces both within and outside its control. Distribution companies mutated and multiplied, home video forced changes in the habits of both audiences and exhibitors, multiplexes became a reality, and the debut of cable television stations created further competition for viewer dollars just as the development of music video accelerated the alteration of their attention spans. Furthermore, the rise of a homegrown art cinema—the independent feature movement—cut into the audience for foreign films further, hijacking hipness into a new made-in-the-USA format ready for subtitle-free absorption. That was the industry profile. Politically, the US was in the grip of the Reagan–Bush, Sr. days. Xenophobia at home was matched by saber-rattling abroad, whether verbal manifestations like the "Evil Empire" speech or actual invasions, into Grenada, Panama, etc. It was an era fueled by MBA dudes with expense accounts doing leveraged buyouts, at one end, and the rise of hip-hop on the other. It was, shall we say, not the most cosmopolitan decade ever. How to fit foreign films into this cultural mix became the new marketing challenge. What was unexpected, perhaps, was the outcome.

3. BAIT & SWITCH

In 1985, the folks at Orion (today Sony Picture Classics) were trying to figure out how to market Akira Kurosawa's *Ran* to US audiences.[1] Co-founder and co-president Michael Barker remembers clearly how he and co-founder/president Tom Bernard saw the dilemma: they thought this was a film that could really appeal to young audiences yet, Barker recalls, "at the time, young audiences wouldn't go to subtitled films." So they did something that was so brilliantly obvious that it's hard to believe it wasn't

1. Personal communication with Michael Barker, April 2003, in person in San Francisco. All subsequent quotes from Michael Barker or regarding early Orion or Sony Pictures Classics films and marketing campaigns are from this same conversation.

already commonplace, something that instantly became the norm: they had a trailer made for *Ran* that omitted the Japanese and thus rendered subtitles unnecessary. They marketed the film, in other words, with the hope that it might be mistaken for an English language picture. "We knew that if we could just get them into the theatre, then they'd love the film," says Barker. Art house distributors had adopted the retailers' bait-and-switch tactics, and they were working.

With Marcie Bloom, Barker and Bernard ran Orion until 1991, when the trio left to found Sony Pictures Classics. The strategy continued: in November 1988, they had a huge success with Pedro Almodóvar's *Women on the Verge of a Nervous Breakdown* after putting out a pumped-up, no-Spanish-here trailer. Barker still chuckles over a story he attributes to New Yorker Films founder Dan Talbot, who went to a movie theatre to see Zhang Yimou's *Raise the Red Lantern*, a Mandarin language film from China that Sony Pictures Classics released with the same, no-dialogue trailer strategy. The audience settled contentedly in their seats until the opening credit sequence ended and the talking—and subtitles—began. Then, Talbot reported to Barker, a sudden burst of groaning was audible. The audience was face-to-face with the ruse and realized it had been duped. But people stayed. And the film became another hit.

In 1986, just a year after the Orion breakthrough with *Ran*, Russell Schwartz was head of marketing for Island Pictures.[2] He was trying to figure out how to position *Dark Eyes* in theatres, given that its stars were multinational talents working in languages including English, yet the film itself was in Italian with subtitles. Marcello Mastroianni could have made an English language film; it just happened, in this case, that he hadn't. The solution? Same thing: a trailer that disguised the language of the film itself and disclosed no subtitles to give pause to a prospective ticket-buyer. Schwartz thinks

2. Email messages, May 2003. All comments on Island and Miramax history and the marketing of subtitled films are from these same emails from Russell Schwartz.

he might have done the same thing even earlier, but *Dark Eyes* is the one that really sticks in his memory. And he isn't proud of it. "I never really believed we were fooling the public, particularly when the only place these trailers ever ran were in the very theatres that played the subtitled versions."

Nonetheless, a trend had begun, and along with his colleagues at other companies, Schwartz remained committed to the new kind of trailer. After Island, he worked for the infamous Weinstein brothers at Miramax. During 1990–2, as their marketing guy, he imported the practice and fine tuned it. In February 1990, *Cinema Paradiso* broke records; in 1992, it was *Meditteraneo*. With the kind of full-on push that Harvey Weinstein is so famous for marshalling, the no-foreign-tongue trailer became a point of entry that Miramax adopted, sanctioned, and would virtually put on steroids for the remainder of the decade, all in the effort to increase the number of bodies (and dollars) for its foreign language films. Like the college guy who gets his date drunk to make sure he gets laid, the marketing departments of many distribution companies in the 1990s, especially the mini-majors, came to believe that if it were only possible to manipulate prospective audiences into the desired position, they'd say yes.

One of the most memorable trailers of this period was the one introducing audiences in the summer of 1995 to *Il Postino* (*The Postman*): it used the voices of movie stars reading Pablo Neruda to imply that the voices declaiming in English were somehow excerpted from the Italian language, subtitled film. The campaign for *Shall We Dance?*, the Japanese film about a salaryman who falls in love with ballroom dancing classes and his teacher, went even further. The trailer showed the couple dancing but made their race indeterminate, sustaining the illusion of the nonexistent dialogue; unlike *Ran*, it didn't allow the audience to peg nationality visually. The poster showed only dancing feet, shorn of nationality. A universal picture, indeed, especially with the characters pictorially decapitated and reduced down to fancy, and of course inherently non-verbal, footwork.

While it's the companies with muscle that have really pushed this strategy, even smaller companies have had to follow suit. Nancy Gerstman and Emily Russo at the boutique distributor Zeitgeist Films admit to giving in to the trend and crafting no-translation-please trailers for films with crossover appeal.[3] Defending the practice as inevitable in the current market, Gerstman points to the necessity of trying every trick possible to increase audiences at a difficult time for the quality films they distribute. Furthermore, Gerstman points out that trailers changed in many ways during the 1990s that accelerated the move to drop dialogue: the pace sped up, the number of cuts increased, and in general trailers adopted a new form that was increasingly incompatible with all dialogue, whether in English or another language. Need I point out that the practice also coincided with the full establishment of music videos? And channel-surfing, a practice that sped up television in an effort to grab viewers before they passed on? The shift away from foreign language trailers was as overdetermined as it was multifunctional.

In 2003, with a surprise success on their hands (the German film *Nowhere in Africa* by Caroline Link had won the Oscar for best foreign language film and taken in nearly $5 million by mid-spring), Gerstman and Russo had to become experts on the current status of subtitling, too. As it turns out, subtitling technologies had improved, first with laser processing and then with new fatter letters, outlined words, and semi-transparent bands that have contributed to increased legibility. The idea was that once the public was seduced into the theatre by the notion that there are no subtitles, at least the subtitles that would meet the presumably resistant audience were better.

3. Personal communication with Nancy Gerstman by telephone, May 2003.

Jack Lechner, today a producer with radical.media, spent the 1990s in the script development department at Miramax. He remains in awe of the effort that Harvey (by now, the first name alone suffices for identification) was willing to make to overcome the famous American resistance to subtitles. It didn't stop with trailers, either. In 1993, when Miramax was distributing the French film *Les Visiteurs* (*The Visitors*), Weinstein decided that a dubbed version would do better business. He hired Mel Brooks to supervise a full American re-cut and dub. Lechner recalled that it wasn't even released on video.[4]

On the other hand, when Miramax acquired *Princess Mononoke*, the Japanese animated film by Hayao Miyazaki, Weinstein went all out: he hired Neil Gaiman to write the English adaptation and secured such notable actors as Claire Danes, Minnie Driver, Billy Crudup, and Billy Bob Thornton to provide voices for the cartoon characters. This time, the strategy resulted in a huge hit. With no real-life characters, audiences were willing to accept the dubbed version. When Miramax tried to repeat the gambit by releasing a dubbed version of *Life is Beautiful*, though, it failed again. And when Miramax crafted a similar campaign for *Pinocchio* in 2002, with advertisements that made it look like an animated film and with another star-studded roster of actors (such as Glenn Close) supplying voices, it was the biggest disaster yet.

If the good news is that American audiences won't accept dubbed movies, the bad news is that they don't seem to accept the alternative, either. According to a recent *Los Angeles Times* article, "even quality subtitles, however, don't bring in the crowds" (Dutka 5). The article quotes Paul Dergarabedian, president of Exhibitor Relations Co., a firm that monitors box office performance, as saying: "American audiences generally don't want to go to the movies to read. They'd rather the experience flow over them, be

4. Personal communication with Jack Lechner by telephone, May 2003. Lechner, who was based in London for a long time working for Channel Four on dramatic films, told an equally instructive story about British films that were ultimately released in the US with subtitles to compensate for their accented English: *Raining Stones* and *My Name Is Joe*.

spoon-fed rather than interactive. Reading dialogue takes them out of the movie, they say, shattering the illusion."

4. ENGLISH, FIRST AND ONLY, PLEASE

Today, Russell Schwartz is the president of domestic marketing for New Line Cinema, which releases only English language films. He's troubled, though, by the duplicitous marketing strategy he helped develop, reflecting that "it was easy to think back then that this was some major marketing ploy. In retrospect, I think acts like this, in their own small way, helped kill the audience for subtitled films—as if any language other than English was dirty and had to be hidden."

I fix onto Schwartz's statement as a sort of talisman, as though it could testify to a long-gone era or deliver knowledge of market forces beyond the reach of even those in charge of manipulating them. For the 1980s, the era that first gave rise to these strategies, was also the decade in which fights over language assumed primacy on the political stage.

Consider the background: "In 1979, the President's Commission on Foreign Language and International Studies released its report on Americans' 'scandalous' lack of foreign language ability. Not one state had foreign language requirements for high-school graduation, and many did not even require schools to offer foreign language instruction."

Then, consider the shocking response. In 1980, the first salvo was fired in a movement not to declare monolingualism a national emergency, but rather to enshrine it as a national value. It occurred, as so many recent momentous US calamities have done, in Florida. "Dade County, Florida, voters approve an 'anti-bilingual ordinance' prohibiting the expenditure of public funds on the use of languages other than English."

By the mid-1980s, when the marketing techniques traced here were being elaborated, the English Only and English First movements were lobbying nationwide and scoring signal success on the state level in much of the United States. California, for example, passed Proposition 63 with 73% of the vote, making it "the first Official English measure passed by ballot initiative" (Draper and Jimenez). And Georgia passed a similar, non-binding legislative resolution naming English the state language in the same year. Indiana, Kentucky, and Tennessee had already done so. The next year, Arkansas, Mississippi, North Carolina, North Dakota, and South Carolina would follow suit. By 1990, Official English measures had been passed in a total of seventeen states. (On the other hand, New York State and North Carolina staked out oppositional positions, passing measures to mandate foreign language education in their schools.)

I fear the correspondence between this nativist political movement and the audience avoidance of subtitled films is neither coincidental nor specious. Rather, I suspect that both are part of an unfortunate trait in American life, a longstanding national narcissism that sees a mythical version of its "own" culture and language as primary and consigns all others to a secondary status of bothersome detritus. The figure of the Ugly American from the past has more than a bit in common with *The Quiet American* seen on screens in late 2002 and early 2003, supposedly the result of a complaint by Michael Caine to Harvey Weinstein over Miramax's delay in releasing a film seen as critical of US global adventures from Vietnam to Iraq.

The doctrine of US "exceptionalism" has long been debated and, for a little while, even nullified. Part of the shock of September 11, 2001, on the American consciousness was the brutality with which it finished off that faith in US inviolability and the long track record of no-battle-on-this-soil smugness that had prevailed since the end of the Civil

War. The style in which George W. Bush insists on going it alone, acting unilaterally, dictating standards and orders to the rest of the world, is the worst manifestation of this same sense of exceptionalism turned into an offensive rather than defensive strategy. Is it surprising, then, to learn that he had never been to Europe, neither "new" nor "old" Europe, before being elected president?

As I made my way through meetings, telephone calls, email missives and websites, seeking the information necessary to gain a perspective on foreign film marketing, again and again I was assured by my friends and acquaintances, all of enlightened attitude, all fighting the good fight for the acceptance of foreign language films, that there was absolutely nothing xenophobic about American audiences' refusal of subtitles. "It's the distinction between work and play," Jack Lechner assured me. "People want to go to the movies for relaxation, but they think that reading subtitles is labourious. It interferes with the entertainment value of the movie." Others insisted similarly that larger messages should not be inferred from the reluctance. Americans, it seemed, just didn't like subtitles, or dubbing, or learning foreign languages.

The result of these inexplicable tastes and habits, of course, is a population ignorant of how the rest of the world thinks and acts and lives and feels. The blinders imposed by monolingualism and cinematic illiteracy (my term for refusing subtitles) have created a nation prone to global illiteracy, bound by linguistic leashes to a univocal universe, impervious to subjectivities not their own.

Toute l'émotion de la V.O. All the emotion of a voice-over. That's the ironic slogan of Titra Film, the Paris-based company that's one of the foremost subtitling companies. To prove its point, Titra Film has produced a series of sponsorship trailers to play at film festivals. In each one, miscommunications occur when a lack of subtitles prevents the audience or even the characters from understanding something crucial. The joke is that we hear plenty of the language we can't fathom before, finally, a subtitle kicks in, proving the indispensability of Titra Film. It's rather like that early Woody Allen movie, but in reverse. In the Titra universe, even characters within the same film need subtitles. When I've watched the Titra shorts in French film festivals, the audience hoots and hollers with delight, applauding the subtitles and with them their own sophistication.

What might be considered the logical end-result of pandering to an American public's refusal of subtitles is a film like Lasse Hallström's *Chocolat* (Miramax again, still seeking the holy grail of audience crossover). In that film, the French actress Juliette Binoche speaks English with a French accent as she inhabits an American fantasy of a French provincial village of an indeterminate vintage. It's the perfect monolinguist's wish-fulfillment, offering up a *soupçon* of sophistication with no linguistic challenges to trouble the surface. "People everywhere are basically the same," a friend's mother likes to say. She rarely if ever travels; my friend flies around constantly, and she doesn't agree. "No, they're all completely different" is her constant refrain and rebuttal. Monolingualism posits a monocultural world, one where "our" values are not merely dominant but genuinely shared and undisputed. A childlike image of the world it is an image of the self unwounded by the other, a self uninformed by the other, oblivious to its status, inured to its needs, cozy in the cocoon of what once upon a time was called ethnocentrism and now, borrowing a term from queer studies in order to change it, might be known instead as imperial normativity.

5. THE WIRED AUDIENCE

In the 2000s, new shifts are ascendant, just now drifting onto the radar of the marketing folks. Here's the question at hand: why would audiences shun subtitles when they are already reading instant messages on their PDAs, typing back and forth to strangers in live chat rooms, communicating with friends through buddy systems, hauling laptops on the road? It simply doesn't make sense. And what about the popularity of karaoke videos, which involve just as much reading as subtitles? No, it doesn't make sense that reading habits are to blame, nor that these new habits of reading text on screens would be left outside the multiplex entrance like some sort of forbidden firearms left outside the saloon.

In fact, the alacrity with which people have taken up keyboard-based communication, from PDAs to AOL, makes me more suspicious than ever of the excuses made for the low attendance at foreign language films. Surely these same people can read there in the movie theatre if they're doing it all day at home and in the office? It was then I began to develop my theory of a cover-up, a refusal to face up to the real reasons that Americans don't want to see these films. My guess is that foreign films function as a rebuke for some viewers, offering up evidence of something that watching television or Hollywood movies cannot yield, namely, evidence that the world is not made in "our" image, and that neither our society or our language is universal. Perhaps the existence of worlds in which we seem not to matter is too great a blow to the narcissistic psyche of the nation.

Alas, it is this same narrow-casting vision that cedes authority to the President and watches with pride as he and his administration wage a war of spurious motives and fraudulent means. It is the public's lack of knowledge, and deficit of cross-cultural understanding, that allows something like the 2003 invasion and occupation of Iraq to take place—with public approval, at least initially, if the polls are to be believed.

Now, maybe if everyone had gone to more foreign language films, public opinion might be otherwise.

Perhaps there is hope, thought. Perhaps distributors are using out-of-date data, some survey with an expiration date that is long past, its information now turned toxic. I turned to Michael Barker and learned that the times, they are a-changin'. Their two great recent successes—*Crouching Tiger, Hidden Dragon* and *Run Lola Run*—have convinced Sony Pictures Classics that a cycle has been completed and it's time to start over. If subtitles are once again hip. then it's about time that distributors, publicists, and the media caught up to audiences.

Crouching Tiger made over $135 million to become the highest-grossing foreign language film ever in history. The fact that it had subtitles didn't put anyone off. *Run Lola Run* had a hugely successful theatrical release, but more to the point, it became the first subtitled film that Barker could recall ever shipping to video stores in a quantity equal to what the order would have been for an unsubtitled film. Both are action movies, the exact genre that was said to have been unworkable with subtitles—which suggests that films promising action may now be able to overcome an audience aversion to subtitles.

The recent Sony Picture Classics' grosses, interpreted properly, seem to provide new evidence for anyone who cares to look. They may be taken as an argument that internet technologies have led to a resurgence of passion for films from other places, accompanied by subtitles. After all, young people are busily scrolling through their messages already; subtitles are just messages sent out to a bigger listserv.

In 2003 Barker reported that Sony Pictures Classics was so convinced of this shift that it decided to release the foreign language film, *The Cuckoo*, from Russia, with a trailer full of subtitles. Perhaps subtitles will now become the new black and white, a favorite of sophisticated directors like Quentin Tarantino, with his pair of *Kill Bill*s wanting to make a statement. Perhaps the new subtitled trailer will be a calling card in its own right, a flare set off on the highway of consciousness, sparkling into the night sky.

I hope it's not too big a leap to imagine the resurgence of subtitles, also, as an incipient anti-war gesture. Subtitles allow us to hear other people's voices intact and give us full access to their subjectivity. Subtitles acknowledge that our language, the language of this place in which we are watching this film, is only one of many languages in the world, and that at that very same moment, elsewhere they are watching movies in which characters speak in English while other languages spell out their thoughts and emotions across the bottom of the frame for other audiences. It gives me hope. Somehow, I'd like to think, it's harder to kill people when you hear their voices. It's harder to bomb a country when you've seen their cities in films that you've loved. It's hard to pretend whole cultures needn't exist when you've entered the space of their own yearning and fear and hope. Subtitles, I'd like to think, are a token of peace. *Toute l'émotion de la V.O.*

Dennis Baron (1990)
The English-only question:
An official language for Americans?
New Haven: Yale University Press

James Crawford (1992)
Language loyalties:
A source book on the official English controversy
Chicago: University of Chicago Press

Harvey Daniels (1990)
Not only English: Affirming America's multilingual heritage
Urbana: National Council of Teachers of English

Elaine Dutka (2003)
It Translates Into Sweat: In a year when two foreign
language films were up for best-screenplay Oscars,
the painstaking art of subtitling is more important
than ever but still misunderstood
Los Angeles Times April 27

Jamie B. Draper and Martha Jimenez (1990)
Official English?
No!—A Chronology of the Official English Movement
TESOL 1996
http://www.shunpiking.com/shun0844/shun0844.html

THE USE AND ABUSE OF SUBTITLES
Amresh Sinha

"Nobody likes to 'read' a movie," claims film scholar Louis Giannetti, "The subtitles are distracting and can absorb much of a viewer's energy" (233–4). Cynthia Joyce echoes the above sentiment: "As anyone with even a mild appreciation for foreign films understands, watching a subtitled film often leaves you with a vague sense that you got only the *Cliffs Notes* version—the crudest signposts are provided for you, but the all-important details never make it into print." Abé Markus Nornes's frustration with bad subtitling makes him so furious that he wants to "kill" the translator. He begins his essay by stating that "all of us have, at one time or another, left a movie theatre wanting to kill the translator. Our motive: the movie's murder by 'incompetent' subtitles." And the paragraph ends with further indictment: "It is likely that no one has ever come away from a foreign film admiring the translation. If the subtitles attract comment, it is only a desire for reciprocal violence, a revenge for the text in the face of its corruption. For as we shall see, all subtitles are corrupt" (Nornes 17).

Reading subtitles can easily polarize the population into those for and against them. People often complain that reading subtitles distracts the viewer from looking/gazing at the image, that it takes away the pleasure of visual consumption and replaces it with the tedious task of reading. More than anything else, a class resentment or bias has set in between the ideologues of popular culture and the liberal, elitist culture. In American popular culture, subtitles have a dubious status, if not an outright *un-American* character. The spectators of foreign films are more tolerant towards the doctrine of multiculturalism than the America-first white majority. Those who think all foreign items are necessarily hostile and harmful to the American way of life inherently view the spectators of foreign films with suspicion. The consumption of popular culture creates a new division between national, local, and global cultures. The subtitles must show the inclination of being completely absorbed in the dominant mode of the visual. Difference must be translated fully into the national language. Subtitles are superimposed, but it is truly an *invisible* superimposition, unlike the traditional superimposition of either sound or image, which have a relative privilege over subtitles. This superimposition exists most prominently on the screen for a certain duration, but its presence is immediately assimilated and inducted into the visual and acoustic matrix.

For us, subtitling does not simply signify replacing the audio with an "invisible" text. It is a phenomenon that is both internal and external, on the borderline between image and voice—an addition, *the third dimension*, to the film itself. The subtitles come from outside to make sense of the inside, but their own genealogy, in relation to the audio-visual mode, is, if anything, spurious. Their status is not simply that of the "offscreen voice" that renders the space outside contiguous to the onscreen space. They remain pariahs, outsiders, in exile from the imperial territoriality of the visual regime. Nothing originally belongs to the cinema, ontologically speaking. We all know that the image on the screen is a gift from another medium, photography. The voice belongs to the actors, who came from the theatre. The music belongs to opera, vaudeville, and melodrama, and the voice-over was traditionally confined to the commentary that normally accompanied the magic lantern or slide show. The writing appeared on the screen in the form of intertitles, inserted between visuals but never superimposed on the visual like the subtitles. Thus, the intertitles, like the visuals, have an intrinsic space in the visual choreography.

Perhaps one of the greatest threats of subtitles lies in the act of reading the text, which bestows a function to the mind that tears it away "from the bodily presence of the film" (Thompson). There are people who staunchly believe that subtitles act as a barrier, as an infringement upon a cardinal rule, between their access to pleasure that extends itself to them and the work of the mind and intelligence required to synthesize the three different kinds of signifiers: visual, audio, and textual. Reading subtitles in a long film could produce both "resentment" and "fatigue" in audience members, because they are "continually faced with difficult choices along the spectrum between translation exactitude and translation impression" (Thompson). The longer the texts, the greater the risks of "fatigue" with the exactitude required for proper translation, which could even lead to "active resentment." Thompson argues that limiting the number of words for translation impression could reduce the audience withdrawal and hostility. But he takes a middle-ground, advocating a balance between translation exactitude and impression. Once we adopt the position that the "subtitles are an intrusion into the visual space of a film," it becomes, more or less, an effort to place the subtitles in the visual field in the least obstructive or obtrusive manner. Habitually, the spatial placing of the subtitles at the lowest spectrum of the screen betrays its almost contemptuously lower status, its inferior origin in the hierarchy of image and sound. Its origin remains an evil necessity, a product conceived as an after-thought rather than a natural component of the film. The "verbosity" of subtitles could even lead to a complete betrayal of the visual dynamics, for they have the potential to "drown" the images in the literal inscriptions of words and sentences that can dominate the intellectual sensibility to the extent that the image might pass without even being seen. Instead of watching images, the audience starts literally to see only the texts. The texts get superimposed over the image, and the reading of the subtitles also takes over the act of seeing. The images on the screen withdraw with the ascendance of the texts. We not only read the subtitles, but the only things to be seen are the texts themselves. There are two possibilities: you either "stop reading the subtitles altogether, or, conversely, see little of the film *except the texts*" (Thompson). Another problem that the filmmaker encounters is the synchronization of subtitles with the dialogue. It is here that we face the difficulties of finding an equivalent translation, and of matching the words with the temporality of utterance and the temporality of reading.

But these issues are not resolved satisfactorily in dubbing either. In fact, dubbing creates a whole different set of problems. "Sound and image are difficult to match in dubbed versions, especially in the closer ranges where the movements of the actors' lips aren't synchronized with the sounds" (Giannetti 233). Is it possible to render properly via translation in subtitles the digitally synthesized voice of Darth Vader? And what does one do with actors like Robert de Niro, or Marlon Brando, or Meryl Streep, "who are chameleons with their voices?" (Gorbman xi). "The goal of dubbing is to outfit a body with an 'appropriate' voice," says Michel Chion (132). Certain actors' voices are rather constant and distinctive. Only a few actors are used in dubbing for the voices of Tom Cruise, Arnold Schwarzenegger, Sylvester Stallone and other popular actors, so foreign audiences who frequent their movies hear the same voice from one movie to another. They are dubbed with voices that become attached to them. The voice becomes closely identified with a particular foreign actor's voice, which lends credibility, ad hoc authenticity, so to speak. The voice takes on the substitutive authenticity of the original voice. It is a replacement, but a replacement that has almost acquired a second nature, an authentic copy.

Historically speaking, it was after the screening of *The Jazz Singer* (1927) that the human voice became central to the cinema. But that didn't mean that characters in silent cinema were mute. Actually they were pretty "chatty"—you *do* see them utter whole sentences through their lip movements, you just don't hear the voices (Chion 8). The characters indeed talk, but they speak in "a vacuum." No one could hear them, but the characters in the film certainly heard each other, because their gestures clearly established that conversations were conducted in a normal fashion. But how did the spectators know what the characters were saying? These speeches were communicated to the audience normally in a thoroughly "abridged manner" through intertitles. The early cinemas had commentators, like the Japanese *benshi*, who freely translated the intertitles to the mostly illiterate spectators. This problem was further compounded when the same audience had to cope with subtitles in foreign films, at which time the commentators became indispensable.

The conventions and practices of subtitling that were set during the age of Hollywood studio system have not changed much since their invention. Meg James explains the technological impasse of subtitling and dubbing processes: "All the major studios continue to rely on a decades-old system of inserting subtitles on film prints that dates back to the 1930s. That's because studios have not invested in technologies to convert English language films for foreign audiences. They prefer to wait until the arrival of digital movie projection, which will eliminate the delays caused by the cumbersome process of etching words on individual frames of film." Unfortunately, thus far, the subtitling apparatus has not lost its antiquated form, nor has the subtitler been able to lift his or her "ancillary" or "servile" status from obscurity.

Luis Manuel Rodríguez, a dentist-turned-translator of hundreds of Hollywood films—including *Star Wars*, *Crooklyn*, and *Primary Colors*—into Spanish, blames bad translations on the fact that translators are last in the assembly-line process of film production. "With American movies, translators don't even get a film credit," he complains in his interview with Cynthia Joyce. "I would imagine a person who is willing to put their name on a film would be much more conscientious about their work. By the time the film gets translated in post-production, the director has already moved on to another project," he says. Joyce also discloses that "not only is it unusual for Rodríguez to get any guidance from the director, it's even rare for him to receive a copy of the film to work from. Instead, he gets a 'spotting list' that tells him how much time, or how many frames, he has for each title—and a week to write about 1,200 to 1,500 snippets of dialogue. If he's lucky he'll watch the movie once before getting started and once after the titles have been printed; but all too often, he must make do without such luxuries. With *Primary Colors*, Rodríguez was under such intense deadline pressure that he had to begin translating without seeing the movie at all." This account of the extremely inauspicious conditions under which a translator operates helps to explain why subtitles are often so badly tarnished.

The spacing of subtitles in the visual field also poses obvious constraints: the subtitles must accommodate the action or be limited to the scene. They cannot spill over to the other image without causing confusion and corruption, and thus the requirement to condense utterances to fit the space available on the screen. The subtitles are also faced with temporal constraints, that is, the time that is allowed for the subtitles to appear on the screen. The problems are complicated when we take into account that the written texts have higher "lexical density" than the spoken words. It arises from the distinction between speech and writing and the requirement to condense utterances to fit the space available on the screen. Zoé de Linde and Neil Kay provide us with a very interesting example of close captioning from the *Oprah Winfrey Show*, demonstrating the problematics of transferring language from one mode to another and illustrating "how the meaning of an utterance is subtly altered by the removal of a few cohesive elements":

> Dialogue: It's what I call the vicious cycle syndrome. You start with drug A and then they put you on drug B, and drug C, and pretty soon you are taking a handful of pills, all because of the first drug.
>
> Subtitle: It's a vicious cycle. You start with drug A, then drug B, then soon you are taking a handful of drugs.

Linde and Kay argue that the subtitles take away the agency of "*they put you on*," and instead put the onus on the patient, who seems to have become a victim of drug addiction on her own volition. And also, by reducing the lexical variety of the synonym "pills" for "drugs," along with the removal of the final clause beginning "*all because*," the subtitles corrupt the "causal sequence" in the original utterance implying the "self-perpetuating nature of medical drugs" (Linde and Kay 50). The corruption of meaning, with its ideological strains, in this intralingual transfer is by no means simply a technical necessity—far from it. In a slightly different context, Trinh T. Minh-ha applies the concept of "suture" to unveil the complicity of subtitles with the ideological apparatus of the cinematic reproduction. She states:

> The duration of the subtitles, for example, is very ideological. I think that if, in most translated films, the subtitles usually stay on as long as they technically can—often much longer than the time needed even for a slow reader—it's because translation is conceived here as part of the operation of *suture* that defines the classical cinematic apparatus and the technological effort it deploys to naturalize a dominant, hierarchically unified worldview. The success of the mainstream film relies precisely on how well it can hide [its articulated artifices] in what it wishes to show. Therefore, the attempt is always to

> protect the unity of the subject; here to collapse, in subtitling, the activities of reading, hearing, and seeing into one single activity, as if they were all the same. What you read is what you hear, and what you hear is more often than not, what you see. (emphasis added; Nornes 18)

Trinh's position is the classical stance of a poststructuralist critic for whom the hegemonic structure of the Hollywood narrative represents a critical genealogy of technological domination. This is a tenable position as long as it is also evident that the subtitled film conforms to the conventions of the continuity system: the overall system of "suture" by which Hollywood movies foster the unity of the subject, while, at the same time, the very device that makes that unity or identity possible in the interest of the logic of causality makes the apparatus invisible. Nornes goes even further, not being satisfied with the indictment of the structural conformity of the cinematic apparatus; he, instead, blames the subtitlers for "hiding" and "suppressing" the ideological content of the subtitles. "Facing the violent reduction demanded by the apparatus," argues Nornes, "subtitlers have developed a method of translation that conspires to hide its work—along with its ideological assumptions—from its own reader-spectators. In this sense we may think of them as *corrupt*. They accept a vision of translation that violently appropriates the source text, and in the process of converting speech into writing within the time and space limits of the subtitle they conform the original to the rules, regulations, idioms, and frame of reference of the target language and its culture. It is a practice of translation that smoothes over its textual violence and domesticates all otherness while it pretends to bring the audience to an experience of the foreign" (18).

The tendency toward invisibility or self-effacement in translation scholarship is a main concern for Lawrence Venuti. By invisibility, Venuti means the self-effacing tendency of the translator who values the sanctity of the original text, that is, the author's voice and the style within the cultural context of its production, over his or her own voice and style. Hence, a successful translation is a translation that does not appear to be a translation at all, for it has managed to transparently incorporate the essence, the universal sense of meaning, of the source language into the target language. Venuti draws attention to the fact that by making the original subservient to the exigency of one's own language, the translator performs an act of domestication, making the experience of the foreign into what is one's own.

The question of fidelity is another seminal issue in translation theory. Its importance cannot be minimized or reduced on any account. Nornes insists that subtitlers—and his criticism, although specifically related to the (corrupt) practice of subtitling in Japanese films, has general overtones as well—have a hard time not violating the sanctity of the original work. There are many reasons why such practices of inflicting violence on the original have continued unabated even today. The strategy deployed by the subtitler depends on whether one defines the task of the translator to communicate to the reader, or to develop a more a critical relationship with the reader and the original text. Take an example of how the "Ketchup" joke told by Mia, Marsellus Wallace's wife, to Vincent Vega in *Pulp Fiction* is subtitled in French:

> Three tomatoes are walking down the street.
> Papa, mama, and baby tomato.
> Baby tomato starts lagging.
> Papa tomato gets really angry…
> goes back and squishes him.
> Says "*Ketchup*."

Now the interlingual subtitles in French:

> *La famille citron se ballade.*
>
> *Papa, maman et bébé citron.*
>
> *Bébé citron est à la traine.*
>
> *Papa citron se met en boule…*
>
> *Le rejoint et l'écrabouille*
>
> *En disant "presse-toi citron pressé."*

This sort of translation poses a few problems, which we need to think about. Is it possible to reproduce the "homophonic pun" on "catchup/Ketchup" in French in a different linguistic system? And in this particular case, Linde and Kay observe, it appears to cause "a content shift," precisely because it is made quite explicit that the two scenes are not homophonic (47). Many of the issues dealing with both the intralingual and the interlingual subtitling of dialogue are predicated upon equivalent text and, therefore, they open themselves to linguistic analysis.

Taking the example from *Pulp Fiction* of interlingual translation from English into French, we find that instead of applying the principle of equivalent translation, which retains the communicative function of the source text, what we have here is an example of "heterovalent translation (content-reworking), where the text takes on a different function in the target language" (Fawcett 122). Most interlingual translations in films are not translations but adaptations. Luis Manuel Rodríguez recalls his experience of translating a double-entendre political joke in *Primary Colors*, "There's one part where John Travolta's character, Governor Stanton, is accused of having an affair with a Paula Jones-type, a hairdresser, and all the TV comedians are making fun of it: 'It all started one day when the governor walked into the hair salon and asked for some longer bangs.' If I translated directly, it just wouldn't have made sense" (Joyce). Exasperated, he made up a totally different joke, this one having to do with the governor having a different kind of "head" trimmed.

This type of translation privileges the mode of intercultural translation over the functional equivalence. But could we assert with the same fervour that this particular kind of translation (communicative rather than semantic), although clearly and without any doubt an act of domestication, a case of familiarization of the foreign in one's own idiom, is, by definition, an act of cultural imperialism? Does this kind of translation betray the original, because the attempt is to communicate the sense of the joke in French, which, at the same time, effectively distorts the original's semanticity? On the other hand, in a different cultural context, if the joke were originally in Swahili or Hindi and was translated into the language of an imperial culture—which maintains and preserves its cultural discourse along with its aggressive defense of economic, political, social, and religious identity—the issue would be treated under the rubric of politics of translation carried out by a colonial power to domesticate the foreignizing elements. But since both English and French are colonial languages, does that mean that the asymmetrical relations of power between the colonial and the colonized is not applicable in this particular case? Or, should we interpret this situation in terms of the cultural imperialism of Hollywood, which is being essentially neutralized by another imperial power that claims the validity of its own cultural expression above all the rest?

Now let us turn our to attention some of the problems "for translators who do not seek the goal of cultural domination" (Fawcett 117). How to give voice in translation to language varieties, such as slang, puns, jokes, sociolects (as opposed to dialects, which are spoken by a distinct group living in a particular region), etc., which are not

THE USE AND ABUSE OF SUBTITLES Amresh Sinha 183

part of the prevalent "correct speech"? It is often not that easy to find equivalents to slang forms in the target language. As a matter of fact, according to Peter Fawcett, "slang seems to be quite regularly expunged from the translation of film" (120). He draws our attention further to the extensive use of back-slang, *verlan* (words written and pronounced "backward"—*femme* becomes *meuf*, head, *deache*, face becomes *essaff*—initially introduced by Arab teenagers in Paris) in the film *La Haine* (1995), which were not subtitled, because of the lack of proper equivalents in English.

Some of the issues of appropriating the foreignness of a film in one's own idiom results in, what Fawcett calls, an "unwarranted cultural transfer." He provides another example from the dubbed version of *Second Chance*, where a French teacher is translated as saying, "Hey, wow, man! You're all meatheads in this class," which most likely is not the way a French teacher would speak to his or her class. The same scene is translated in German as *Eine brilliante Klasse habe ich da*, which fails to evoke the sardonic expression of the German language in the facial expression (Fawcett 120). Mishandling sociolects and dialects in translation can lead to laughable situations. I recall watching the 1980s Hong Kong "sword" and "ghost story" films. Not only did they feature incredible gravity-defying stunts and special-effects, but they also included the most outrageous English translations, which bent and broke every possible syntactic and grammatical rule of the English language, to comical effect. "But," warns Fawcett, "the results of inept handling of sociolect and dialect can be far worse than laughable: they can lead to offensive stereotyping and to whole groups of people being gratuitously insulted" (120–1). A particularly gratuitous example of stereotyping an entire nation's speech pattern is Peter Sellers's portrayal of an Indian actor in Blake Edwards's *The Party* (1968). The British Raj films and Steven Spielberg's *Indiana Jones and the Temple of Doom* (1984) are also examples of films in which the native tongue is always drowned in the babble of noises in the background. Indian voices are stereotypically rendered with a thick accent (most notorious of all is the accent of the character Apu in *The Simpsons*), suppressing the vast linguistic diversity of the highly balkanized subcontinent, which has little if any common identity and many divergent subcultures.

Let us take an example, from Mira Nair's award-winning film *Monsoon Wedding* (2001), which testifies to the complicated linguistic and social hierarchy of Indian life, as well as its bilingual or multilingual capacity to interact simultaneously with various dialects, national and colonial languages. There is a scene in the film in which a young boy makes fun of his older relative who has just missed the chance to sleep with a young woman.The boy uses a Hindi slang, "KLPD," an English acronym, to tease his relative. The English subtitles translate the acronym fairly accurately as "betrayal of the erect dick" but suppress the full connotations of the "abusive" appropriation of the English letter, "K," "L," "P," "D" to form a Hindi word. The letter "K" stands for Khade, which could be translated as "standing" or "erect;" "L" for "Ling," derived from Sanskrit Lingum," meaning phallus or penis; "P" is the preposition "of" or "on," and "D" for dhoka, meaning "betrayal." Hardly anyone in the West got it. People laughed at the content, but the form of the word, although in English, escaped the viewer's attention, and there was nothing in the subtitles to indicate the trace of the acronym. The subtitles of the film also benevolently neglect to translate in full the following vulgarity from Hindi to English: "There is not enough shit in your asshole."

In "The Politics of Translation" Gayatri Chakravorty Spivak intones that the task of the translator is to "facilitate" love between the original and its shadow (181). This love must come from the translator's desire to acknowledge the realm of memory, of love, and the trace of the other. For Spivak, "translation is the most intimate act of reading" (180). To translate is to "surrender" to its charm—"More erotic than ethical," she claims (183). In her political analysis of a Third World feminist translator, both reading and surrendering take on new meanings. "The translator earns permission to transgress from the trace of the other, before memory, to the closest places of self" (180). In other words, transgression in translation is invoked at a time when the memory of the other takes precedence over the forgetting of the self. Translating is an act of loving, of transgression, of fraying, based upon the surrendering (here we can conjure Trinh's "suturing" as fundamentally complicit in ideological exercise) and not renunciation of the self, that is, in love for the other. The hierarchical difference between the original and the copy is substituted by the agency of love and surrender. An intimacy without fidelity and full of "transgressions," as opposed to the responsibility of conveying or communicating the meaning and the sense adequately, is the frayage, the breaching, the pathway, to the "rhetoricity" or the "stylistics" of the language, which, in other words, is to expose its limits. The rhetorical aspect of the text reveals itself in "the silence of the absolute fraying" of the language that text demands to be intimately acquainted with in order for the limits of language to be disclosed. To translate is to surrender oneself to the text.

Moreover, speaking of the "site" of translation from a postcolonial perspective, the question of fidelity (as opposed to love) between the source and the translated text takes on multiple resonances. First of all, it ought to be recalled that the relationship between the original and the translation is not only based on linguistic or literary theory, but also on the repressive asymmetrical relations between the "subjection" of the colonized language to the colonial discursive practices, a project of historicity that continues to emerge in the heterogeneous discourses of postcoloniality. Spivak considers the difference between "migrant" and "postcolonial" as an example of "catachresis," and how that difference cannot be fully appropriated by a term like "hybridity"—an important concept in postcolonial theory, referring to the integration (or, mingling) of cultural signs and practices from the colonizing and the colonized cultures (243). Taxonomically speaking, the difference between migrancy and postcoloniality refers to a difference in kind, which is to say that the latest restructuring of global politics in the name of New World Order has created a migrant reality that may not coincide with the systemic difference of postcoloniality. *Sammy and Rosie Get Laid* (1987) is a film that points to the discontinuity between the urban migrant (the son) and the postcolonial subject (the father). It is also a film that does not marginalize the issue of lesbian politics (as does *My Beautiful Launderette* [1985], where the gay theme acquires, according to Spivak, an almost incidental value).

We critique *Sammy and Rosie Get Laid* as a film that touches upon the issue of lesbianism in a manner that is no longer governed by the specific difference between migrant and postcolonial, insofar as the focus of lesbianism, its interraciality, is also a site that marks the failure and command of language use. In a poignant scene, the postcolonial subject and the migrant lesbian come face to face with each other's alterity.

Rafi (Sammy's father), incensed after finding the lesbian couple in his son's bed, lapses into his mother tongue, Urdu, as he hurls abuses at them.

Rafi: *Lahol vilakubat, yeh kya kar rahe ho yahan tum log? Haramjadion, randion, pata nahin khanha se ayie ho...nikal jao yanha say.*

Subtitles: God save my eyes from the sight I am seeing. You perverted, half-sexed, God accursed lesbian.

> My translation: God forbid! What are you two doing? Bastards, whores, no idea where you have come from...get out of here.

The translation of "bastards" (in feminized form) and "whores" into "perverted, half-sexed, God accursed lesbian" is only an example of supplementary excesses of translation from one language into another that lacks the equivalent word. It is this "Other" model, the figure of lesbian, feminine subalternity, that renders Rafi speechless: for there is no such word as lesbian in Urdu lexicon. For the migrant lesbian, on the other hand, hurling abuses in Punjabi/Urdu gives her the control of an entire "spectrum of language use" (Spivak 249). What she says to Rafi in retaliation is, however, almost incomprehensible due to the cacophonous environment of the scene, and all we can hear are a few excerpts like, "Who the hell do you think you are? Fucking (substituted for the Hindi *Sala*, which literally means 'brother-in-law,' an endearing term of common abuse) bastard!" But the subtitles perform quite an imaginative free translation of the range of her abuse:

> Subtitles: Fuck off old bastard. I'll tin-opener [sic] your foreskin.... I'll shove live rats up your canal.... Pig-shit bastard! I'll crush his balls! Let me get that withered sperm factory.

In short, the recourse to *Ur*(du) language becomes the site for both the breakdown and the flexibility of a language command through which we witness the limit of postcolonial understanding of sex and gender, forcing its subject to a state of speechlessness that can only be articulated by a return to the mother tongue.

The strength of subtitles lies in *abuses*, in the *Klang*—the ringing at the origin of language that Hegel discerns in the statue of Colossi of Memnon (*Klangstatue*)—of foreignness.[1]
The idea of "abusive" translation originates in Derrida's famous remark in "The Retrait of

1. The "colossal sounding statue" (*Klangstatue*) of the Memnons in ancient Thebes, emitted a sound when struck by sunlight at sunrise. The Colossi of Memnon actually portray Amenhotep III. Due to an earthquake in 27 BC, these statues became known for a bell-like tone that usually occurred in the morning due to rising temperatures and humidity. The Roman emperor Septimius Severus, seeking to repair the statues, inadvertently silenced them forever.

Metaphor"—"a 'good' translation must always commit abuses" (*Une 'bonne' tradution doit toujour abuser*), and its subtle complexities are the subtext of his "White Mythology." The notion of abuse in translation is, arguably, best articulated by Philip E. Lewis. By translating the title of his essay *Vers la traduction abusive* as "The Measure of Translation Effects," Lewis claims that his translation itself becomes an effect or meditation on translation. Since a faithful translation of *Vers la traduction abusive* is quite possible in English as "Towards an Abusive Translation," why does he translate the title as "The Measure of Translation Effects" then? According to Lewis, "the English word 'abusive' (meaning wrongful, injurious, insulting, and so forth) does not immediately pick up another connotation of the French cognate: false, deceptive, misleading, and so forth." But the reason is not limited to that, as Lewis goes on to elaborate the choice of his title in English. He claims that the slant of his translation, which, of course, also reveals his strategy towards an abusive turn for translation to which he would subject his own essay, is a measure "to achieve more than a stilted transfer of meaning, to make it 'work' in English, to endow it with texture of a piece written in English for an English-speaking audience" (33).

If we are willing to force a compromise as far as the subtitling processes go, then it might be a good idea to adopt some of Lewis's insights. Lewis advocates the interpretive model, which is not simply an imposition of one interpretation; instead it offers a model beyond the "contradictory exigency" of the classical paradigm of the translator's task, and asks for "a double interpretation requiring . . . a double writing." The double interpretation remains "faithful both to the language/message of the original and to the message-orienting cast of its own language" (37). Lewis's model of the translator remains faithful both to the original and translation, and it seems to recall Rosenzweig's characterization of translator, who must face the predicament "to serve two masters": The foreign work and the foreign language and one's own public and one's own language (Berman 35).

So what is at stake in abusive translation? "How far can the abuse be carried?" At stake is the practice of translation that resists "the movement of domestication or recuperation by which rhetoric—and analogously, philosophy—bring the abusive forces of catachresis back under the control of a reigning interpretation, of meanings supposed to be already present in the storehouse of language" (Lewis 58). The task of the translator is to render the traditional concept of translation, in which the meaning of the foreign words and sentences are made comprehensible within the reader's linguistic *milieu*, incomprehensible in such a way that the familiar sight of the reader's own language turns radically different in its foreignness. The foreignness is not made ours, on the contrary, in subtitles, what is ours, our own language, is made foreign.

Antoine Berman (1992)
The Experience of the Foreign:
Culture and Translation in Romantic Germany
S. Heyvaert, trans.
Albany: SUNY Press

Michel Chion (1995)
The Voice in the Cinema
Claudia Gorbman, trans.
New York: Columbia University Press

Zoé de Linde and Neil Kay (1991)
Processing Subtitles and Film Images:
Hearing versus Deaf Viewers
The Translator 5.1

Jacques Derrida (1978)
The Retrait of Metaphor
Enclitic 2

——(1982)
White Mythology
Margins of Philosophy
Alan Bass, trans.
Chicago: University of Chicago Press

Peter Fawcett (1997)
Translation and Language:
Linguistic Theories Explained
Manchester: St. Jerome Publishing

Louis Giannetti (1999)
Understanding Movies
New Jersey: Prentice Hall

Claudia Gorbman (1995)
Editor's Note
The Voice in the Cinema
New York: Columbia University Press

Meg James (2001)
Language Barrier Slows Movie Releases
L.A. Times August 25

Cynthia Joyce (1998)
Why Do Movie Subtitles Stink?
http://www.salon.com/media/1998/03/23media.html

Philip E. Lewis (1985)
The Measure of Translation Effect
Difference in Translation
Joseph F. Graham, ed.
Ithaca: Cornell University Press

Abé Markus Nornes (1999)
For an Abusive Subtitling
Film Quarterly 52.3

Gayatri Chakravorty Spivak (1993)
The Politics of Translation
Outside in the Teaching Machine
New York: Routledge

——(1993)
Sammy and Rosie Get Laid
Outside in the Teaching Machine
New York: Routledge

Peter Thompson (2000)
Notes on Subtitles and Superimpositions
http://www.chicagomediaworks.com/2instructworks/
3instruct_writings/wrsubtit.doc

Lawrence Venuti (1995)
The Translator's Invisibility: A History of Translation
London: Routledge

ALTÉRITÉ: THE D-IMAGE EFFECT
Trinh T. Minh-ha

JIKANDES–IT'S TIME

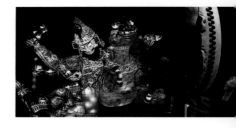

tell me, is it the fog or is it me?

show a country, speak of a culture, in whatever way,
and you'll enter into fiction while yearning for invisibility

ravers' madness
a new form of kindness

how tall is Japan?
height, weight, age?

                    AGE

             PASS

       OF

RITES

RITES OF PASSAGE

MACHINE TIME

Japanese written on every facet of life
calligraphied in the thousand plays of neon signs

the speed of light

where are you now?
    in a train
    facing the window-screen
    second-class seat
    speeding through Japan's likeness

Kogo tokitsukusazare
    As people say here, "in a good talk, don't explain everything"

GISHIKI

Rituals

    and the formation of identity

the skill of behaviour, the craft of framing time, the art of paths

why travel, I would say, if not to be in touch with the ordinary in non-ordinary
ways; to feel and think ordinarily while experiencing what can later become the
extra-ordinary in an ordinary frame

SHINKANSEN

the bullet train
part of a new class structure
the luxury of going faster
while sitting in one place

start in a room sealed with darkness
and a door or a window immediately etches itself onto the viewer's mind

again, it's that unbearable fellow
traveller who won't stay behind,
whom one cannot get rid of

opening at dawn, closing at dusk

sorrows forming and falling away
heavy
like drops of water from a lotus leaf

every day from a blossoming lotus
something's emerging
every day from deep in the mud
someone's being reborn

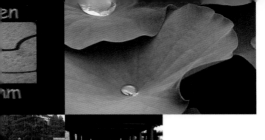

SUKURIN RIZUMU—SCREEN RHYTHM

painting, photography, and cinema used to offer different realms of images
today the gap becomes the bridge,
what tends to separate film from video can offer a passage
a world, not of motion pictures, but of images on the move

     pushing, no piercing
     the match lasts the times it takes
     for horns to unlock
     no crisis, no bloodshed
     when "gravity is the root of lightness" (Tao te-ching)

the seated interface carries with it a danger
both geophysical and spiritual:
that of body losing touch with body

everyday, controlled by a computer brain in Tokyo
over 150 bullet trains crisscross Japan
their whereabouts neatly mapped in tiny lights on wall panels

the truly real world is there where you see trains. For Soseki Natsume, nothing represents better the civilization of the twentieth century than the train. Hundreds of people crammed in a box that rumbles along heartlessly. All taken at uniform speed to the same station.... He wrote: "Modern civilization uses every possible means to develop individuality, and having done so, tries everything in its power to stamp it out. It allots a few square yards to each person, and tells him that he is free to lead his life as he pleases within that area. At the same time it erects railings around him, and threatens him with all sorts of dire consequences if he should dare to take but one step beyond their compass.... The railway train which blunders ahead blindly into the pitch of darkness is one example of the very obvious dangers which abound in modern civilization."

    inside outside, host guest
    the role assigned like the role assumed
    at first seems fixed
    carefully enforced, scrupulously performed
    but once the initiation rites have passed
    from one closure to another
    the inside surreptitiously draws its elements from outside
    without being any less inside
    meticulously adapted, extended, and transformed

nothing is natural, for the natural in its most natural is carefully created

in the matted room
a solitary painting
barely line, barely shape
that frail shadow
of a *bodhisattva*
shading its human frame

the mask: what makes a face into a molding of society and history

performing one's gender is part of the boring social contract
commenting on the sexual ambivalence in girls' comic books, Imaizumi Fumiko
insists that girls' "deepest desire is to be neither male nor female"—they take on
a sexless role that departs from the adult women's subservient role in life,
feeling that reality and dreams can be reversed by changing male and female
appearances.

only when behaviour carefully rehearsed becomes collective
do differences fully take on their individual colour

the relentless pressures to conform
the endless demand for freedom

GISHIKI

like nature, human nature itself is carefully molded

GISHIKI

the choreography of everyday activities
and of every stage role
has been kept alive for centuries

GISHIKI

suddenly here I am
carried by the cadence and the swift metamophoses of the line
its continuity, tensions, improvisations, and repetitions

the exact train system mirrors the structure of the society it serves
machines and people work in mutual accord
once the choice for a destination is made
it can be altered any time in any way during the journey
for the fare registered by the machine
can always be readjusted by the human hand

HUMAN TIME—MACHINE TIME

itineraries are modified as so desired
without any fuss or distrust
for no one seeks to beat the system
when treated with mutual respect
human and machine share the same devotion to duty

the infinite lines of railways regulating the urban space

traveler's heart
er settled long in one place
like a portable fire
—Basho

It is said that
when Shakyamuni lost his ordinary sight
one branch of a plum tree blossomed in the snow

"the principle underlying [Japanese] cultural forms," says Nyozekan
Hasegawa, "is the control of feeling"
a control ideally meant to intensify emotion without flooding the
recipient

bridge, train, passenger
what's in motion?

windows closed
muted soundtrack
no body movement
only the erotic rocking
of human against machine

landscape, image, wagon, viewer
what's moving in the midst of stillness?

travelling anew
with video images
put online
displayed on screen

from one spectacle to the next
mobility of human sets
procession of window images
the landscape wired
now glimpsed
now no longer seen
morphing changing
from one minute to the next

shooting in rural Japan
one often shoots in corporate mentality
collective highlights, collective shots, collective climax
collective photography...

the other dimension: gaseous and liquid
because what appears evident to the eye is the straight line
normal perception is solid, geometric, clear-cut, and divisive

WOMEN'S TIME—JAPAN'S TIME

Japanese women of old are said to have this impassive look of the mask and to live like masks, with their deepest energies turned inward

(according to Enchi Fumiko)

surface is surface
and yet,
boundless is the depth of the surface
that neither conceals nor reveals

what if, in this journey, like Enchi and Soseki, I were to regard events as parts of a Noh play and the people as its actors? Curbing my emotions to get near to the Noh atmosphere; no, not to probe the whys and wherefores of the characters' behaviour and to pry into their daily worries, but to let them move about and come to me in full lines from a two-dimensional picture

video: a delight
for the drowsy body
the seated interface
screen against screen
mutually accessed
mutually processed
activated and shut off

trains, processions, parades,
time organized in sequences

the time of light

the San-mon gate of Nanzen-ji
massive, unique
one among the thousand gates

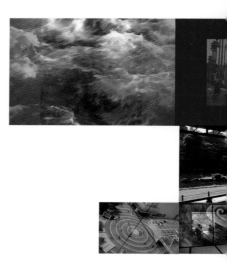

    gates, bridges, corridors
    intricate passages in time
    sequences of infinity

in the Nihonshoki, the introduction of the art of gardens is linked to the arrival in the year 612 of a Korean refugee who, in order to gain residence in Japan, called attention to his talent for representation and was put in charge of tracing the figures of Mount Sumeru and the Bridge of Wu in the southern garden of the palace. People called him then the "pathmaker" (*michiko no takumi*)

    all lie uncomfortably between
    fact and fancy
    there where
    in the heart of an insular culture
    even the mobile world
    of invisible narrators
    of uneven times and odd rhythms
    finds its place
    in the precise framing of daily activities

Upon looking at how time is expressed in writing and how a death can express the passing of a historical age and its people, Kenzaburo Oe particularly recalls the death of Tsuburaya Kokichi, a young runner in the Olympics, who committed suicide in 1968 because, in his own words, the man was "too tired to run" for national prestige.

But, in the history of women's resistance and of women pathmakers of the sixties, it is the name of Kamba Michiko that comes to many women's lips as I inquire about the one political figure that strikes their memory.

Kamba Michiko's death may be said to have marked the turning point for the image the world had of Japan. With the repression of a civic society, what was then launched was a new image of Japan as a corporate society for which the only way to progress was the Western way.

Highly advanced and yet not independent

a global economic power struggling today to re-orient itself
to turn toward Asia without turning its back on the West

"Ambivalent Japan": isolated from other Asian nations and confined to Her half-scrutable strangeness by the West. In America, the very nation with which She signed the Security Treaty, suspicion is always lurking at the slightest sign of trade competition

FUTSU

the ordinary

IJO

the extra-ordinary

part-time women's labour, the million-yen wall
full-time family shadow work
the issue of homemaking
indispensable but invisible

Japan's stigma: the lot of its millions of outcasts and others—natives, exiled and
immigrants discriminated against (the Ainu, the Okinawan, the Burakumin, the
ethnic Koreans, and also the Chinese, the workers from Southeast Asia and the
Middle East)—all essential to Japan's progress and identity as a modern nation,
but confined to the underpaid, underprivileged margins

sliding open the blinding screens
I find myself stepping suddenly into the fourth dimension

speeding: everywhere one turns, someone is trying to sell speed
the fast species

the peculiar vibrations of graphic space, graphic time
the whole of visual environment finds its dynamism in the graphic line

keep to the time as required by tele-vision
screen space, say TV programmers
is always, always limited
but, as novelist Hisashi Inoue once said,
"I don't like bonsaiism...it's perfectly alright for some trees to grow big and wild"

the journey unfolds through the unseen but dominant framing of time

three times in one
present past future

as soon as one is in time
time no longer flees
standing still, it opens out

TRAIN TIME—NOH TIME
NO
NO TRAIN

Noh performance, as Soseki affirmed, is "three-tenths real emotion, seven-tenths technique" layers upon layers, clad with "art" to weave a tapestry of gestures of serenity that is to be found nowhere else in this world
yet, for Enchi Fumiko, we are Noh actors moving in the screen space of ritual, ethical life

the skill of behaviour, the craft of framing time, the art of paths
what else but the shape of living caught in the unfolding course of a digital play?

The determination to never wage a war again, as Kenzaburo Oe remarks, is a resolve adopted not by innocent people but people stained by their own history of territorial invasion

video time: a temporal trap
remote control and the law of least action
individual inertia as the result of ever-increased speed
of programmed agency

from inside the train
looking up
at the wired sky
moving on
wireless, rootless, unplugged

Kisho Kurosawa spoke of Japanese aesthetics as being primarily two-dimensional and gray. He laid focus on temporal intervals, intermediary zones and silent spaces; on the necessity to create with the ma of things and events, for a person without ma is scorned as a stupid fellow, one who lacks calm and is unable to tune in with the grey zone of Japanese culture

      images have come upstream towards the traveller
they appear on the screen with each step
front foot back foot
one moves with them
one stops by the road to chat with them
and they know how to show certain things
but cannot always tell why they show things the way they do

The fourth dimension: to be attentive to the infra-ordinary
an intrusion of eternity

"The entire world is our mind, the mind of a flower." —Dogen zenji

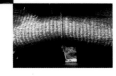

Text and stills excerpted from
The Fourth Dimension (87 min. digital
film by Trinh T. Minh-ha, produced by
Jean-Paul Bourdier, Japan−USA, 2001).
Original visual layout by Ellen Gould.

FILMIC FOREIGNESS, FILMIC HOMECOMING: ON GARINÉ TOROSSIAN'S *GIRL FROM MOUSH*
Marie-Aude Baronian

In what follows, I would like to consider the question of "foreignness of film" as a filmic experience of being/feeling foreign. What I mean by this is not the feeling of strangeness in the reception of filmic material, or the mimetic depiction of foreign matters in film, but rather the extraneous identity experienced through and within filmic texture. Filmic texture can be a place of foreignness—in terms of exile, diaspora, exoticism—and/or "homecoming." This filmic foreignness is at stake in *Girl from Moush* (1993, 16 mm), a five minute film made by Gariné Torossian, a Canadian experimental filmmaker of Armenian origin.[1] This film relates to the Armenian diaspora or, more specifically, to the feeling and experience of foreignness that result from such a diasporic situation.

By representing the original homeland, Armenia, through images, Torossian expresses not only a sense of belonging to these images, but also sense of their foreignness, their exoticism. The film proposes a journey where all kinds of visual materials intermingle. *Girl from Moush* invites the filmmaker, as well the spectator, on a voyage: a literal, a virtual, an actual, and a dreamt one. This pictorial "pilgrimage" to Armenia reflects the memory of diasporic Armenians. As Gregory Goekjian has argued in his pertinent article entitled "Diaspora and Denial: The Holocaust and the 'question' of the Armenian Genocide":

> Put simply, the Holocaust constituted a symbolic end to the Jewish diaspora, whereas the Genocide is the symbolic origin of the Armenian diaspora. In actuality, of course, an enormous and powerful Jewish diaspora remains after the Holocaust, and Armenia had a significant diaspora for centuries before the Genocide. But whereas the Holocaust resulted in the creation of a concentrated, modern center for Jewish historical discourse, the Armenian genocide erased that center, creating a "nation" that has had to exist in exile and memory-in diaspora. (3)

1. I want to make use of this opportunity to express my gratitude to Gariné Torossian who kindly supplied me with all the visual materials I needed.

Although Torossian does not address directly or perhaps even intentionally the issue of the Catastrophe, I do think that the Armenian Genocide is "present" (though never visible) in/outside of the film. This tragic Event "floats" in the shadows of the film. I do not want to raise the essentialist idea that the Armenian Genocide is automatically an issue for every Armenian artist, but I do believe that because of the overwhelming power of this denied historical event and because of its diasporic consequence, it is somehow unavoidable to think about Armenian identity without at least a slight allusion to 1915. One such allusion is found in Torossian's title. Moush, which is located in present day Turkey, was part of historical Greater Armenia. Moush was also the main site of the massacres and deportations of the Armenian people during the 1915 Genocide. Nevertheless, I admit that *Girl from Moush* is not *about* the Genocide, in that it does not address it as such. Furthermore, Torossian's work is neither a victimologic keen of homelessness, nor an ethnocentric promotion, nor an epistemological or psychoanalytic need to comprehend and define fully oneself. Still, it is remarkable that the persistent non-recognition of the Genocide dispossesses the Armenian diaspora of the appropriate language to properly or explicitly recount their slaughtered ancestors and their lost patrimony.

Girl from Moush consists of blurry found footage, a hand-made collage of images and various reproductions from picture books, calendar images, still photographs depicting churches and other Christian signs, landscapes, (family) portraits, and all kind of artwork such as manuscripts, Armenian graphics, and architectural details. The images are grainy, and many frames are scratched giving an impression of "agedness" and archive. Actually, the images are photos of photographs copied onto Super 8 and then shot on 16 mm. Most of the images move repeatedly and quickly; they are dynamic, disturbing, and quite shaky. This contrasts with some of the Christian images, which convey tranquillity and are sometimes represented fully as complete objects on the screen. In order to distinguish and identify every detail of the film, the viewer must be attentive and concentrated.

Torossian's film concentrates on iconic figures of Armenia, including the Christian churches of the homeland. Some of these visuals remind me of "postcard images" of the ancestral country—images that are preciously shared throughout the (Western) Armenian diaspora. These images appear somehow as nostalgic and even fetishistic. It is well known how fetishistic images can connote absence and death. Indeed, let us keep in mind that the destruction of Armenian churches was a logical consequence of the genocidal policy and its denial. Over one thousand churches were destroyed during the Genocide. Churches, as overly visible traces, constituted much too representative a proof of the Armenian existence as a Christian culture and civilization. Torossian, by the combination and reshaping of her images, emphasizes the auratic and spiritual value of those churches.

Armenia is depicted by Torossian as a timeless, spiritual, desired, and idyllic place, but the film also suggests that it exists as an aesthetic reality and inspiration—more specifically, a "real" place that nourishes her aesthetic language and intuition. In this regard, it is significant that in the film she pays homage to great Armenian artists. On the sound track, we hear Gariné Torossian naming important Armenian artists, such as the poet Sayat Nova and the composer Komitas. We also hear Armenian music in the background. The collage effect, or the "second-hand" aspect of the images, refers not only to Torossian's own memories but also to filmic memories: some of the images are portraits of the exiled Armenian filmmaker Sergueï Paradjanov, while others recall Paradjanov's *Color of the Pomgranates* (1971) (also titled *Sayat Nova*). Another Armenian artist is invoked in Torossian's recurrent use of church images from Atom Egoyan's *Calendar* (1993). Torossian incarnates herself in the film; she seems to be "in front of" the camera, part of the visual scene. It is as though she realizes that being part of Armenia is a complex matter: she is bound to Armenian roots, but only through images. The film puts visual memories *together*: personal, intimate (childhood) souvenirs and memories transmitted through the filmmaker's Armenian filiation and history, but also souvenirs and memories of images that belong to the history of film (Paradjanov). Both memories are part of the same process of image and identification.

The photographs in the film refer, to a certain extent, to the primary function of photography, which is to leave traces, tracks of what was once there. Photographs, in many diasporic communities, are seen as relics. But the indexical function of the photographs Torossian reproduces and reshapes quickly becomes iconic. In addition to this, we can say that the iconic aspect of these images appears through the filmic collage because their indexicality (their physical existence) is not taken for granted: the images are iconic because they exist as images in the Armenian imaginary and because they result from an imaginary act: the one of making images. As Torossian stated,

> I'm shown thinking of Armenia, wanting to be a part of it. After making the film I realized this is just a dream, a fantasy about a country I could never visit. No one could. You make it because you're blind to something. Afterwards you see what's there. I needed to make the film to grow up, to become wiser. (Hoolboom 151)

The way Torossian constructs and assembles the different images is like a reminder of her Armenian family: "My grandmother and all my aunts were knitters, and when I was making my experimental films it reminded me of that meticulous kind of work"

(Hoolboom 149). If the film takes the form of a collage, it evokes for me as well another typical Armenian cultural object: the Armenian carpets made out of assemblages of colours and graphs.

Torossian de-constructs and re-constructs, cuts and pastes, physically reshaping the images as she redefines her bond with and fascination for her Armenian ancestors. Her experimental style not only underscores the presumption that filmic images are unable to represent such an overwhelming heritage but, furthermore, it reflects the different shades and shadows of a (tragic) past that escapes inscription and recognition, and can only be localized in the imaginary. If these (sacred) images are part of the collective memory of Armenians, they are still kept secret and not transmitted to the mainstream field of vision.

The foreignness in *Girl from Moush* is thus not only the subject matter represented as such, but is at stake *by* and *with* the medium itself. By saying so, I not only highlight the experimental genre of the film, but also attention on its origin as an act of transmission, an act of connection and re-placement. The film becomes a "homecoming," even if film means an imagined place. It would be wrong, then, to state that the filmic image is the illusory substitute for an absent reality, but rather that it expresses the only possible state of the imaginary (Rollet 103). The filmic texture Torossian creates evokes the possibility (or impossibility?) of reconstituting or recreating a sense of "community" out of amnesic events and fragments, a kind of aesthetic *Ersatz*. This sense of community can easily lead to idealization, nostalgia, or even fetishization. And yet the memories of the original homeland are inseparable from its History—the one that obviously resists official archive. The collage style of the film assumes, to a certain extent, that there is no transparent, intact, homogeneous, and official history waiting to be fully and mimetically depicted.

The film raises issues that are part of a contemporary debate concerning cultural identity. One perspective (considered classical and historical) argues that (ethnic) identity is always primordial, given, received, and transmitted, while another point of view (usually considered postmodern) conceives of identity as constructed, re-invented, and interpreted anew. *Girl from Moush* combines both. To be Armenian is certainly something inherited, transmitted (it can even be felt as a burden), but it also stands for a process, a movement of self-recreation. Armenia is not a fantasy, but for most diasporic Armenians their identity is actively recreated in an act of identification with the ancestral homeland. This film seems to visually address the slight or ambiguous difference between identity and identification: Am I *really* an Armenian, or am I identifying with those images that "constitute" Armenian collective memory? Actually, the film outlines that to "be" Armenian is to identify with—in this case—the homeland and the visually transmitted memories inherited by Armenians in the diaspora.

"I feel connected to every Armenian I meet," Torossian says in the film. This reflects a certain naïveté that is quite specific to the diaspora: the only thing Armenians have in common is this imagined land and its tragic history. What is meaningful is that, in contrast to other diasporic communities (Black or Jewish), the Armenian homeland is today identifiable on the map and exists spatially. However, it remains somehow "imagined," because most Armenians in the Western diaspora, like Torossian, have never lived or been there; they have only been there through the process of a "visual" journey. In the film we see Torossian day-dreaming as she walks. We also repeatedly see a superimposition of her face on images of Armenia. This emphasizes the fact that the images of her dreamt homeland are definitely felt from the inside.

Girl from Moush also deals with issue of translation. Translation here should not be understood as a matter of subtitles, as a cultural translation of the object of the film, or as a matter of adaptation for universal reception. The film does not belong to those visual productions that stimulate ethnographic fascination with the exotic. "Armenianness" is not depicted as an exotic decorative element; on the contrary, the exoticism is felt by the viewer when he or she realizes the foreign "untranslatability" of those visual signs. If the film deals with exoticism at all, it is the exoticism of the fragmented memories and not the exoticism that could delight the spectator looking for escapism. Put differently, exoticism and foreignness are not to be found in the literal depiction of another culture, but in the foreignness that emanates from Torossian's own vision and from her experience of feeling/being foreign to herself. The film does not aim to translate foreignness or to fully grasp it as something evident. Rather, it maintains a certain untranslatability that Torossian expresses in her pictorial re-compositions. The viewer experiences untranslatability when he or she perceives those images coming from a definitely foreign "out there."

Throughout the film, we hear in the background the distant voice of a woman—Torossian herself. She is speaking on the phone, first in Armenian and then in English, repeating the same words. Since nobody answers her, the call remains an internal monologue. This call without an answer expresses Torossian's longing for an (imaginary) land without a real destination. The words express her profound and passionate emotional attachment to the legacy of Armenian roots:

This is partially what she says:

> . . . Armenia will always be in my heart . . .
>
> It will always make me feel . . .
>
> make me feel . . . complete knowing that I have this wonderful culture

> even though I haven't been there...
> I feel that I have been there because it is always with me
> and so wherever I go, wherever I fly I am always Armenian and I will always
> have my...culture
> and I always tell everybody whenever I hear an Armenian piece or music
> or the words of an Armenian poet,
> it always make me feel that there is something inside...
> that something...

She continues to speak until the end of the film interrupts the monologue. Speaking two languages is not only a question of translating from a foreign language into a "mainstream" one. Here, it highlights the diasporic experience or the fragile shift between origin (cultural roots) and assimilation, between the private, intimate language, and the public one.

Does Torossian want us to recognize, identify, and translate her language, in order to actually comprehend it? Not especially, as the "background" effect of her voice, which is almost inaudible, seems to indicate. Yet, do we actually need a translation to overcome foreignness? *Girl from Moush* cannot function through a linguistic or ethnic translation. The only translation that occurs here is not the one of language or of cultural context, but one of transmission as an act: to translate memories, to translate the Memory of what is to some (the Armenian diaspora) an "over-remembered" land, and to others an "over-forgotten" one. In both cases, foreignness remains: for the Armenians who feel "stuck" in a foreign or exotic position, and for the viewers of such a film to whom the Armenian signs could appear foreign.

If the film gives us an impression of being spread, covered, and promulgated with images, it nevertheless recalls the absence or the forgetting of many other images; some images are omitted because they are non-representable, historically absent, or neglected. The images that remain refer to absence, but they also indicate an "over-present" kind of obsession especially because of this absence. The iconic figures of Armenia are especially iconic because they have been particularly cherished in the experience of diaspora, an experience that is inseparable from its tragic history. Again, I must stress, as I did before, that *Girl from Moush* does not aim to discuss at length this history or to call into question or recall its historical circumstances. The film is, in Laura Marks's words, "not sanguine about finding the truth of a historical event so much as making history reveal what it was not able to say. . . . A film can recreate, not the true historical event, but at least another version of it, by searching into the discursive layers in which it was found" (29, 60–2).

If the film can be experienced as foreign by the viewer, and as a place of foreignness by Torossian, it is also simultaneously experienced as a homecoming by her. Diasporic identities are not just represented in a film through the filmic material, but they exist or they allow themselves to exist with the film, as film. Metaphorically, we could draw a parallel between the work of (re-)making images and the work of mourning, that is to say the process resulting from the loss of something or someone we are attached to, which allows us to progressively detach ourselves from it.

Girl from Moush reveals that if foreignness can seem "uncomfortable," because some-how obsessively ongoing or ungraspable and un-representable, the only comfort that remains is that of the making and re-making of images.

Gregory Goekjian (1998)
Diaspora and Denial:
The Holocaust and the "question" of the Armenian Genocide
Diaspora 7.1

Michael Hoolboom (1997)
Inside the Pleasure Dome: Fringe Cinema in Canada
Toronto: Gutter Press

Laura U. Marks (2000)
The Skin of the Film:
Intercultural Cinema, Embodiment, and the Senses
Durham: Duke University Press

Sylvie Rollet (1997)
Le Lien imaginaire. Une poétique cinématographique de l'exil.
Positif N° 435

THOUGHTS ON BALKAN CINEMA
Fredric Jameson

For many people "the Balkans" means two closely identified, even superimposed historical images: the horrendous civil and ethnic wars of the last decade in what we are now supposed to call "the former Yugoslavia"; and the regional wars that accompanied the slow disintegration of the Ottoman Empire over the last two centuries. What these two images of history share is something called violence, a suspiciously imprecise and ideological concept about which any philosophical analysis would raise concerns, but which movies are supremely equipped to dramatize. Movies don't simply show us all kinds of violence more vividly than we could privately imagine; they also function to prove that such a thing exists in the first place. So movies are pre-eminently the place in which the Balkans can be shown, not only to have been violent at two crucial moments of their history, but to be the place of violence itself—its home and its heartland. This would be the meaning of the eruption of rage, infectious rage, at the end of Slobodan Sijan's *Marathon Family* (1982), a violence so intense it ends up burning up the film in the projector. Such movies seem to offer eyewitness proof that the people in the Balkans are violent by their very nature; they seem to locate a place in which culture and civilization—the law, civility, the most elementary forms of compassion and cooperation—are the thinnest veneer, at any moment capable of being stripped away to show the anarchy and ferocity underneath. The inhabitant of this landscape is the wild man of the Balkans (more specifically, of the Southern Slavs), to whom we will return later.

But is this stereotypical language ("veneer of civilization" and the like) not reassuring to the rest of us, whose veneer is supposed to be a good deal thicker—a veritable rhinoceros-hide of civilization, with deeply engrained habits of the law, of civilized behaviour and the like? One might at first think so, and perhaps in an older bourgeois class culture this would be the case. We would find our middle-class pride flattered by such glimpses of anarchy, that might, to be sure, take many stereotypical forms, not only the Balkans, but poor people, black people, the immigrant workers with their accents and cursing, and so on and so forth.

That bourgeois class culture does not really exist any more, I think, or not with the social power and influence it once had: perhaps there are parts of Europe that harbour more significant remnants of the older bourgeoisie (I think of West Germany, for example), but for the most part it is an endangered species. And this is why the wild man of the Balkans is likely to have an effect more potentially subversive and metaphysical than reassuringly stereotypical and confined to this or that Other. The spectacle of the "veneer of civilization" being stripped away can now hit home, and make us wonder whether everyone is not potentially subject to just such a reversion: whether the sub-human aggressivity we have hitherto attributed to specific national and racial groups may not in fact be part of human nature itself and a real possibility for any human group, for our own neighbours and fellow-citizens, for example (for it is never really something we imagine to threaten ourselves). Now we understand that human nature is itself evil, in some more fundamental way: and as the old Augustinianisms and Calvinisms are perhaps a little too antiquated and quaint for present-day tastes, we go back to Hobbes, and revel in his deeply satisfying pessimism. Yes, the most genuine emotion we can all feel is fear; yes, we really do need law and order and a strong Leviathan-type state to protect us against ourselves; yes, if we want a religion, let it be neo-Confucianism, with its cult of authority and the family, and the cosmic order of the universe, which we must reinstall in our gated communities, a lesson to be relearned even by our more exuberant businessmen. So the wild man of the Balkans has some ideological functions for the rest of us as well: but ideology can always think two thoughts at once, and is perfectly willing to harmonize the stereotype that the southern Slavs are naturally violent and aggressive with the other idea that we are all naturally violent and aggressive: the conclusion to be drawn being that both groups need order, whether imposed from the outside or from within.

I have been struck by the degree to which much of the recent writing by Balkan authors about the Balkans seem to turn defensively around the matter of stereotypes.[1] It is Sartrean: the Other alienates me by way of the look, which is to say by way of thinking something about me, reducing me to a stereotype, confining me within a racial or ethnic slur, something I am supposed to *be*, along with all the rest of my tribe.[2] But in the Sartrean scheme of things, there is no way of escaping this form of alienation: we are always looked at, we are always stereotyped, all our reactions to this situation—pride or shame—are so many vain struggles which change nothing in the fundamental alienation itself. We are only free to conceal it from ourselves as best we can, something a big and powerful country can do, but that smaller and more vulnerable countries are less able to achieve, whose citizens are constantly encountering the judgements of others and of foreigners on a daily or an existential basis. So one might argue that for Third World and other small countries the political and the existential coincide much more often than for those of us living in wealthy and autonomous life-areas.[3] This is to say that the illusions of private life, of existential experience, go hand in hand with a certain protection from the political (both internally and externally). For the unprotected, however, private experience—love, individual human relations, desire, and ambition—is interspersed and entangled with group and political/ethnic experiences, inseparable from judgements on me as the allegorical representative of this or that stigmatized

1. See, for example, Maria Todorova, Vesna Goldsworthy, and Dusan I. Bjlic and Obrad Savic.
2. Jean-Paul Sartre, *Being and Nothingness*, Part III ("Being-for others").
3. This is the argument of my essay, "Third World Literature in the Era of Multinational Capitalism."

group. But this situation ought to be an advantage for the art of such countries, which is able to register the group-political as an existential fact and not as some external, extrinsic, foreign-policy-type contingency. Balkan art, then, ought to be able to register the alienation of being "from the Balkans" in a different way than those rare American political works devoted to showing what the "ugly American" looks like to the outside world. And indeed, I think that much recent film production does bear this external gaze within itself in a constitutive way and includes the external look of foreigners, of the West, of the US, in the image thus presented. We are like this, and in fact, we're even worse than you thought we were, and we love it! This is the image of the wild man reassumed and reasserted, comically in *Black Cat, White Cat* (Emir Kusturica, 1998), and with its full quotient of horror in *Wounds* (Srdjan Dragojević, 1998), which retranslates such alienation by the other into the more contemporary language of the media and of spectacle society.

Slavoj Žižek has proposed a rather different notion of these ethnic stereotypes, recalling Freud's doctrine of the "narcissism of minor differences." Here our identification with our "neighbours" (in the Biblical sense of the *prochains* and the *semblables*, those almost exactly like us) is reduced to a small individual trait of some kind whose significance thereby comes to be magnified in an excessive and indeed obsessive and ominous persistence and omnipresence.[4] But Žižek also argues that in the older federal situation (of Yugoslavia) these ethnic differences—and for example the ethnic jokes which expressed them—were not the occasion for tension, conflict, insult, disrespect or discrimination, but rather opened up a space in which affectionate inclusion and solidarity could be ritually reaffirmed. This idea suggests at the very least that we need to return to the history of Yugoslavia over a long period and to interrogate the various

4. Sigmund Freud, *Civilization and its Discontents*, Standard Edition, volume XVIII, chapter V. See also Slavoj Žižek, *Tarrying with the Negative*, chapter 6, "Enjoy your Nation as Yourself."

kinds of works that history has enabled there, rather than to confine ourselves to the short, violent, and by now already thoroughly stereotyped memory of Bosnia and the Kosovo war.

I have felt it was useful, as a foreigner, for foreigners to the Balkans to recall some of the things Yugoslavia also meant to us, if only to make Yugo-nostalgia more vivid and actual for all of us:

> Here we built new houses with red roofs and chimneys where storks will nest, with wide-open doors for dear guests. We'll thank the soil for feeding us and the sun for warming us and the fields for reminding us of the green grass of home. With pain, sorrow, and joy, we shall remember our country as we tell our children stories that start like fairy tales: once upon a time, there was a country. . . .[5]

For that, we do not need to go back as far as the interwar period, with its monarchies and nascent fascisms: for the West, of course, that was the Balkans of espionage, of Eric Ambler novels and of numerous films (such as Hitchcock's *The Lady Vanishes* of 1938), whose dynamic was very different from the later Cold War forms of what I would call an almost theological spy narrative (as in Graham Greene and LeCarré). The older 1930s variety tended to include Turkey in the Balkans, and thus to slip over into a well-nigh Levantine vision of sinister and terrifying Mediterranean merchant multiculturalism, of the kind still deployed in Orson Welles's masterpiece *Monsieur Arkadine* (1955).

This semi-comical Balkans, then, in the war, gives way to the most immediate pictures of anti-Nazi movements, which, like the French Resistance, are autonomous and show heroic left or communist militants in their own right, without the taint of subservience to Stalin. These are famously home-grown movements which owe little or nothing to

5. The ending of Emir Kusturica, *Underground* (1995–7).

Soviet direction, and which offer the ultimate alternatives in what is as much a civil war between fascists and communists as it is a struggle against the external Hitlerite invader and occupier. In France, we witness an ambiguous ending, in which the left Resistance triumphs over the right-wing revolution of Vichy, but is then itself betrayed in the immediate postwar Liberation period by the onset of a Cold War in which France is torn between the two external and equally alien superpowers of the US and the Soviet Union. In the Balkans, success and failure are more clearly demarcated: we have on the one hand the triumph of the partisans in Yugoslavia, and on the other hand, the tragedy of Greece, with its British and later American repression of the revolution. The latter ironically makes for more interesting art and filmic representation than the former, for what are perhaps self-explanatory reasons: you celebrate a triumph rather than represent it, and in that sense perhaps the greatest work of art celebrating the Yugoslav victory, or better still, the victory that became Yugoslavia as such in its modern postwar sense, is not to be found in any particular aesthetic text but rather in the construction of the figure of Marshal Tito himself, with Fidel one of the few great revolutionary leaders to come through demarxification and the triumph of capitalism without serious revision or post-traumatic vilification and the posthumous revelation of clay feet or worse.

But in Greece, with the interminable agony of its counterrevolutionary repression, the immense artistic monuments are the early films of Theo Angelopolos. These are far more stunning, in my opinion, than the later humanist, more generally Balkan and, if I may say so, post-Greek statements of which *Ulysses' Gaze* (1995) is only the best known. But *The Traveling Players* (1975), *The Hunters* (1977), and *Alexander the Great* (1980), are among the greatest political films ever made—and haunting narrative constructions which "Balkan film," if there is such a category, must necessarily be proud to include within its pantheon.

We then necessarily move on to the construction of socialism in Yugoslavia, a period which, to be sure, and, as is the case in most other peoples' democracies, produces a multitude of what will come after the fact to be identified as dissident statements. But I think we must be very careful with these categories. The "dissident" no longer exists as a social type, in the East or anywhere else; but I believe that this representational category is more appropriately to be compared with the existential hero or anti-hero of an older period in the West than with any narrative or representational character with genuine political content. Besides this, we must take into account a different type of political art, only for the West or for a capitalist public indistinguishable from dissidence; and that is what surely must be called the critique of bureaucracy from a socialist point of view. In the West we have always been inclined to feel that there never was such a thing as a socialist point of view and that nobody ever really supported the construction of socialism, that such an idea was mere communist or Stalinist propaganda. Perhaps the current wave of nostalgia for socialism sweeping across the Soviet East and China may provoke a certain rethinking of this Western doxa. At any rate, much of what we take to be a critique of communism was in fact a constructive and socialist critique of the errors or flaws, the human failures, vices and misjudgements, at work in the construction of the communist system itself—most notably, of course, the negative features of bureaucracy. But the critique of bureaucracy is only anti-communist if bureaucracy is grasped as the inevitable end product of any socialism. If you take a different perspective, for example that of Max Weber, modernity is grasped in all its forms as being necessarily bureaucratic, and an inspection of any corporation would reveal it to be as profoundly bureaucratic as government itself. In that sense, then, the task of warning about the excesses and deformations of bureaucracy becomes a permanent function of socialist art as such, and should not be confused with a dissident repudiation of socialism. But the only Eastern works I know to confront these paradoxes directly and overtly are rather to be found in Poland, in the early films of Krystof Zanussi—great Platonic debates between realists and idealists, bureaucrats and young altruists, within the system[6]—as well as in that political masterpiece of what we may call the Zanussi school, namely Kieslowski's early film *Camera Buff* (1979), in which a well-meaning amateur film-maker imagines himself to be unmasking the lies of the communist bureaucracy, when he is in fact destroying the very humane and progressive projects concealed behind those official lies. Dusan Bjelic has suggested to me that this category is in Yugoslavia exemplified by so-called black film, or, in other words art films of which Dusan Makavejev's *W.R. or the Mysteries of the Orgasm* (1971) is only the most famous. But unlike what takes place in the other Eastern countries, black films combine existentialism with Godard—or *nouvelle vague* type experimentation, including a good deal of 1960s extreme leftism along with the sexual politics of Wilhelm Reich, around which Makavejev's film turns.

But the slippage from a socialist critique of socialism to a dissident anti-communism is something that not only takes place in the mind of the critic, as when the Khrushchevite and socialist critiques of early Solzhenitsyn, such as *A Day in the Life of Ivan Denisovitch*, are read in the spirit of his later anti-communism. Such slippage can also take place within the work itself, something I take to be the case with Grlic's 1981 film *You Love Only Once*, weirdly distributed as *The Melody Haunts My Reverie*, starring Miki Manojlovic. Parenthetically, Manojlovic might well be a leading candidate for the very paradigm

6. See for example *The Structure of Crystals* (1969).

of the Yugoslavian wild man, something on the order of the young James Woods for the American 1960s and 1970s. At any rate, Grlic's film dramatizes the situation of a prototypical wild man, whose arbitrary and aberrant decisions epitomize everything dangerous about a bureaucratic system and a party made up of cronies with the aura of a partisan past: so far the film is a critique of socialism, if we read it right. But these situations are difficult for the outsider to read. Few foreign spectators, for example, will have realized that the "victim" of repression in Kusturica's 1985 *When Father Was Away on Business* (yes, it is Miki Manojlovic again) has been condemned and sent to prison not because he is a liberal but rather precisely because he is a Stalinist and anti-Titoist, and has been arrested in the great anti-Soviet purge of 1948 (after the break with Stalin). So Western pro-dissident sympathies suddenly find themselves turning into the proverbial mixed feelings. But then, as the wild man of *The Melody Haunts My Reverie* is tamed by love and then institutionalized in a version of the Soviet dissident mental hospital, he becomes a rather different and more existential figure, somewhat on the order of *Pierrot le fou* (1965); and I take it his ultimate suicide is meant as a dissident condemnation of the system as a whole.

Now I want to say two more things about the old Yugoslavian federal system before moving on to modern times. One of the nastier things said today about Tito (as about Stalin himself for the Soviet federation) is that he repressed the identity of the various "nationalities" and thus—the image is that of the explosion of a pressure cooker—caused their tensions to build up to the later explosion. The most illustrious use of this wholly conventional figure can no doubt be attributed to President Clinton, who, in a 1994 speech, said that the Cold War's end "lifted the lid from a cauldron of long-simmering hatreds" (Woodard 426). (One can add to that the historical myth Žižek is never tired of denouncing, namely that of the age-old enmities of the various peoples, the battle of Kosovo in 1389, and so forth.) One can only conclude that if Tito really suppressed all this, he did a good thing. But what I do feel it is necessary to read into the record is a very different interpretation of the Yugoslav civil wars—that of Susan Woodard in her essential book, *Balkan Tragedy*, in which she sees this bloody explosion, not as a Balkan matter, but rather as the result of globalization. It is, in other words, a postmodern tragedy rather than a premodern one, and in order to understand it we need to have a closer look at the way the Yugoslav federal system operated and must also be mindful of the unique historical moment at which that operation was most successful. That moment was of course the Cold War, and it is not necessary to remind anyone of the exceptional position of Yugoslavia between the three worlds, with all of whom it traded and whose diplomatic equilibrium assured the country's external economic and military security, at least until imports from the West became increasingly attractive and generated ever greater loans and debts.

But it is the internal situation which is less well known, and which Susan Woodard has observed "was not held together by Tito's charisma...but [rather] by a complex balancing act.... Far from being repressed, national identity and rights were institutionalized—by the federal system, which granted near statehood to the republics, and by the multiple rights of national self-determination for individuals" (Woodard 45). Thus a first balance existed between the federal (or central or national) government, and the six republics; a second kind of balance then existed between the territorial organization of these republics (largely ethnic, that is to say, Croatian, Serbian, Slovenian, and later on, Bosnian or Muslim) and the actual "national" or "ethnic" identity of individuals, which could of course, in law as well as in fact, be different from the national or ethnic affiliation of the republic in which he or she lived. This is an attempt to resolve the age-old dilemma of the opposition between territory and family affiliation, in a way that avoids either ethnic cleansing or the dictatorship of the majority. As for the tensions, that is the whole point; and any reflection on the physical process of balancing or equilibrium makes clear that tension is necessary to it and is, as it were, the raw material of the balancing itself. Tension is, in other words, necessary for the equilibrium to be maintained: it does not menace the equilibrium so much as it allows it to exist in the first place.

This political and juridical account needs to be supplemented by an economic one. On the one hand, the Yugoslav system offered a startling variety of property forms, and not merely the stark opposition between private and public as we imagine it over here. On the other, one of the fundamental roles of the federal system was to balance—a word it seems impossible to avoid in the Yugoslav context—the needs and demands, as well as the natural resources, of the various republics against one another. We are less aware of this process in our own federal system, where it is concealed by the appearance of personal deals and seemingly suspicious or corrupt trade-offs between politicians (a form I'm sure it sometimes had in Yugoslavia as well). In any case a policy of redistribution is always certain to arouse resentment and opposition, unless reinforced by a fundamental national commitment to achieving economic equality and to a federal system whose reason for being is precisely such a policy.

The weakening of federal authority, however, comes from the outside. Clearly enough, with the end of the Cold War, Yugoslavia loses its strategic position and ceases to be of much interest to its wealthier former partners (in any case now reduced to the US and the new European Union, since both the Second and Third Worlds are by now a shambles). But it is important that we not confuse the pressure of the international situation with the kinds of knee-jerk market propaganda only too frequently peddled in the West and reaffirmed without question in the latest history, where "economic reform" always means privatization: "In 1987 a reform-minded federal premier, Ante Markovic, began to implement just the kind of economic reforms that were necessary...but the trickle of the good news proved to be too little, too late" (Cox 133). On the contrary, the fateful sapping of the federal system begins earlier, and precisely with privatization and Reaganite neo-liberalism and with our old friend the International Monetary Fund (IMF). For the price of loans whose interest has skyrocketed is now, as always, the extraction from the borrowing country of promises about fiscal responsibility, balancing the budget, cutting inflation, austerity, and the reduction or elimination of social services and the like—a dogmatic neo-liberal policy whose disastrous consequences the anti-globalization movement has certainly made known today, but which you can examine in detail in the revealing book by the Nobel-Prize-winning Clinton economist Joseph Stiglitz, called *Globalization and its Discontents*. These policies were no less destructive twenty years ago in Yugoslavia than around the rest of the developing world yesterday and today. In Yugoslavia their implementation meant not only that the federal government could no longer sustain its balancing act between the republics, but also that the very essentials of socialist prosperity, full employment and extensive social services in health and education, had to be scrapped. But these unpopular measures, forced on the central (federal) government, are reinforced by an even more horrendous policy, namely the shift to more direct relations between foreign financial institutions and the individual republics. After this, the dissolution of the federal system is only a matter of time; the systematic dismantling of socialist institutions under IMF pressure is the cause of that dissolution, whose results were, as we know, even more disastrous than the "transition to capitalism" encouraged in the former Soviet Union. Milosevic may well be a war criminal, but the IMF gave him the historical opportunity to become one and deserves a special kind of indictment and opprobrium in its own right.

I have not until now mentioned that feature of Yugoslav socialism which was most important for the West in the earlier and more prosperous years, and that is the famous idea and practice of workers' self-management, which constituted the central claim of the Tito regime to a unique tradition of Marxism and socialism unlike any other (the idea of "national communism" was apparently an American foreign-policy propaganda invention). But maybe self-management was also a feature of Titoist propaganda? I know that in later years, as many of my Slovenian friends assure me, self-management became an official propaganda slogan for Yugoslav communist party (The League of Communists) in its intellectual and discursive struggle against other political tendencies. Meanwhile, there is also the practical and historical question of the degree to which autonomy was ever realized or put into practice: did not the various authorities still control quotas and investments, and to what degree, within that complex and interactive economic network I have been describing, could any individual factory set its policy in the first place? Well, we do not have to decide that here: it is as an ideal that workers' self-management functioned in Western left politics and as an ideal that we may still consider it now. So I am delighted to quote one of my Slovenian comrades against himself: indeed, this is an important reflection in our context in general, and bears on the distinction between historical inaccuracy and Utopian truth in the cultural area. I quote it now at some length, with the reminder that Žižek is here talking about Stalinism and Soviet culture rather than about the Yugoslav situation:

What we are dealing with here is the old structural notion of the gap between the space and the positive content that fills it in: although, as to their positive content, the communist régimes were mostly a dismal failure, generating terror and misery, they at the same time opened up a certain space, the space of utopian expectation which, among other things, enabled us to measure the failure of really existing socialism itself. What the anti-communist dissidents as a rule tend to overlook is that the very vital assumptions which they themselves drew on to criticize and denounce the everyday terror and drudgery were generated and sustained by the communist breakthrough, by its attempt to escape the logic of capital. In short, when dissidents like Havel denounced the existing communist régime on behalf of authentic human solidarity, they (unknowingly, for the most part) spoke from the place opened up by communism itself—which is why they tend to be so disappointed when the "really existing capitalism" does not meet their high expectations. Perhaps Vaclav Klaus, Havel's pragmatic double, was right when he dismissed Havel as a "socialist."

The most difficult task is thus to confront the radical ambiguity of even the most "totalitarian" Stalinist ideology. While the universe of Stalinist politics undoubtedly was the universe of arbitrary terror and unheard-of hypocrisy, one should bear in mind how, for spectators across Europe in the late 1930s, the great Soviet films (say, the Maxim Gorky trilogy of Mark Donskoi) epitomized the authentic sense of human solidarity.

He then cites a key scene from a film about the Civil War:

It is easy to claim, in a quick pseudo-Marxist way, that such scenes were simply the ideological legitimization of the most brutal terror. However, no matter how manipulative this scene of the revolutionary trial is, no matter how contradicted it was by the arbitrary harshness of actual "revolutionary justice," it nonetheless bears witness to a new sense of justice; as such, such scenes install in viewers new ethical standards by which reality is measured—the shocking outcome of this exercise of revolutionary justice, the unexpected resignification of "severity" into severity towards social circumstances and generosity towards people, cannot but produce a sublime effect. In short, what we have here is an exemplary case of what Lacan called the "quilting point" (*point de capiton*), of an intervention that changes the co-ordinates of the very field of meaning: the old Bolshevik does not plead for generous tolerance against severe justice, he redefines severe justice itself in terms of excessive forgiveness, and generosity. Even if this is a deceptive appearance, there is, in a sense, more truth in this appearance than in the sad social reality that generated it. (Žižek 1999, 46–7)

Still, we have little enough from this period in the way of historical representations of Yugoslav socialism which might be compared either to the Kieslowski film already mentioned or to something like Wajda's 1977 *Man of Marble* (the later *Man of Iron* from 1981, despite the virtuoso performance of the unforgettable Krystyna Janda, is a far more tendentious and ideological affair). In any case, the reconsideration of Titoist communism—a national home-grown matter—has to be rather different than that of Polish reconsideration of their local Stalinism (to be sure, itself a far milder and more benign phenomenon than those in many of the other Eastern countries).

It is, however, surprising that as yet so little of current cultural production in the East, and not only in the former Yugoslavia, has come to terms with the socialist past. At a time when it seems impossible to escape discussions of trauma, national memory, monuments, and everything connected with the coming to terms with the past, I feel entitled to say my piece on the subject: in my opinion, the great psychoanalytic discoveries (the talking cure itself) have encouraged a pop-psychological idea that collectivities can somehow "work through" their past and undo its grip in some positive and healthy fashion. I think this is a ridiculous idea, and that on the collective level it simply amounts to a call for a new national-propagandistic version of the national history to replace whatever older one. There is no coming to terms with the past: human beings unfortunately face a stark alternative between forgetting it and reliving it traumatically. The idea of reconciliation with the past is simply another way of forgetting it, by turning it into an image, or inserting it into a fairy tale, or in some other way drawing its sting by way of aesthetization. One of the great functions of art is indeed to offer just such aestheticizing anaesthesia (one of its other functions being rather to restore and sharpen memory and trauma—in fact, art has many possible functions, none of which can be judged good or bad in the absolute). I take it that for most people, the conventional ethical choice would be for confronting something rather than escaping, repressing, or forgetting it—but in my opinion that's also just a standard humanist reflex and not any genuine existential leap.

So I cannot deplore the repression of the socialist past in ethical terms, nor in those of a psychology of memory and trauma which I believe to be false in the first place. Rather I do so from another vantage point—that of the Other. I think that this avoidance corresponds to the interiorization of a Western, perhaps even American, gaze and judgement within the national mind (if I can use shorthand like that). It is thought that for the US the socialist past is something shameful, and a kind of stigma on the order of cannibalism, group marriage, bad plumbing, and the like: something you do not want outsiders to know about. So you pretend it never existed, and you deeply bury any idea that it was something to be proud of and a rare social achievement which groups in the future will want to return to and to learn from. Globalization and the world system today are built on complex networks of envy, in which just such a surrender to supposed Western values and attitudes—and just such an interiorization of them—are part and parcel of Western hegemony as such. In my opinion things like Russian Sots-art, in which Stalinism is ironized with all the trappings of a grotesque nostalgia art, is a far more original reaction to the problem of the past and of the gaze of the Other on that past, than simple omission or oblivion. I realize, of course, that the problem is not just cultural but political to the degree to which *ostalgie*, a nostalgia for the socialist past, is also for much of the population a very real indignation at the loss of the structural advantages of the socialist or communist system, and at the subsequent impoverishment of their own lives.

The new Balkan wars have effectively wiped many of these concerns away. Before I offer a few concluding thoughts on that final period and on the reification of violence, I want rapidly to recapitulate my theory of national cinema,[7] if only as a checklist against which to measure our various options here, which are not necessarily national in the limited sense, and which range from Croatian, Serbian, or Bosnian cinema, through Yugoslav cinema as such, all the way to some generalized notions of a Balkan cinema which could include Bulgaria and Greece and perhaps even Turkey. It is not, I hasten to add, a fully developed and systematic theory. I first wanted to make the point that a genuine national cinema will also tend to include its form within itself as content: not as nationalistic themes or some ethnic jingoism, as rather in the presence of collective assemblages—masses of people moving together, groups as agencies rather than individuals, a decentering combined with unusual kinds of multitudes and numerous bodies interlinked. The numerous orgies and popular festivals in Balkan films is quite enough to document the presence of this particular feature (I've already quoted from

7. "Preconditions of a National Cinema," unpublished paper.

the feast at the end of *Underground*), but even more than that I think one can single out the thematics of Gypsy or Romany life as a kind of *mise en abysme* of this feature. The microcosm of Gypsy life is a kind of insert, smaller but more sharply detailed as in a telescopic reduction. Attracting both persecution and cultural envy (which are in any case the two sides of the collective coin), Gypsy life becomes the reduced symbol of the larger collectivity as a whole, held at a distance and defamiliarized, offering possibilities for the twin investment of attraction and repulsion (similar in that to anti- and philo-semitism in other areas). What happens later on, when the Gypsy becomes the gangster, and the outsider takes his revenge and reorganizes his small collectivity into a mafia, is to be sure dramatized in Kusturica's famous film, *The Time of the Gypsies* (1989); but I would also like to step across the geographical border for a moment and recommend to you an extraordinary Hungarian film, translated as *The Midas Touch* (1983), by Géza Bereményi, which reaches new heights in this thematic.

I take it that this collectivity is also designated within the form by a kind of repertory company aesthetic, in which the same actors return again and again, sometimes in minor roles, sometimes in starring ones: but in such a way that there is no real star system, and very often this kind of ensemble playing is developed out of a vibrant theatrical life (about which, in connection with Yugoslavia's multiple capital cities, I know very little). In our present context, one would wish to know something about the intermingling of actors from various nationalities (on the other hand, as with Tito himself, and on a lesser level Kusturica, on ethnic mingling and intermarriage which becomes its own kind of symbol).

Then there is the question of the individual filmmakers: for, in the case studies I alluded to, there seems always to be one dominant director or auteur who emerges from a variety of talented ones—in the case of the French 1930s, Jean Renoir; in that of the Polish 1960s, Wajda; in the case of more recent Taiwanese films, Hou Hsiao-hsien. The "great director" does not blot out the multiplicity of other filmmakers but rather confirms their existence and directs attention to those around him. I suppose one must also here also reckon in the politics of film festivals, access to foreign markers and foreign tastes, indeed in some cases the very production of films that cater to foreign audiences and their stereotypes and prejudices. This is why I would hesitate a good deal to promote Kusturica to this status, even though he is certainly the best-known abroad. Indeed, it could be argued that the eminence of the single great auteur is always as much a matter of historical luck, of international conjunctures, world taste, festival culture, and so forth, as it is due to merit. From that perspective, then, the Kusturica phenomenon would certainly repay analysis, because, whatever his own strength as a filmmaker (not necessarily superior to other filmmakers less well known abroad), his celebrity is a real media and historical fact.[8] My sense is that a certain degree of abstraction is today necessary for world cinema fame: at least in the US, if not in Hollywood itself, we are not interested in the specificities of other national situations, nor do questions of distinctive individual adult relationships arouse any curiosity either. They must either be eternally human or else sexy; thus, US, Hollywood, Academy Award interest has primarily gone to foreign movies about children (who are, of course eternally human); but I suggest that in this instance Gypsies can run a good second, being an exotic closed community with much human eccentricity, particularly when the more specific and sometimes even tragic features of their unique historical trajectory can be ignored. Nor does the question involve having to pick "the best" Balkan film, although here I would be tempted to mention my favourite, Slobodan Sijan's *Who's Singing Over There* (1980),

Now see two excellent recent books: Goran Gocić, *The Cinema of Emir Kusturica* and Dina Iordanova, *Emir Kusturica*. I also need to acknowledge my fundamental debt to two indispensable histories of this cinema: Dina Iordanova, *Cinema of Flames* and Daniel J. Goulding, *Liberated Cinema*.

and will come to a few more works that interest me in a moment. At least one might want to argue that Sijan is the most considerable Balkan auteur unknown or ignored in the West.

I also included a third feature in my general theory of national cinema. This has to do with stylistic distinction, and I should initially and insistently make a very strong differentiation between this matter of style and any vague notion of cultural difference or identity. I wish to argue that the latter are spurious concepts, of an external or tourist nature; nowadays, under globalization, musical preferences, physical decorations or clothing, religion and the like, are all essentially Disneyfied matters. When any of these details is parleyed into a philosophical issue and becomes part of a national program, then it has become a political issue and a symbol of something else. Is it possible that national culture survives only in pre-modern areas? I do think that the persistence of what is often called national culture in that sense is always a peasant matter. But there is no continuity or inheritance of values here; this or that kind of cultural fanaticism is dependent on social relations (i.e., as in the lynch mob, or the xenophobic village), and is of course a crucial feature of recent Yugoslav history as well.

Film style is something else; we may consider it either from a formalist or a commercial angle—in either case it is characterized by the attempt to do something altogether different and distinctive that differentiates the product from the norm or the mainstream. So obviously that norm will have to be in some sense interiorized, in order for the style to be able to negate it. There must, in other words, exist an Other to be thus cancelled and negated; and for the most part, from the 1930s to the present, but at whatever historical level of international distribution or (today) of globalization, that other has been Hollywood. Prolonged and infrequent takes (Ozu), jerky hand-held camera movement (*nouvelle vague*), plot developments which are not laboriously explained for the public (European narrative generally), etc., all these things are generally aimed against the dominant Hollywood or classical style; but they can occasionally also betray the use of Hollywood against the national norm (as famously with other features of the *nouvelle vague* in France). The question today, notoriously articulated by David Bordwell, is whether any stylistic opposition to Hollywood is any longer possible: this owing to the dependence on an essentially international (or festival) public and the colonization of the national public by Hollywood itself (378–85). It is perhaps the general equivalent of the specifically postmodern formal conviction that anything goes, and that therefore nothing is particularly shocking or distinctive any longer; and I leave the question open here.

I want to conclude with a juxtaposition of two films which seem to me remarkable and yet antithetical meditations on the phenomenon named violence, and therefore which, each of them, define and articulate it in a specific way and rescue the word from the realm of myths and vague ideas. Both of these films are remarkable achievements, which hold their own with anything currently being produced in the West (or anywhere else, for that matter; given the serious deterioration of American film it would scarcely be an achievement to overtake and surpass it). On the other hand, whether either of these films could be considered to be in any sense the sign of a national cinema either in the restricted or the generalized sense is doubtful; and perhaps in the age of globalization and the omnibus financing of individual film projects, such a thing is no more conceivable than the autonomy of the nation state itself (let along the chances for the reinvention of a new kind of federal system).

The two films I want to single out particularly are Goran Paskaljevic's *Cabaret Balkan* (originally titled *The Powder Keg*) and *Wounds*, by Srdjan Dragojević (both 1998). Both of these auteurs, from different generations, already have important achievements to their credit. I believe that one can take these films as two antithetical perspectives on violence, which I will call the mimetic or emulatory and the providential; or if you prefer, the diachronic and the synchronic. The two films might thus be said to correspond to something like the opposition between *Goodfellas* (Martin Scorsese, 1990) and *Pulp Fiction* (Quentin Tarantino, 1994) in the American tradition. The one—*Goodfellas* or *Wounds*—stages violence as something like a process of imitation or emulation, what René Girard calls mimesis in his earlier work. In Scorsese, the young inherit the behaviour of the older brothers or fathers, which they try to imitate on a new level and in a new historical situation, no longer appropriate to it. Thus ancient Mafia codes, already distant and degraded, are ill-adapted to the contemporary world, and at the end even the old wooden Massachusetts houses seem strangely archaic in the light of the new suburbs to which the protagonist is protectively transferred. Meanwhile, authority seems ever more distant; the older "brothers" are marginal rather than central; they would like to join the inner circle, but are dismissed from it by unseen authorities. And the different but equally unseen and distant authorities of the state then lift the protagonist out of his previous "familial" milieu into the new and anonymous one.

In *Wounds*, the immigrant inheritance is replaced by the more objective or external history of war itself, as the older generations are transformed by it. The mafia-style corruption that emerges from the wars is then itself devoid of legitimacy and becomes a laughable and pitiful caricature of the older authentic wild man: a drug-dealing would-be chieftain outgrown by the two boys, whose historical situation is comparable to the French youth of Musset's *Confessions d'un enfant du siècle*, born too late for the great Napoleonic adventure and seeking some appropriately heroic substitute for it in imitative violence which can no longer merely be classified as crime since it has outgrown all its utilitarianism. But now in Dragojević's film, a new technological mediator appears: it is the media itself, which by way of its real-life interview programs—emulations of American TV which far outdo their models since the people interviewed are real gangsters—now takes in charge the transformation of act into gesture and the production of images and the representation of violence, which however in this case is the same as violence itself. Or perhaps the philosophical inquiry here turns on the difference, in the case of violence, between appearance and reality, a difference that can presumably be verified in other, more normal settings. Yet it seems to me that *Wounds* takes the meditation on image or spectacle society and on the simulacrum farther than the tradition that has grown up around these phenomena in the West; and that it has invented a style of grotesque comic-book figures on the order of immense destructive babies stamping on Lilliputian realistic figures and flinging about elements of a realistic world in a fashion quite unlike the Hollywood cartoon style, and reminiscent in the West only of achievements like Oliver Stone's *Natural Born Killers* (1994) or the monstrous mechanic (Billy Bob Thornton) from the director's later *U-Turn* (1997).

Cabaret Balkan is quite different from this, and stages a totality of interrelations on the order of what I will call the providential narrative—the synchronic network or web of social and personal relationships, a narrative developed from George Eliot on down to its filmic variants in works like those of Altman or, later on, of Tarantino. Here a trajectory of chance movements and encounters suddenly projects an immense synchrony of seeming accidents which is in fact a vivid tableau of providential violence, of violence predestined by whatever absent force governs the explosive potential of this "powder keg" (the film's original title). We can certainly understand this potential from the outset as that of sheer rage, a pent-up frustration that any chance encounter—the initial (very minor) car accident caused by the young driver's inattention—can set off. I believe that rage in this form—well-known in the US from its newer forms (also associated with cars, as in road rage)—is rather distinct from the tradition of the wild man which is somehow definitively laid to rest in *Wounds*. The Wild Man can also know rage: he is also all by himself a kind of powder keg; but his principal attribute is unpredictability and capriciousness, rather than anger: if you expect an outburst of anger from him, he will be duty-bound to turn back your expectation by mildness or sympathy. As with so many Sartrean characters, his prime motivation is freedom, and in particular his own freedom from the forecasts and judgements of other people: he is "uncivilized" specifically in the sense in which he does not want to be alienated or imprisoned by other people.

The heroes of *The Powder Keg* are, on the contrary, still imprisoned, already imprisoned, in the network of the others, in the synchronic totality of destinies that makes up society itself; and it is this that leads to their explosive rage. You may well, if you like, consider this synchronic and providential pattern itself a figure for the national community or collectivity as such, as were the great multiple plots of Altman or indeed the web of destinies of George Eliot herself. We should also note the latency, within this pattern, of the synchronies in time itself and in chronology—what in science fiction is called time travel. The loops of the various destinies that criss-cross each other can in other words sometimes regress in time, give characters another chance, or on the contrary determine unexpected reversals. This is well brought out in another excellent film from the Balkans, *Before the Rain* (1994, by Milcho Manchevski), which is also to be numbered among the providential forms we are considering here. Providential does not here mean anything necessarily good or salvational; it can mean the opposite, namely death; or indeed both all at once, as in Tarantino's explicitly theological *Pulp Fiction*, or in the Mexican film *Amores perros* or the Brazilian *City of God*. But whatever the interpretive outcome—and I myself think that it is the pattern that is important and that is somehow beyond the good and evil of personal destinies—*Cabaret Balkan*, like *Wounds*, offers yet another extraordinary testimony to the ongoing vitality of cinema from the former Yugoslavia.

Dusan I. Bjlic and Obrad Savic, eds. (2002)
Balkan as Metaphor:
Between Globalization and Fragmentation
Cambridge: MIT Press

David Bordwell, Janet Staiger,
and Kristen Thompson (1985)
The Classical Hollywood Cinema:
Film Style and Mode of Production to 1960
New York: Columbia University Press

John K. Cox (2002)
History of Serbia
Westport: Greenwood Press

Sigmund Freud (1961)
Civilization and its Discontents
Standard Edition, volume XVIII
London: Hogarth Press

René Girard (1965)
Deceit, Desire and the Novel: Self and Other in Literature
Baltimore: John Hopkins University Press

Goran Gocić (2001)
The Cinema of Emir Kusturica
London: Wallflower Press

Vesna Goldsworthy (1998)
Inventing Ruritania: The Imperialism of the Imagination
New Haven: Yale University Press

Daniel J. Goulding (2002)
Liberated Cinema: The Yugoslav Experience, 1945–2001
Bloomington: Indiana University Press

Dina Iordanova (2001)
Cinema of Flames: Balkan Film, Culture, and the Media
London: British Film Institute

——(2002)
Emir Kusturica
London: British Film Institute

Fredric Jameson (1986)
Third World Literature in the Era of Multinational Capitalism
Social Text 15

Jean-Paul Sartre (1966)
Being and Nothingness, Part III ("Being-for others")
New York: Washington Square Press

Joseph Stiglitz (2002)
Globalization and its Discontents
New York: W. W. Norton

Maria Todorova (1997)
Imagining the Balkans
New York: Oxford University Press

Susan Woodard (1995)
Balkan Tragedy: Chaos and Dissolution After the Cold War
Washington: The Brookings Institution

Slavoj Žižek (1993)
Tarrying with the Negative:
Kant, Hegel, and the Critique of Ideology
Durham: Duke University Press

——(1999)
When the Party Commits Suicide
New Left Review 238

(DE)REALIZING CINEMATIC TIME
Mary Ann Doane

As you spin the Zoetrope, your eye fixed in position in front of small slits that it must ignore, the still images seem to come to life or to movement which, in the Zoetrope, is the same thing. The flicker (anticipatory of the cinema) and the gaps must disappear in order for motion to emerge as representation. The Zoetrope is only one of a number of "optical toys" produced in the nineteenth century (others include the Thaumatrope and the Phenakistoscope) which revealed the popular and scientific obsession with the phenomenon of movement and, in particular, with the representation, reproduction, repetition, or construction of a movement which does not really exist. Subtended by the still image, the "movement" of these toys is illusory, ethereal. Perhaps this is why, for Max Ernst, the Zoetrope was, above all, surreal. In a collage published in *Rêve d'un petite fille qui voulut entrer au Carmel* (Paris, 1930), a young girl, caught within the circular structure of a Zoetrope, covers her face with one hand in a move seemingly born of desperation as the pigeons inscribed on the inside of the circle disengage themselves and one escapes to the "outside." In Ernst's surreal vision, the Zoetrope becomes a prison, confining and constraining movement at the same time that it apparently seeks to liberate it from the deadly stillness of the pose.

This radical tension between stillness and movement and their relation to the representability of time haunts all the optical toys of the nineteenth century as well as the work of Étienne-Jules Marey, Eadweard Muybridge, and the emerging cinema itself. Marey's aim was the dissection and analysis of movement—its breakdown into a series of still poses—and entailed the obsessive search for the smallest unit of movement. He was famously opposed to the cinema, claiming that it added nothing to our senses, simply reaffirming and reconfirming ordinary vision. Marey's goal, on the contrary, was to produce a foreign vision, an unfamiliar vision of movement that would be synonymous with its scientific understanding. This was movement as it "had never been seen before," movement frozen in its various stages, bodies suspended in mid-air in positions unimaginable in previous eras. However, despite Marey's opposition to the cinema, his work of analysis was the condition of possibility for the production of cinematic movement as synthesis. Both are completely dependent upon instantaneous photography, and the clarity and legibility of motion in the cinema is based on the separability of moments in individual frames. Paradoxically, movement could only be represented by reducing it to its opposite—stillness. In this way, movement became subject to circulation and legibility by halting its vertiginous trajectory.

Instantaneous photography (or what we call instantaneous, which is only ever an aspiration) became possible around 1880 with the introduction of gelatin-silver bromide emulsions. Yet, these suspended and awkward movements, unfamiliar and uncanny, would not necessarily have struck the viewer as more "true" or more aesthetic for, as Roland Barthes has pointed out, beauty is always dependent upon a prior code, and these "instants" would have seemed to exist outside of codification, as pure contingency. Critics used words such as "bizarre," "unattractive," and "ungracious" to describe them and one writer of a handbook on photography, E. Giard, claimed that, "The real can sometimes be unreal" (Gautrand 241). It is perhaps impossible to overemphasize the potential strangeness of these moments in the late nineteenth century, particularly in contrast to the earlier daguerreotype, in which the stiff pose necessitated by the extended duration of the exposure was long familiar from portraiture in painting.

From one point of view, the cinema would seem to restore to things their continual happening—their familiarity, in effect—by obliterating awareness of the stillness that inhabit its movement. Still, there are two limits to this aspiration to fullness, originality, and continuity as the mark of movement's successful capture and domestication. One of these limits is internal, effectively invisible—the inevitable loss of time/movement necessitated by the camera's and projector's intermittent motion. The shutter blinds the spectator for almost 40 percent of the running time of any film. Much of the movement or the time allegedly recorded by the camera is simply not there, lost in the interstices between frames. In this sense, movement is still strange, alien. The second limit is an external (and visible) one, imposed by the necessity of an ending which is always yoked to the arbitrary, given the fact that things go on, while the film cannot. This limit is mirrored or mimicked internally (and still visibly) by the cut, which disrupts and shatters the continual unfolding of the real time of the shot and which, in its turn, reiterates the frameline and its signalling of absence. This series of Chinese boxes, by means of which the cinema represents time and movement, allows for the disengagement of temporality and its circulation as a commodity. Leisure time entails the consumption of time. What the film presents to its spectator is an experience of time, both familiar and strange.

The compatibility of this curious dialectic of stasis and mobility that subtends cinematic representation with the ancient problem posed by Zeno's Paradoxes (of the arrow, of the stadium, of Achilles, and the tortoise) was recognized very early. In the 1920s, Jean Epstein wrote of "the transmutation of the discontinuous into the continuous, negated by Zeno, but accomplished by the cinematograph" and claimed that "the cinematic image carries a warning of something monstrous" (23, 21). For Zeno, the infinite mathematical divisibility of movement—its separability into distinct static moments—proved its impossibility. For some writers, such as Epstein, the cinema undermined Zeno's argument. For others, such as Henri Bergson, the cinema's understanding of movement was as false and culpable as Zeno's.

Up until this point, I have deliberately left vague the relation between movement and time. At the philosophical level, they are frequently addressed as inseparable issues, indeed as the same ontological problem. If Zeno can disprove the possibility of movement, he can demonstrate that there is no change, hence, effectively, no passage of time. When Bergson argues for the indivisibility of movement as a continuous whole, he is arguing the same for duration. Movement is often represented as the embodiment of time and it is difficult to conceive of an access to time which is not mediated by movement or change (which itself seems ineluctably wedded to movement). The early cinema seems to corroborate these assumptions by foregrounding movement as the guarantee of cinema's ability to capture or store time; time becomes visible as the movement of bodies through space. Nevertheless, theoretically, time and movement are distinguishable as concepts. Gilles Deleuze, in what he claims is "the style of ancient philosophers" refers to time as the "number of movement"; it is sometimes dependent upon what it measures (that is, movement) and sometimes an entirely independent instance (Deleuze 1989, 35). Classical cinema, according to Deleuze, maintains the subordination of time to movement, but modernist cinema (primarily of the 1960s and 1970s) demonstrates that the cinema is capable of producing an image of pure time, liberated from movement. While even classical cinema disengages movement from bodies through processes of montage and camera movement, the "primitive" cinema, in Deleuze's analysis, does not extract movement "for itself," but leaves it attached to "elements, characters and things which serve as its moving body or vehicle" (Deleuze 1986, 24). Hence, in his argument, the primitive cinema could not realize the full potential of the cinematic representation of time.

This suturing of movement and time to the body, which Deleuze aligns with inferior or less desirable forms of cinema, is, in fact, the dominant tactic of mainstream film. The loss or lack which subtends cinema and which is exemplified in Zeno's Paradoxes can be masked by an emphasis on the sheer presence of the body in motion. While it is true that even classical cinema produces its own autonomous temporality/movement through editing and camera movement, the real time of the shot acts as an anchor, grounding time in the emphatic materiality of bodies. Slow motion, fast motion, step printing—all of which could be perceived as the perversion of time and bodies—are produced as a marginal rhetoric, confined to the realm of the exception, the special effect. They become explicit signs, read as such, in opposition to the alleged transparency of real time.

The concept of real time seems to be ubiquitous at the moment—used primarily to convey a sense of the capabilities of new media, of new computer technologies with specific and distinctive relations to temporality. These relations hinge on the concept of "instantaneity." Television news anchors frequently exhort their viewers to keep up with the news in real time by visiting the station's or network's website. "Real time" here connotes immediacy, continuity, an intolerance for delay, and most of all, a certain solidity associated with the guarantee of the real. It would seem that the only remaining residence of the real, in an age of simulation, the virtual, and the artificial, is time.

How did time come to assume such a heavy burden? More specifically, perhaps, how did immediacy and instantaneity come to signify our understanding of the reality of time? Although the *Oxford English Dictionary*'s first example of the use of the term "real time" dates back to only 1953 (and its last example is 1979), the phrase has been in use for a much longer period of time, dating back to the emergence of the cinema and, more particularly, to the development of editing as one of its central signifying strategies. For the term "real time" can only take on meaning when there is a sense of the possibility of an "unreal time," the time, for instance, of an edited temporal flow, which is capable of reducing days to minutes, years to an hour. Variations of the concept of real time have consistently attached themselves to mechanical and electronic forms of reproduction, which from the outset have always embodied a veiled or explicit promise to represent, store, or reproduce time. It is illuminating to observe how the contours of the concept mutate when it is applied to film, television, and digital media, across the span of the twentieth century. The term has a history which may shed light on current understandings of temporality and instantaneity.

In the technical language of filmmaking, the term "real time" refers to the duration of a single shot (assuming the shot is neither fast nor slow motion). If the physical film is not cut and its projection speed equals its shooting speed (usually somewhere between 16 and 24 frames per second), the movement on the screen will unfold in a time which is isomorphic with profilmic time, or what is generally thought to be our everyday lived experience of time—hence, the term "real." The time of the apparatus matches, is married to, the time of the action or the scene. This real time is marked by an apparent plenitude. No lack or loss of time is visible to the eye or accessible to the spectator. But this temporal continuity is, in fact, haunted by absence, by the lost time represented by the division between frames. These interstices, crucial to the representation of movement, must themselves remain unacknowledged. The cinema presents us with a simulacrum of time. Nevertheless, knowledge of the indexicality of the cinematic image sustains a belief that something of time, something of movement or its imprint, or at the very least, its adequate representation, is there. This idea is embodied most fully in the concept of real time, in the duration of the single shot. Real time here signifies pure continuity, without breaks of any kind.

Television displaces this concept of real time with the notion of "liveness"—which pinpoints the technical specificity of the medium and its advantage over film. "Liveness" refers to the (virtual) simultaneity of production, transmission, and reception. As a time that embodies the essence of instantaneity, liveness is particularly crucial to the representation of catastrophe, disaster, or accident, moments which seem to disrupt irrevocably the banal flow of everyday time. Catastrophe's liveness, which is in actuality preeminently about death, functions as a denial of the commodification of time and corroborates television's access to the momentary, the discontinuous, the real. The death associated with catastrophe ensures that television is felt as an immediate collision with the real in all its intractability—bodies in crisis, technology gone awry. In television, it is above all liveness that insures the reality of time.

The term "real time" re-emerges with a vengeance in the description of the capabilities of digital media. The *Oxford English Dictionary* defines "real time" as "the actual time during which a process or event occurs, esp. one analyzed by a computer, in contrast to time subsequent to it when computer processing may be done, a recording replayed, or the like." In other words, real time is the time of the now, of the "taking place" of events—it is specifically opposed to the subsequent, the *after*. Ideally, in real time, there would be no gap between the phenomenon and its analysis. Current definitions of real time tend to emphasize speed of response or reaction time, suggesting that interactivity, or the aspiration to interactivity, is what distinguishes computer real time from film or television real time ("real time operating systems are systems that respond to input immediately" [*Webpoedia*]; "Real time is a level of computer responsiveness that a user senses as sufficiently immediate or that enables the computer to keep up with some external process...[*WhatIs.com*]). However, these definitions of computer real time also expansively include those of film and television. Real time in digital terms would then include both continuity (the one-to-one relation between film time and everyday time promised by the cinema) and instantaneity (the speed of access, the simultaneity of event and reception promised by television). But in addition, digital real time, through the concept of interactivity, welds the user's time to the concept of real time. The lure of the internet is the lure of connectivity, of being in touch, of synchronicity, and of availability—24/7/365: 24 hours a day, 7 days a week, 365 days a year. Although the space of the internet may be superbly virtual, its time lays claim to the real.

The twentieth century, through a succession of forms of mechanical and electronic representation, appears to have witnessed a striking intensification of the articulation of reality with time. Thomas Levin has compellingly argued that there has been a shift in postmodernity away from the discredited and anachronistic spatial indexicality of the photographic image (dislodged by the digital image) and toward temporal indexicality as a guarantee of the real (the recent film *Time Code*, with its use of digital video and its claim to be the first film shot entirely in real time, would be symptomatic of this). Given the viewer's heightened knowledge of the manipulability of the visual image—its status as a simulacrum with no origin or referent—time rather than space becomes the residence of the real. However, I would argue that this apparently recent phenomenon has a much longer history, an examination of which can elucidate the embrace of the seemingly contradictory attributes of continuity and instantaneity by the concept of real time. It is a history which coincides with that of the intensification of capitalism and its investment in a commodification inseparable from the notion of innovation—it is the pre-history of real time.

The primary fascination of the cinema, after all, in contradistinction to photography, was its ability to inscribe time, manifested by its primary signifier—movement. The emerging cinema participated in a more general cultural imperative—the structuring of time and contingency in capitalist modernity. New technologies of representation such as photography, phonography, and cinema were critical to modernity's reconceptualization of time and its representabilty. There are two central and intersecting structuring oppositions in this rethinking of time: abstraction/rationalization versus contingency and discontinuity versus continuity.

At the birth of modernity, both time and money exemplify a process of dematerialization and abstraction that fuels a capitalist economy. As time becomes a value it begins to share the logic of the monetary system—a logic of pure differentiation, quantifiability, and articulation into discrete units. The capitalist buys a certain quantity of the labourer's time in order to produce surplus value. That time must be measurable and therefore divisible. Similarly, the world-wide standardization of time, prompted by the development of railroads, requires the generalized acceptance of minimal units of time for calibration. If the trains are to run on time, there must be only one time—the homogeneous, empty time of Walter Benjamin's "progress." But the rationalization and abstraction of time generally recognized as imperative to capitalism pose certain problems which make their tolerability less assured, two of which I would like to isolate here. The smooth narrative of a successful and progressive rationalization is disturbed by an insistent fascination with contingency, indexicality, and chance which manifests itself at many different levels—in aesthetics, debates about photography, physics, biology, and the growth of social statistics and statistical epistemologies in general. Rationalization must entail a reduction or denial of contingency. In Taylorism, each of the labourer's movements must be meaningful—ideally, there is no loss or excess in the system. The body's movements are efficient, purposeful, and time becomes the measure of that efficiency. But modernity is also strongly associated with epistemologies which valorize the contingent, the ephemeral, chance—that which is beyond or resistant to meaning. While in classical thought meaning precedes and determines embodiment, in modernity meaning is associated with immanence and embodiment—it is not predetermined in ideal forms but in a process of emergence and surprise. Impressionism, for instance, has been described as the concerted attempt to fix a moment, to grasp it as, precisely, fugitive. And new technologies of representation—photography in particular—are consistently allied with contingency and the ability to seize the ephemeral. Photography is allied with a *thisness*, a certainty in the absolute representability of things and moments. The promise of indexicality is, in effect, the promise of the rematerialization of time—the restoration of a continuum of space in photography, of time in the cinema. Here, time appears to be free in its indeterminacy, reducible to no system or hierarchy (any moment can be the subject of a photograph, any event can be filmed). The technological assurance of indexicality is the guarantee of a privileged relation to chance and the contingent, whose lure would be the escape from the grasp of rationalization and its system.

The second difficulty posed by capitalism's embrace of processes of abstraction and differentiation is linked to the concomitant necessity of thinking time in discrete units, as discontinuity. The notion of time as abstract differentiation of a homogenous substance, as eminently divisible for purposes of calculation, clashes with the long-standing philosophical and phenomenological assumption that time is, as Charles Sanders Peirce has put it, "the continuum *par excellence*, through the spectacles of which we envisage every other continuum" (65). Its divisibility is difficult to think. In modernity, time becomes uncanny, alienated, strange—no longer experienced but read, calculated. For Benjamin, the shock factor characteristic of modernity guarantees that impressions do not "enter experience (*Erfahrung*)," but instead "remain in the sphere of a certain hour in one's life (*Erlebnis*)" (163). Time is, in a sense, externalized, a surface phenomenon, which the modern subject must ceaselessly attempt to repossess through its multifarious representations. The rationalization of time ruptures the continuum *par excellence* and generates epistemological and philosophical anxieties exemplified by the work of Henri Bergson, in his adamant reassertion of temporal continuity in the concept of *durée*.

Are the two tendencies within modernity outlined above—abstraction/rationalization and an emphasis upon the contingent, chance, and the ephemeral—irreconcilable? Do they simply represent two different modalities or attitudes operating independently during the same time period, each undisturbed by the other? I would wager that it is possible to demonstrate their profound connection, their interdependence and alliance in the structuring of temporality in modernity. What is at stake is the representability of time for a subject whose identity is more and more tightly sutured to abstract structures of temporality. The theory of rationalization does not allow for the vicissitudes of the affective, for the subjective play of desire, anxiety, pleasure, trauma, apprehension. Pure rationalization excludes the subject, whose collusion is crucial to the sustenance of a capitalist system. In the face of the abstraction of time, its transformation into the discrete, the measurable, the locus of value, chance, and the contingent are assigned an important ideological role—they become the highly cathected sites of both pleasure and anxiety. Contingency appears to offer a vast reservoir of freedom and free play, irreducible to the systematic structuring of leisure time. What is critical is the production of contingency and ephemerality as graspable, representable, but nevertheless, anti-systematic. The rationalization of time characterizing industrialization and the expansion of capitalism was accompanied by a structuring of contingency and temporality through emerging technologies of representation—a structuring which attempted to insure their residence outside of structure, to make tolerable an incessant rationalization. Such a strategy is not designed simply to deal with the leakage or by-products of rationaliza-tion—it is structurally necessary to the ideologies of capitalist modernization.

Yet, the structuring oppositions delineated above—rationalization versus contingency and discontinuity versus continuity—are unstable in another sense as well. Both the lure of contingency and the insistence upon continuity as the reality of time are allied in countering or contesting the rationalization of time. But continuity and contingency are in tension as well, if not flatly opposed, troubling the neatness of the binary structure. The prerequisite of contingency is discontinuity—contingency must be unpredictable, pure difference and uniqueness, the product of a moment, not a continuum. Peirce attempted to solve this problem by claiming that the present instant differed dramati-cally from any other instant, past or future, for time, in his view, was a true continuum everywhere except at the moment of the punctual present, the now. This understanding of the present's absolute difference and uniqueness allowed Peirce to sustain the dream of modernity, to embrace the possibility of the emergence of the truly new.

This discursive tension is, in a sense, embodied or materialized within film form itself. For film is divided into isolated and static frames—instants of time, in effect—which when projected produce the illusion of continuous time and movement. The intensifica-tion of interest in dissecting and reunifying time in the nineteenth century, in manipulating it in order to produce both the possibility of its record/representation and the opportunity to construct alternative temporalities, is not some reflection of a perennial psychical order, but of a quite precise historical trauma. The subject is no longer immersed in time, no longer experiences it as an enveloping medium. Through its rationalization and abstraction, its externalization and reification in the form of pocket watches, standardized schedules, the organization of the work day, and industrialization in general, time becomes other, alienated. The desire to package or commodify time, to represent and distribute its experience in a highly controlled medium which nevertheless seems to be structured by a free, unsystematic alliance with contingency, is simultaneously a revolt against rationalization *and* its extension. What film archives, then, is first and foremost a lost experience of time as presence, time as immersion. This experience of temporality is one which was never necessarily lived, but emerges as the counter-dream of rationalization, its agonistic underside—full presence.

Hence, time's reality in the cinema is both that of continuity and rupture. Similarly, the real time of digital media refers both to adequation to the time of a process and an homage to the notion of instantaneity. Perhaps the difference lies in the stress of the *OED* definition of "real time" as, specifically, "computer time": "the actual time during which a process or event occurs, esp. one analyzed by a computer, in contrast to time subsequent to it when computer processing may be done, a recording replayed, or the like." This definition explicitly opposes real time, as the actual time of the event, to recorded or reproduced time. In it, real time emerges as pre-eminently anti-archival. While film, unlike both television and computers, is not capable of a representation simultaneous, or nearly simultaneous, with the event, and must struggle with the impossible dream of recording or re-presenting the present, digital media—like television before it—paradoxically foils or obstructs memory. Despite the consistent and relentless expansion of computer memory and the insistent association of digital media with the perfect archive, the concept of computer real time transforms storage into its antithesis and relegates it to an afterthought or by-product of the technology, the primary purpose of which is to "keep in touch" with the event.

The conceptualization of time which emerges, however, continues to conjoin continuity and instantaneity, and in much the same manner as the cinema. For it is the continuous time, the real time of the long take which allows for the possibility of contingency, the unforeseen, the unexpected, in the cinema. In digital media, despite the limitations of its technology, it is the webcam site which seems to embody this aspiration. The webcam operator relinquishes, abdicates, even banishes control by situating the camera in place, allowing it to record whatever happens to happen within the frame, 24 hours a day, 7 days a week, 365 days a year. In this sense, the webcam site, like photographically-based media, has a privileged relation to contingency, to chance. The attraction is precisely the *lack* of control, the possibility of the unintended, the unshaped, the felicitous or infelicitous accident. As such, the webcam site offers the spectre of exemplifying both the nightmare and the promise of photography—an accidental representation, a representation without an author, without a human agent, produced by a camera with no operator. For Baudelaire, this was the evil of photography, the cause of its enslavement to the real. For Roland Barthes, this was the fascination of photography—the contingency and absolute particularity of the punctum, the point which marked the evacuation of cultural signification, the escape from meaning. Whatever the inadequacies or obscure qualities of the image, the semiotic expectation induced is that of an access to the referent, to what happened or is happening in front of the camera.

The curious dialectic between continuity and instantaneity, which has informed the cinema from its inception and indeed all time-based forms of visual representation developed in the twentieth century, continues to haunt and fascinate. The contemporary cinema, attempting to embrace and assimilate the digital in conjunction with its cultural struggle with the latter, has made the special effect, formerly localized and marginalized, more prominent in its discourse. Particularly striking in this respect is *The Matrix* (1999) with its concept of "bullet time," a veritable meditation on cinematic intermittent motion and its concomitant loss of time. Bullet time is a fantasy of both the fullness of represented time and the body's surreal malleability and agility in the face of technological threat (aligned with the motif of the body versus the machine). A short documentary available on the DVD, in the genre of *The Making of* _____, entitled *What is Bullet-Time?*, describes the technical difficulties in the production of this technique. In a strategy reminiscent of Marey's and Muybridge's dissection of movement into individual poses, scores of both still and movie cameras were arranged in a pattern around the filmed movement. Despite the fact that the movie cameras ran at speeds as high as 500 frames per second, the technicians found it necessary to interpolate moments between the frames, in effect to "fill in" the missing time. As the primary technical advisor points out, "interpolation is the creation of frames digitally that are the by-product of real frames." "Real frames" are analyzed in order to create "new frames of moments in between the captured frames." He claims that this is a "new way to photograph things." It is also a way of annihilating the indexicality of the cinematic image, of producing purely digital moments which might seem to contest the very idea of real time. On the other hand, the gesture of "filling in," of incrementally reducing Zeno's Paradox, reveals a persistent investment in continuity. And the images of the documentary emphasize the massive array of cameras—cameras whose function is still to capture time and whose presence seems to contest the cinematic image's embrace of the virtual. The bodies are there, in a space which may be a non-space but which retains the vestiges of real time. In addition and perhaps more to the point, the perverse time of the special effect in *The Matrix* is still dominated by the real time of the narrative's "real world," a haven from the special effect, where matter continues to constitute a limit.

I would argue that it is not the digital accoutrements or high-tech special effects of the new mainstream cinema that truly contest the rationalization of time which is the continuing legacy of modernity. That challenge is instead found in the more marginal but insistent interrogation of cinematic time by the avant-garde. The normalization of cinematic vision conceals an intense epistemological work of fragmentation. The reconstitution of a naturalized movement is a laborious process subject to certain standards for the reconstruction of time. The ease and obviousness of cinematic movement are deceptive. Much avant-garde work in film from the 1960s on no longer takes this reconstitution for granted but, instead, works to defamiliarize this motion and time. Bill Brand's *Demolition of a Wall* (1973), in the manner of the structural/materialist films of the 1970s, activates the frame as a minimal unit. Brand takes 6 frames from Lumière's *Démolition d'un mur* (*Demolition of a Wall*, 1896) and organizes them successively in each of the 720 permutations possible in their ordering. The result is a series of jerky and disorienting movements. But I would like to focus briefly on two more recent attempts to denaturalize cinematic time and movement, both utilizing found footage and both concerned with what one might call (following Quetelet) a "social physics" of the body: Leslie Thornton's 1999 *Another Worldy* and Martin Arnold's *Cinemnesis* series: *pièce touchée* (1989); *passage à l'acte* (1993); and *Alone. Life Wastes Andy Hardy* (1998).

Thornton's *Another Worldy* is a surreal ethnography of dance which locates rhythmic movement as always already foreign, as ritualized excess. It is a compilation film made up of footage from musicals of the 1940s, ethnographic documentaries about the role of dance in "primitive" cultures, and various markers of the filmic including titles, leader with a synchronizing countdown, copyright notices, and scratches and marks on black leader. The estrangement effect of the film is largely a function of the subtraction of most of the original soundtracks and the resynchronization (through editing) of the dance movements to techno-pop music (selections from *The Tyranny Off the Beat*, produced by Cleopatra and OFF BEAT, 1995). The movements of the dancers appear uncannily and anachronistically to match the rhythms of the techno-pop music, and the constant juxtaposition of Hollywood musicals with ethnographic footage of native dances works to denaturalize and exoticize all gesture. A description of the montage in one section of *Another Worldy* gives a sense of the extent to which movement begins to function as a citation from elsewhere: a sequence of a Hollywood version of a Middle Eastern belly dance, an ethnographic documentary scene of bare-breasted women pounding the ground with large sticks, a series of markings on film leader, a backwards title for a film entitled *Daddy*, another Hollywood scene of a waitress and a busboy dancing, an Edison Kinetoscope film of Eugene Sandow, a famous Austrian bodybuilder (1894), three men dressed in seventeenth-century costume dancing rather stiffly, a title—"Strange rhythms of trained bodies"—preceding ethnographic documentary footage of two very young dancers in traditional costume in Sri Lanka, a shot of a bare-breasted woman from an ethnographic film, a title reading "Mystic Movements," a return to the two Sri Lankan dancers, interspersed with another title—"Erotic music." All of these are set to the techno-pop selection, "Why me?" (by the band Dorsetshire).

Most of the Western musicals already invest in the lure of the foreign and exotic (the Middle Eastern belly dance, a Polynesian show, women in white Cossack-like uniforms in *Russian Revels* with the Lucky Girls). It is as if some supplemental significance were required to rationalize fascination with movement. Through its disconcerting juxtapositions, the film effects a levelling or flattening of strangeness so that what are presented as norms of Western movement become invested with the pathological. Movement, which in the Hollywood cinema normalizes the representation of time through anchoring it to the body, becomes disengaged, a sight to behold. Although *Another Worldy* does not directly address the dependence of cinematic movement upon the dialectic of stasis and mobility, it succeeds in denaturalizing that movement—indeed, rendering it absurd, dismantling its racial and sexual edifice, removing it from the realm of the unquestionable time of real time.

Martin Arnold's trio of films, on the other hand, directly engages the radical tension between stillness and movement which subtends the cinema. Arnold uses a home-made optical printer to dissect motion into its smallest cinematic components and to experiment with varying speeds and with the repetition of frames so that movement seems to vibrate, pulsate, stutter. In *pièce touchée*, for instance, an 18 second shot from *The Human Jungle* (Joseph M. Newman, 1954) is stretched to fill the 15 minute duration of the film. Arnold deliberately chose one of the most banal and familiar of Hollywood domestic scenes—a husband returning home from work, greeting and kissing his patiently-waiting wife. But the work of the optical printer translates each movement into a potential catastrophe, a neurotic gesture revealing a profound psychic disequilibrium. Arnold describes the experience of watching another scene from this film on a computerized projector, "At a projection speed of four frames per second the event was thrilling; every minimal movement was transformed into a small concussion" (4). In dislocating the frame from its normalized linear trajectory, *pièce touchée* reasserts the explosive instantaneity at the heart of cinematic continuity. Similarly, *passage à l'acte* reworks, at the level of both image and sound, a well-worn and commonplace familial breakfast scene characterized by sibling rivalry and the exercise of paternal authority (this scene is taken from *To Kill a Mockingbird* [Robert Mulligan, 1962]). Using the same strategies of delay, deferral, and the disarticulation of movement and time, *Alone. Life Wastes Andy Hardy* decomposes cinematic affect and pathos. Arnold's work, in its perverse re-embodiment of the desire of Marey and Muybridge, seems to literalize Benjamin's "optical unconscious." The goal here is to see differently, to see *more*. It is crucial that both Thornton's *Another Worldy* and Arnold's trio of films utilize found footage, recycling the overly familiar and banal, producing a discourse of meta-movements—movements which take as their raw material the recorded movement of popular culture—and, in effect, exposing the profound rupture underlying the apparently seamless continuity of real time.

These films emerge in the midst of what many have labelled a digital revolution, an era of the computer and its embrace of instantaneity and real time. However, the webcam site, in some ways the archetypal instantiation of computer real time, makes palpable temporal lack. One can wait anywhere from seconds to minutes to hours for a change in the image. In the cinema, the illusion of movement was celebrated in early reviews as the ability to preserve life itself—to defy death. The discontinuities foregrounded by the webcam site are displaced by the continuity of accessibility—again 24/7/365.

There is still the promise of the accident, the unintended, but here it is a function not so much of representation as of access to it. Contingency is that of choosing the right moment to look. The everydayness of the webcam site, together with its constant accessibility and sheer banality, are what make possible a glimpse of the catastrophic, the unscripted. What the alliance of temporal continuity and instantaneity in technologies of representation makes palpable is the intricate dialectic between banality and catastrophe that haunts contemporary time. As Susan Sontag has pointed out, "We live under continual threat of two equally fearful, but seemingly opposed destinies—unremitting banality and inconceivable terror" (227). The hyperlocal banal event of the webcam site can act as a response or even antidote to the trauma of the accident or catastrophe, which seems to be the media's only other way of conceiving the event.

The dialectic of banality and catastrophe, together with that of continuity and instantaneity, are the reverberations of the dialectic fundamental to commodification—that of repetition and novelty. A basic repetition glossed by the lure of innovation produces the fascination of the commodity. For Benjamin, this dialectic of repetition and novelty characterized technical reproducibility and underwrote the exchange value of the photograph and film. The problem for Benjamin was how to disengage authentic newness or change from this dialectic subtending the logic of capitalist consumerism. For Jean-François Lyotard, it is the avant-garde that has the potential to resist this logic by concerning itself with the question, "Is it happening?" as opposed to the constantly renewed declarative "This is happening" of commodity capitalism. However, in his analysis, the avant-garde can succeed only if it does not succumb to the seductive rule of the new that characterizes the art market. The seduction "exerts itself thanks to a confusion between innovation and the *Ereignis* [the occurrence], a confusion maintained by the temporality specific to contemporary capitalism." Lyotard writes,

> The occurrence, the *Ereignis*, has nothing to do with the *petit frisson*, the cheap thrill, the profitable pathos, that accompanies an innovation. Hidden in the cynicism of innovation is certainly the despair that nothing further will happen. But innovating means to behave as though lots of things happened, and to make them happen. Through innovation, the will affirms its hegemony over time. It thus conforms to the metaphysics of capital, which is a technology of time. The innovation "works." The question mark of the *Is it happening?* stops. With the occurence, the will is defeated. The avant-gardist task remains that of undoing the presumption of the mind with respect to time. (106–7)

The discourses of real time participate in the logic of innovation, insofar as immediacy and instantaneity allow access to the ever-new, the ever-unique, the ever-different. Real time is the rope connecting us to the "what happens" deprived of all interrogation. It is our assurance that something is happening and this guarantee is our access to it. The simulacrum of real time allows the will to once again affirm its hegemony over time.

The question then becomes how to disrupt this logic of real time. For Lyotard the answer lies in the avant-garde because it is able to demonstrate or embody the submission of the mind, of analysis, before the sublime idea of an uncontrollable and unknowable time, composed of events which precede all meaning. Yet, in a sense it is this construct—of time as simply there, unquestioned and unquestioning, outside or before the attribution of meaning, going on—which forms the basis of real time's appeal to the ground of the real. A more productive question, it seems to me, would entail asking how time's reality became a function of a lack of distance between the duration of an event and the duration of its representation, of immediacy, instantaneity, and accessibility. Why is the real no longer a matter of being there, but of being then? And why is it so crucial that this "then," is in fact a "now"? Such an erasure of memory and history would be the zero degree of the logic of innovation, a form of commodification in which the commodity itself, always already out of date, would be superfluous.

Around 1895, the cinema solidified a growing fascination with represented movement and change, the very marks of time. It did so by harbouring within itself the frozen moment, the still frame, the antithesis of that which it so laboriously strove to reconstruct. At the heart of the machine designed, like photography, to reproduce and distribute an intensified access to contingency—here the very contingency of time itself—lay a monumental arrest of time, one mirrored at a higher level by the film's more expansive commodification of time. If the mainstream cinema is in collusion with the processes of commodification, it is so at a much more profound level than that of the tie-in, or of any object within the frame. In continually assuring us that "Something is happening," through the ceaseless erasure of its own petrification of time, the cinema prepared the way for the various reincarnations of real time in television and digital media. The lust for real time persists. And it is to the credit of a certain tendency within the avant-garde that it forces a recognition of this contemporary dilemma of movement's paralysis, and hence of the profound unreality of technology's real time.

Roland Barthes (1974)
S/Z: An Essay
Richard Miller. trans.
New York: Hill and Wang

Charles Baudelaire (1964)
The Painter of Modern Life and Other Essays
Jonathan Mayne, trans.
New York: Da Capo

Walter Benjamin (1969)
Illuminations
Harry Zohn, trans.
Hannah Arendt, ed.
New York: Schocken Books

Gilles Deleuze (1986)
Cinema 1: The Movement-Image
Minneapolis: University of Minnesota Press

——(1989)
Cinema 2: The Time-Image
Minneapolis: University of Minnesota Press

Mary Ann Doane (1990)
Information, Crisis, Catastrophe
Logics of Television: Essays in Cultural Criticism
Patricia Mellencamp, ed.
Bloomington: Indiana University Press

Jean Epstein (1977)
Magnification and Other Writings
Stuart Liebman, trans.
October no. 3

Max Ernst (1982)
A Little Girl Dreams of Taking the Veil
Dorothea Tanning, trans.
New York: George Braziller

E. Giard (c. 1902)
Le Livre d'Or de la Photographie.
Paris: C. Mendel

Jean-Claude Gautrand (1998)
Photography on the Spur of the Moment:
Instant Impressions
A New History of Photography
Michel Frizot, ed.
Köln: Könemann

Thomas Y. Levin (2000)
"You Never Know the Whole Story": Ute Friederike Jürß
and the Aesthetics of the Heterochronic Image
Ute Friederike Jürß: You Never Know the Whole Story
Ursula Frohne and Dörte Zbikowski, eds.
Hamburg: Museum für Neue Kunst, Hatje Cantz Verlag

Jean-François Lyotard (1991)
The Sublime and the Avant-Garde
The Inhuman
Geoffrey Bennington and Rachel Bowlby, trans.
Stanford: Stanford University Press

Scott MacDonald (1994)
Sp...Sp...Spaces of Inscription:
An Interview with Martin Arnold
Film Quarterly 48.1

Oxford English Dictionary, 2nd. ed. (1989)
s.v. "real time"

Charles Sanders Peirce (1935)
Collected Papers of Charles Sanders Peirce
vol. 6, *Scientific Metaphysics*
Charles Hartshorne and Paul Weiss, eds.
Cambridge: Harvard University Press

Susan Sontag (1961)
Against Interpretation
New York: Dell Publishing Company

Webopedia
s.v. "real time"
http://sbc.webopedia.com/TERM/R/real_time.html

Whatis.com
s.v. "real time"
http://whatis.techtarget.com/definition/
0,,sid9_gci214344,00.html

THE FOREIGN GAZE WHICH SEES TOO MUCH
Slavoj Žižek

1. FIRST IMPRESSIONS ARE RIGHT

When we are witnessing an intense religious ritual, it is commonplace to claim that we, outside observers, cannot ever properly interpret it, since only those who are directly immersed in the life-world—part of which is this ritual—can comprehend its meaning. Or, more precisely, they do not reflexively "understand" it; they directly live its meaning. Here one should take a step further: even the religious belief of those who participate in such a ritual is a rationalization of the uncanny libidinal impact of the ritual itself. The gap between understanding and living is not the same as the gap between the participants directly involved with the thing and our external interpretive position—it resides already in the thing itself, i.e., it splits the participants themselves from within. The participants who need a rationalization of meaning in order to be able to sustain the Real of the ritual itself. Along the same lines, the basic interpretive operation of psychoanalysis is not to move deeper than the superficial interpretation, but, on the contrary, to be attentive to the perplexing first impressions. One usually says that the first reading is always deceptive, and that the meaning only discloses itself in a second reading—however, what if the meaning that arises in the second reading is ultimately a defense formation against the shock of the first reading? Terry Eagleton interpreted T. S. Eliot's "The Waste Land" along these lines: the first impression of the poem—the fragments from common daily occurrences, mixed with the impenetrable texture of references to an inconsistent multitude of artistic and religious phenomena, IS the poem's message. This direct short-circuit between the fragments of alienated contemporary daily life and the confusing multitude of metaphysical references is, for Eliot, in itself the best diagnosis of where we stand today: lacking a firm religious-metaphysical foundation, our daily lives are fragmented into bits of empty and vulgar social rituals.

When we pass this threshold and endeavour to discern a consistent spiritual edifice beneath the confusing multitude of references (is Eliot a Buddhist? does he propagate a pagan myth of resurrection?), we have already missed the crucial point.

And, perhaps, the gaze fascinated by the perplexing first impression, the awareness that there is in this first impression more than any later rationalization will reveal, is the very model of the cinema spectator. This is also why Alfred Hitchcock is the film director *par excellence*: the gaze fascinated by the perplexing first impression is one of the axes of his universe. About one third into *Shadow Of a Doubt*, there is a brief passage which fully bears witness to Hitchcock's genius: the young FBI detective investigating Uncle Charlie takes his young niece Charlie out for a date; we see them in a couple of shots walking along the streets, laughing and talking vivaciously. Then, unexpectedly, we get a fast fade-out into the American shot of Charlie in a state of shock, gaping with a transfixed gaze at the detective off screen, blurting out nervously "I know what you are really! You are a detective!" Of course, we expect the detective to use the opportunity provided by the date to acquaint Charlie with Uncle Charlie's dark side, though we expect it will be a gradual revelation: the detective should first break the cheerful mood and address the serious issue, thus provoking Charlie's outburst when she realizes how she was being manipulated (i.e. she realizes the detective asked her on a date not because he liked her, but as part of his professional work).

Instead of a gradual revelation, however, we are directly confronted with the trauma-tized Charlie. It is only AFTER this shocking discontinuity that the detective voices his suspicions about Uncle Charlie's murderous past. To put it in temporal terms: it is as if, in this scene, *the effect precedes its cause*. We are first shown the effect (the traumatized gaze) and then given the context responsible for this traumatic impact...or are we? Is the relationship between cause and effect really inverted here? What if here the gaze is not merely the recipient of the event? What if it somehow mysteriously generates the perceived incident? What if the conversation that follows is ultimately an attempt to symbolize or domesticate this traumatic incident? Such a cut in the continuous texture of reality, such a momentous inversion of the proper temporal order, signals the intervention of the Real: if the scene were to be shot in the linear order (first the cause, then the effect), the texture of reality would have been left undamaged. That is to say: the Real is discernible in the gap between the true cause of the terrified gaze and what we are given to see later as its cause: the true cause of the terrified gaze is not what we are shown or told afterwards, but the fantasized traumatic excess projected by the gaze into the perceived reality.

Such a perplexed gaze sustains what is one of the archetypal Hitchcockian scenes, that of a couple—just outside the scope of a public place within sight of a group of naive observers—arguing on a small half-barren hill with a couple of trees and bushes, usually windy. For Alain Bergala (on whose magisterial analysis I rely here), this scene stages Adam and Eve in the Garden of Eden, just prior to being chased from it, in the process of tasting the forbidden knowledge. If one discounts a couple of minor references and variations (from *Notorious* to *Topaz*), there are three main versions of it: *Suspicion*, *The Birds*, *Torn Curtain*. In *Suspicion*, it is the brief shot of Grant and Fontaine struggling on a windy hill near the church, observed by Fontaine's friend from the entrance to the church; in *The Birds*, it is the scene, just prior to the first bird attack on the group of children, in which Mitch and Melanie withdraw to a small hill above the picnic place with children celebrating the birthday party; finally, in *Torn Curtain*, it is the scene in which Paul Newman and Julie Andrews withdraw to a small hill, out of hearing of the East German secret police officials who can only observe them—there, Newman explains to his fiancée the truth about his mission. The key feature is that, in all three cases, the couple on the hill is observed by an innocent/threatening/naive observer below the hill (the friends close to the church; Mitch's ex-lover and mother; the East German secret policemen) who merely watches the scene and is unable to discern the meaning of the intense exchange of the couple. The traumatic character of the scene, the excess of the Real that pertains to it, hinges on this gaze: it is only from the standpoint of this gaze that the scene is traumatic—when the camera later jumps closer to the couple, the situation is again normalized. Bergala is right to emphasize how this scene reproduces the basic coordinates of the child's primordial sexual encounter: witnessing the parent's love-making, unable to decide what the scene he sees is, violence or love. The problem with his account is that it appears all too close to the standard, archetypal, reading, trying to identify the kernel of the scene's meaning, instead of conceiving of it as a meaningless *sinthom*, or "a knot of excessive enjoyment."

Among the contemporary directors whose work intimately relates to Hitchcock's, the greatest of such shocking encounters is David Lynch. It suffices to mention the night-club scene from *Mulholland Drive*, his new masterpiece: in the nightclub, a Latino girl sings a passionate love song and, after she collapses, her singing GOES ON—a rendering of the Real of the Voice similar to that at the beginning of Sergio Leone's *Once Upon a Time in America*, where we see a phone ringing loudly, and when a hand picks up the receiver, the ringing goes on. This image of the voice continuing to sing even when its bodily support collapses is an inversion of the famous Balanchine ballet staging of a short piece by Anton Webern: in this staging, the dancing continues even after the music stops. We have thus, in one case, a voice that insists when deprived of its bodily support, and, in the other, bodily movements that insist when deprived of their vocal (musical) support. The effect is not simply symmetrical, because, in the first case, the vocal drive is undead signifying immortal life, while in the second, the figures are "dead men dancing," shadows deprived of their life-substance. However, in both cases, we witness is a dissociation between reality and the real—in both cases, the Real insists even when perceived reality disintegrates. This real, of course, is the fantasmatic Real at its purest.

Of course, in all these cases, the shock-effect is followed by an explanation which relocates it back into ordinary reality: in the nightclub scene in *Mulholland Drive*, we are warned at the very outset that we are listening to a pre-recorded music, that the singers simply mimic the act of singing (in this case, Rebekah del Rio belting out "Llorando," a Spanish version of Ray Orbison's "Crying"); in the case from Leone, the phone we continue to hear ringing after the receiver is picked up is another phone, etc. However, what is nonetheless crucial is that, for a short moment, part of reality was (mis)perceived as a nightmarish apparition—and, in a way, this apparition was more real than reality itself, since in it the Real shined through. In short, one should discern which part of reality is "transfunctionalized" through fantasy, so that, although still part of reality, it is perceived in a fictional mode. Much more difficult than to denounce/unmask what seemingly appears to be reality as fiction is to recognize the fictitious part of "real" reality. Is this not what happens in transference, where, while we relate to a "real person" in front of us, we effectively relate to the fiction of, say, our father? Recall also *Home Alone*, especially part 2: in both parts, there is a cut two-thirds into the film; although the story seems to take place in a continuous diegetic setting, it is clear that, with the final confrontation between the child and the two robbers, we enter a different ontological realm: a plastic cartoon-space in which there is no death, in which my head can explode, yet I go on as normal in the next scene.... Again, a part of reality is here fictionalized.

Symmetrical to this short-circuit between fiction and reality is another (obverse) case of the dialectic of semblance and Real. It makes clear how the "returns of the Real" in our culture (our obsession with the intrusions of the "raw real" of sex or bodily violence) cannot be reduced to the rather elementary fact that the virtualization of our daily lives, the experience that we are more and more living in an artificially constructed universe, gives rise to the irresistible urge to regain the firm ground in some "real reality." THE REAL WHICH RETURNS HAS THE STATUS OF A(NOTHER) SEMBLANCE: *precisely because it is real, i.e. on account of its traumatic/excessive character, we are unable to integrate it into (what we experience as) our reality, and are therefore compelled to experience it as a nightmarish apparition.* This is what the captivating image of the collapse of the World Trade Center was: an image, a semblance, an "effect," which, at the same time, delivered "the thing itself." This "effect of the Real" is not the same as what, way back in the 1960s, Roland Barthes called *l'effet du réel*: it is rather its exact opposite, *l'effet de l'irréel*. That is to say, in contrast to the Barthesian *effet du réel* in which the text makes us accept as "real" its fictional product, here, the Real itself, in order to be sustained, has to be perceived as a nightmarish irreal specter. Usually we say that one should not mistake fiction for reality—recall the postmodern doxa according to which "reality" is a discursive product, a symbolic fiction, which we misperceive as a substantial autonomous entity. The lesson here is the opposite one: *one should not mistake reality for fiction*—one should be able to discern, in what we experience as fiction, the hard kernel of the Real which we are only able to sustain if we fictionalize it.

2. THE DRAMA OF FALSE APPEARANCES

The penetrating power of the perplexed foreign gaze pertains not only to cinema practice, but also to cinema theory. Let us take one of the exercises of cinema theory and historicism at its best, Marc Vernet's rejection of the very concept of *film noir*. In a detailed analysis, Vernet demonstrates that all the main features that constitute the common definition of *film noir* ("expressionist" *chiaroscuro* lightning and askew camera angles, the paranoiac universe of the hard-boiled novel with corruption elevated to a cosmic metaphysical feature embodied in the *femme fatale*, etc.) as well as their explanation (that a threat was posed to the patriarchal phallic regime by the social impact of the Second World War, etc.) are simply false. What Vernet does apropos of *noir* is something similar to what the late François Furet did with the French Revolution in historiography: he turns an Event into a non-Event, a false hypostasis that involves a series of misrecognitions of the complex concrete historical situation. *Film noir* is not a category of the history of Hollywood cinema, but a category of the criticism and history of cinema that could have emerged only in France, for the French gaze immediately after World War II, inclusive of all the limitations and misrecognitions of such a gaze (the ignorance of what went on before in Hollywood, the tension of the ideological situation in France itself in the aftermath of the war, etc.).

This explanation reaches its peak when we take into account the fact that poststructuralist deconstructionism (which serves as the standard theoretical foundation of the Anglo-Saxon analysis of *film noir*) has in a way exactly the same status as *film noir* according to Vernet: in the same way that American *noir* doesn't exist (in itself, in America), since it was invented for and by the French gaze, one should also emphasize that post-structuralist deconstructionism doesn't exist (in itself, in France), since it was invented in the US, for and by the American academic gaze with all its constitutive limitations. (The prefix post- in "post-structuralism" is thus a reflexive determination in the strict Hegelian sense of the term. Although it seems to designate the property of its object—the change, the cut, in the French intellectual orientation—it effectively involves a reference to the gaze of the subject perceiving it: "post" means things that went on in French theory after the American [or German] gaze perceived them, while "structuralism" *tout court* designates French theory "in itself," before it was noted by the foreign gaze. "Post-structuralism" is structuralism from the moment it was noted by the foreign gaze.) In short, an entity like "post-structuralist deconstructionism" (the term itself is not used in France) comes into existence only for a gaze that is unaware of the details of the philosophical scene in France: this gaze brings together authors (Derrida, Deleuze, Foucault, Lyotard, etc.) who are simply not perceived as part of the same episteme in France, in the same way that the concept of *film noir* posits a unity which did not exist "in itself." And in the same way the French gaze, ignorant of the ideological tradition of American individualist anti-combo populism, misperceived through the existentialist lenses the heroic cynical-pessimistic fatalist stance of the *noir* hero for a socially critical attitude, so, too, did the American perception inscribe the French authors into the field of radical cultural criticism and thus conferred on them the feminist etc. critical social stance for the most part absent in France itself. In the same way *film noir* is not a category of American cinema, but primarily a category of the French cinema criticism and (later) of the historiography of cinema, "post-structuralist deconstructionism" is not a category of French philosophy, but primarily a category of the American (mis)reception of the French authors designated as such. So, when we are reading what is arguably the paradigmatic example and topic of (cinema) deconstructionist theory, a feminist analysis of the way the *femme fatale* of *film noir* renders the ambiguous male reaction to the threat to the patriarchal "phallic order," we effectively have a non-existing theoretical position analyzing a non-existing cinematic genre. . . .

However, is such a conclusion effectively unavoidable? Even if we concede that, at the level of data, Vernet is right? Although Vernet effectively undermines much of the standard *noir* theory (say, the rather crude notion that the *noir* universe stands for the paranoiac male reaction to the threat to the "phallic regime" embodied in the *femme fatale*), the enigma that remains is the mysterious efficiency and persistence of the notion of *noir*: the more Vernet is right at the level of facts, the more enigmatic and inexplicable becomes the extraordinary strength and longevity of this "illusory" notion of noir, the notion that haunts our imagination for decades. What if, then, *film noir* is nonetheless a concept in the strict Hegelian sense: something that cannot simply be explained, accounted for in terms of historical circumstances, conditions and reactions, but acts as a structuring principle that displays its own dynamics? What if *film noir* is actual as a concept, as a unique vision of the universe that combines the multitude of elements into what Louis Althusser would have called an articulation? So, when we ascertain that the notion of *noir* does not fit the empirical multitude of *noir* films, instead of rejecting the notion, we should risk the notorious Hegelian rejoinder "So much worse for reality!"—more precisely, we should engage in the dialectic between a universal notion and its reality, in which the very gap between the two sets in motion the simultaneous transformation of reality and of the notion itself. It is because real films never fit their notion that they constantly change themselves, and this change imperceptibly transforms the very notion, the standard by which they are measured: we pass from the hard-boiled-detective *noir* (the Hammett-Chandler formula) to the "persecuted innocent bystander" *noir* (the Cornell Woolrich formula), from it to the "naive sucker caught in a crime" *noir* (the James Cain formula), etc.

We are thus tempted to designate the two foreign misrecognizing gazes whose askew point of view was constitutive of their respective objects (*film noir*, "post-structuralist deconstructionism") as precisely the two exemplary cases of the so-called "drama of false appearances"[1]: the hero or heroine or both are placed in a compromising situation, either because of their sexual behaviour or a crime; their actions are observed by a character who sees things mistakenly, reading into the innocent behaviour of the heroes illicit implications; at the end, of course, the misunderstanding is clarified and the heroes absolved of any wrongdoing. However, the point is that through this game of false appearance, a censored thought is allowed to be articulated: the spectator can imagine the hero or heroine enacting forbidden wishes, but escape any penalty, since he knows that despite the false appearances, nothing has happened, i.e. they are innocent. The dirty imagination of the onlooker who misreads innocent signs or coincidences is here the stand-in for the spectator's "pleasurably aberrant viewing" (Maltby 455). This is what Lacan had in mind when he claimed that truth has the structure of a fiction, the very suspension of literal truth, opens up the way for the articulation of the libidinal truth. This situation was exemplarily staged in Ted Tetzlaff's *The Window*, in which a small boy effectively perceives a crime, although nobody believes him and his parents even force him to apologize to the murderers for the false rumours he is spreading about them. . . .

1. See Wolfenstein and Leites.

It is, however, Lillian Hellman's play *The Children's Hour*, twice filmed (both times directed by William Wyler), that offers perhaps the clearest, almost laboratory example of this "drama of false appearances." As is well known, the first version (*These Three*, 1936) provided the occasion for one of the great Goldwynisms: when Sam Goldwyn, the producer, was warned that the film concerns lesbians, he supposedly replied: "That's okay, we'll turn them into Americans!" What then effectively happened was that the alleged lesbian affair around which the story turns was effectively turned into a standard heterosexual affair. The film is set in a posh private school for girls run by two friends, the austere domineering Martha and the warm and affectionate Karen who is in love with Joe, the local doctor. When Mary Tilford, a vicious pre-teen pupil, is censured for a misdeed by Martha, she retaliates by telling her grandmother that late one evening she has seen Joe and Martha (not Karen, his fiancée) "carrying on" in a bedroom near the student's quarters. The grandmother believes her—especially after this lie is corroborated by Rosalie, a weak girl terrorized by Mary—removes Mary from the school, and also advises all of the other parents to do the same. The truth eventually comes out, but the damage has been done: the school is closed, Joe loses his post at the hospital, and even the friendship between Karen and Martha comes to an end after Karen admits that she, too, has her suspicions about Martha and Joe. Joe leaves the country for a job in Vienna, where Karen later joins him. The second version, from 1961, is faithful to the play: when Mary retaliates, she tells her grandmother that she has seen Martha and Karen kissing, embracing, and whispering, implying that she does not fully understand what she was witnessing, but that it must have been something "unnatural." After all, the parents remove their children from the school and the two women find themselves alone in the large building, Martha realizes that she effectively does love Karen in more than just a sisterly fashion. Unable to bear the guilt she feels, she hangs herself. Mary's lie is finally exposed, but it is far too late now: in the film's final scene, Karen leaves Martha's funeral and walks proudly past Mary's grandmother, Joe, and all other townspeople who were gulled by Mary's lies....

The story turns around the evil onlooker (Mary) who, through her lie, unwittingly realizes the adult's unconscious desire: the paradox, of course, is that prior to Mary's accusation, Martha was not aware of her lesbian longings—it is only this external accusation that makes her aware of a disavowed part of herself. The "drama of false appearances" is thus brought to its truth: the evil onlooker's "pleasurably aberrant viewing" externalizes the repressed aspect of the falsely accused subject. The interesting point is that, although in this second version the censorship distortion is undone, the first version is as a rule hailed as far superior to its 1961 remake because of the way it abounds with repressed eroticism: not the eroticism between Martha and Joe, but the eroticism between Martha and Karen. Although the girl's accusation concerns the alleged affair between Martha and Joe, Martha is attached to Karen in a much more passionate way than Joe with his rather conventional straight love.... The key to the "drama of false appearances" is thus that, in it less overlaps with more. On the one hand, the standard procedure of censorship is not to show the (prohibited) event (a murder, a sex act) directly, but the way it is reflected in the witnesses; on the other hand, this deprivation opens up a space to be filled in by fantasmatic projections, i.e. it is possible that the gaze which does not see clearly what is effectively going on sees MORE, not LESS.

And, in a homologous way, the notion of *noir* (or "post-structuralist deconstructionism," for that matter), although resulting from a limited foreign perspective, perceives in its object potentials invisible to those who are directly engaged in it. Therein resides the ultimate dialectical paradox of truth and falsity: sometimes, the aberrant view which misreads a situation from its limited perspective, can, on account of this very limitation, perceive the "repressed" potentials of the observed constellation. It is true that, if we submit products usually designated as noir to a close historical analysis, the very concept of *film noir* loses its consistency and disintegrates; however, paradoxically, we should nonetheless insist that Truth is on the level of the spectral (false) appearance of *noir*, not in the detailed historical knowledge.

And, furthermore, sometimes the external misperception exerts a productive influence on the misperceived "original" itself, forcing it to become aware of its own "repressed" truth (arguably, the French notion of *noir*, although the result of misperception, exerted a strong influence on American movie making). Isn't the supreme example of this productivity of the external misperception the very American reception of Derrida? Did it not—although it clearly was a misperception—exert a retroactive productive influence on Derrida himself, forcing him to confront more directly ethico-political issues? Was the American reception of Derrida in this sense not a kind of *pharmakon*, a supplement to the "original" Derrida himself—a poisonous stain-fake, distorting the original and at the same time maintaining it alive? In short, would Derrida be still so much "alive" if we were to subtract from his work what undoubtedly is its American misperception?

3. ". . . FROM MY LIE THIS DID COME TRUE"

There is, however, an additional "turn of the screw" to be added to this dialectic: if only a foreign gaze can perceive that which is "in ourselves more than ourselves," our own repressed or decentered truth, this means that the true foreigner does not come from outside, but is located in our very heart—the point brilliantly made by Atom Egoyan's masterpiece *The Sweet Hereafter*, arguably THE film about the impact of trauma on a community. Mitchell Stephens, a lawyer, arrives in the wintry hamlet of Sam Dent to sign up the parents of children who died when their school bus plunged into an ice-covered lake. His motto is "there are no accidents": there are no gaps in the causal link of responsibility, there always HAS to be someone who is guilty. (As we soon learn, he is not doing this due to professional avarice. Stephens's obsession with the complete causal link is rather his desperate strategy to cope with private trauma, to sort out responsibility for his own daughter Zoe, a junkie who despises him, although she repeatedly calls him demanding money: he insists that everything must have a cause in order to counteract the inexplicable gap which separates him from Zoe.) After Stephens interviews Dolores Driscoll, the driver of the bus, who says the accident was a fluke, he visits the families of the dead children, and some agree to file a lawsuit with him. Among them are the parents of Nicole Burnell, a teenager who survived the crash as a paraplegic but remembers nothing. Stephens's case depends on proving that the bus company or the school board were at fault, not Dolores's driving.

Nicole, estranged and cynical since the accident, sees her parents succumbing to greed through Stephens's dark influence. Her father has been molesting her for years; where she once believed in his love, she now sees only exploitation. At the inquest, she decides to lie, testifying that Dolores was driving too fast—Stephens's case is thus ruined. While Nicole is now forever isolated from the community, she will now be able to guide her own future. In the film's final scene, which occurs two years later, Dolores, now driving a minibus at a nearby airport, meets Stephens on his way to rescue his daughter yet again; they recognize each other, but prefer not to speak. In the film's final lines, Nicole's voice-over accompanies this encounter of Stephens and Dolores: "As you see each other, almost two years later, I wonder if you realize something, I wonder if you realize that all of us—Dolores, me, the children who survived, the children who didn't—that we're all citizens of a different town now. A town of people living in the sweet hereafter."

At first glance, Stephens seems to be the film's protagonist: the film begins with his arrival in town, he is involved in the climax, and much of the first half of the film is seen from his point of view. It is Stephens's passion which drives the lawsuit, the dramatic spine of the story—it thus seems that we shall get the standard Hollywood narrative in which the larger tragedy (the bus accident) offers the background for the true focus, the protagonist's coming to terms with his own trauma. However, halfway through, Egoyan thwarts our expectations with a major shift in the point of view: when Nicole leaves the hospital as a paraplegic, the story becomes *hers*, and Stephens is re-positioned as her antagonist. Is, then, Nicole's lie an act of saving the community, enabling the townspeople to escape the painful judicial examination which would have torn apart their lives? Is it not that, through her lie, the community is allowed to absolve itself, i.e. to avoid the *second* trauma of having to symbolize the accident, and to enter the fantasmatic bliss of the "sweet hereafter" in which, by an unspoken pact among them, the catastrophe is silently ignored? Is it in this sense that her lie is an ACT in the strict sense of the term: an immoral lie that answers the unconditional call of Duty, enabling the community to start again from nothing?[2] Is this not the basic lesson of the film, namely that our social reality as such is a "sweet hereafter" based on constitutive lies? A young incestuous girl, through her lie, enables a community to reconstitute itself—we all live in a "sweet hereafter," social reality itself is a "sweet hereafter" based on the

2. I owe this point to Christina Ross, McGill University, Montreal.

disavowal of some trauma. The townspeople who survive as a community connected by a secret bond of disavowed knowledge, obeying their own secret rules, are not the model of a pathological community, but the very (unacknowledged) model of our "normal" social reality, like in Freud's dream about Irma's injection, in which social reality (the spectacle of the three doctors-friends proposing contradictory excuses for the failure of Freud's treatment of Irma) emerges as the "sweet hereafter" following the traumatic confrontation with the trauma of Irma's deep throat.

However, such a reading simplifies the film's texture. Does the traumatic accident derail the idyllic life of the small town community? It seems that the opposite is the case: before the catastrophic accident, the community was far from idyllic—its members indulged in adultery, incest, etc.—so that the accident, by way of localizing the violence in the external/contingent traumatic bus accident, by way of displacing it onto this accident, retroactively renders the community edenic. However, such a reading also misses the point. The key indication of the community's life is provided by the way the daughter/father incest (which went on before the accident) is presented: strangely, this ultimate transgression is rendered as totally *non-traumatic*, as part of everyday intimate relations. We are in a community in which incest is "normal." Perhaps, then, this allows us to risk a Lévi-Straussian reading of the film: what if its structuring opposition is the same as the one which Lévi-Strauss identifies in his famous analysis of the Oedipus myth? Namely, the opposition between *overvaluation* and *undervaluation* of kinship ties, and concretely: between the excessive proximity of father and daughter (incest) and their estrangement (losing children in an accident, or, in the case of Stephens, losing ties with a junkie daughter). The key insight of the story concerns the link between the two opposites: it is as if, since parents are so attached to their children, following the proverbial obsessional strategy, they prefer to strike preemptively, i.e. to stage themselves the loss of the child in order to avoid the unbearable waiting for the moment when, upon growing up, the child will abandon them. This notion is expressed clearly by Stephens in an episode in Banks's novel (not used by Egoyan), when he muses on his disavowed decision to let go of his young daughter after forgetting her in a store: "I must have known that if my child was indeed to be lost to me, then I would need all my strength just to survive that fact, so I had decided ahead of time not to waste any of my strength trying to save what was already lost" (Banks 54).

The reference of the film is, of course, Robert Browning's famous poem "The Pied Piper of Hamelin," quoted repeatedly through the film by Nicole, with the longest quotation occurring when her father takes her to the barn for sex. And the ultimate Hegelian paradox (the "identity of the opposites") of the film is that it is Stephens himself, the angry outsider, who is the true Pied Piper in the film. That is to say, the way the community survived the loss was by replacing the dead child with a dreamed one: "It's the other child, the dreamed baby, the remembered one, that for a few moments we think exists. For those few moments, the first child, the real baby, the dead one, is not gone; she simply never was" (Banks 125–6). What the successful litigation pursued by Stephens would have brought about is the disturbance of this fragile solution: the pacifying spectre of the dreamed child would have disintegrated, the community would have been confronted with the loss as such, with the fact that their children DID exist and now NO LONGER DO. So if Stephens is the Pied Piper of the film, the threat is that he will snatch away not the real children, but the dreamed ones, thus confronting the community not only with the loss as such, but with the inherent cruelty of their solution which involves the denial of the very existence of the lost real children. Is this, then, the reason Zoe lied? In a true stroke of genius, Egoyan wrote an additional stanza in the style of Browning, which Nicole recites over a close-up of her father's mouth after she has falsely implicated Dolores:

> And why I lied he only knew
> But from my lie this did come true
> Those lips from which he drew his tune
> Were frozen as the winter moon.

These frozen lips, of course, stand not only for the dead children, but also for Nicole's rejection of continuing the incestuous relationship: only her father knew the truth about why she lied at the hearing—the truth of her lie being a NO! to her father. And this NO! is at the same time a NO! to the community (*Gemeinschaft*) as opposed to society (*Gesellschaft*). When does one belong to a community? The difference concerns the netherworld of unwritten obscene rules that regulate the "inherent transgression" of the community, the way we are allowed/expected to violate its explicit rules. This is why the subject who closely follows the explicit rules of a community will never be accepted by its members as "one of us": he does not participate in the transgressive rituals which effectively keep this community together. And society, as opposed to community, is a collective that can dispense with such a set of unwritten rules—but since this is impossible, there is no society without community. This is where the theories that advocate the subversive character of mimicry get it wrong; according to these theories, the properly subversive attitude of the Other—say, of a colonized subject who lives under the domination of the colonizing culture—is to mimic the dominant discourse, but with distance, so that what he does and says is like what the colonizers themselves do…almost like it, with an unfathomable difference which makes his Otherness all the more palpable. One is tempted to turn this thesis around: it is the foreigner emulating faithfully the rules of the dominant culture he wants to penetrate and identify with, who is condemned forever to remain an outsider, because he fails to practice, to participate in, the self-distance of the dominant culture, to follow the unwritten rules that tell us how and when to violate the explicit rules of this culture. We are "in," integrated in a culture, perceived by its members as "one of us," only when we succeed in practicing this unfathomable DISTANCE from the symbolic rules—it is ultimately only this distance which exhibits our identity, our belonging to the culture in question.

Therein resides the radical character of Nicole's ACT: she does something incomparably more radical than simply breaking the explicit rules of her community—rather, she breaks the very unwritten rules which tell us how to relate to these explicit rules, which rules we are allowed to break, and when we are effectively not allowed to make a step, though this step is permitted, solicited even, by the explicit rules. This latter situation is that of the *forced choice*: we are allowed the freedom of choice—*on condition that we make the right choice*.[3] (In our ideological universe, sexual prohibitions as a rule function as a secret endorsement to do it; on the other hand, in political democracy, we are free to choose—on condition that we do not use this freedom to disturb the existing power relations. . . .) This paradox is exemplified by one of the classic scenes from a Hollywood screwball comedy, in which the girl asks her boyfriend: "Do you want to marry me?" After he answers "NO!" she shouts angrily: "Stop dodging the issue! Give me a straight answer!" In a way, the girl's underlying logic is correct: the only acceptable straight answer for her is "Yes!" so anything else—inclusive of a straight "No!"—counts as evasion; the boy

3. For a more detailed analysis of this forced choice, see Chapter 1 of Slavoj Žižek, *The Plague of Fantasies*.

is free to decide, on condition that he makes the right choice. Would a priest not rely on the same paradox in the dispute with a skeptic layman? "Do you believe in God?" "No." "Stop dodging the issue! Give me a straight answer!" Again, in the eyes of the priest, the only straight answer is to assert one's belief in God: far from standing for a clear symmetrical stance, the atheist's denial of belief is, in his eyes, an attempt to dodge the issue of the divine encounter.

This brings us back to Nicole: her lie has such a traumatic impact precisely because, in stating it, she rejects the ideological game of the forced choice and usurps the right to make the wrong choice. The true foreigner in the film is thus not Stephens, the outsider who intrudes on the closed community, but Nicole herself, who voluntarily excludes herself from it by violating its unwritten rules.

Russell Banks (1992)
The Sweet Hereafter
New York: Harper

Alain Bergala (2001)
Hitchcock and Art. Fatal Coincidences
(accompanying volume to the
Centre Pompidou exposition)
Dominique Paini and Guy Cogeval, eds.
Paris and Milano: Centre Pompidou and Mazotta

Terry Eagleton (1970)
Eliot and Common Culture
Eliot in Perspective
Graham Martin, ed.
New York: Humanities Press

Claude Lévi-Strauss (1963)
The Structural Analysis of Myth
Structural Anthropology
New York: Basic Books

Richard Maltby (1996)
"A Brief Romantic Interlude": Dick and Jane Go to
3 ½ Seconds of the Classic Hollywood Cinema
Post-Theory
David Bordwell and Noel Carroll, eds.
Madison: University of Wisconsin Press

Marc Vernet (1993)
Film Noir on the Edge of Doom
Shades of Noir
Joan Copjec, ed.
London: Verso

Martha Wolfenstein and Nathan Leites (1950)
Movies: A Psychological Study
Glencoe (Ill.): The Free Press

Slavoj Žižek (1997)
The Plague of Fantasies
London: Verso Books

WHERE ARE KIAROSTAMI'S WOMEN?
Negar Mottahedeh

The overwhelming focus on the question of censorship in the Iranian cinema of the 1980s and 1990s has left few critics unaware that the inspiring vision, the spectacular rhythm, and the poetic language by which Iranian cinema addresses its audiences all reference, in some way, the limitations placed on the medium by the theocratic government. For, since the revolution that established the Islamic Republic of Iran in 1979, governmental regulations have forced cinema to take on the specificity of the national. In the 1980s and early 1990s especially, compliance with governmental dictates radically affected the representation of women on screen. Modesty laws imposed the veil on all women at all times. Censorship laws prohibited close-ups that would place the female gaze in direct interaction with the non-familial gaze of the male seated in the theatre or that would create emotive relations between the sexes on screen.

Film critic Godfrey Cheshire suggests that both liberals and religious hardliners may have been all too willing to comply with the restrictions placed on the industry and that, indeed, both sides understand the consequences of this acquiescence. He writes that the remarkable difference of Iranian films "owes in large part to Iran's deliberate isolation, its sense of its own cultural separateness and its suspicion of Western influence, a wariness which cuts across the political spectrum: where hard-liners worry about the incursion of anti-religious values, liberals worry about Iranian cinematic culture being molded according to Western viewpoints and prejudices" (Chesire 1998, 277).

Both sides complain, however: censorship sets limits on the artist's freedoms. The pre-framed face and body of the veiled woman is difficult to light, difficult to frame, and difficult to move realistically in and out of private and public spaces. Iranian cinema cannot represent urban reality like other cinemas can. The veiled woman unframes the realist frame. Thus a realist cinema, and the cinema of Iranian everyday life, must place itself outside the city—and sometimes even outside national boundaries—in more "exotic" rural, spaces where women can be fabulated and represented in nature, framed in fields of rice or wheat. Their "naturalized" colourful outfits are an added bonus.

VILLAGE FILMS AND THE ORIENTALIST GAZE

In truth, Kiarostami's cinema could be included in this category of film. He has made so-called "village films" that make the representation of real women possible by transporting the narrative and hence the veiled subject to a rural and exoticized location. Here, she can be filmed constantly labouring outdoors, relieving the filmmaker from the awkward task of placing her in a familial context where the veil is deemed unnecessary, even inappropriate.

One may be tempted to call these representations Orientalist in style. Watching for Kiarostami's women it becomes evident, however, that Kiarostami is resistant to any posture that attempts to situate his characters as ethnographic tallies of dress and custom among primitive cultures in the Third World. We find the most obvious instance of this wariness in *Through the Olive Trees*.

Through the Olive Trees (1994) is a fiction film that is presumed to document the circumstances behind the making of the previous film in the Koker trilogy, *Life and Nothing More*. Rather than proceeding in documentary form, the film delves into a detailed exploration of a developing love affair between the young set-assistant, Husayn, and a local student, Tahirih.

In an early scene, the assistant director, Shiva, goes to pick up Tahirih. She has been selected to perform the role of the new bride in *Life and Nothing More*. Given that *Through the Olive Trees* merely parades behind the genre of documentary, Tahirih ends up acting out her own love affair in the film—a love affair that is at the heart of the fictional world of our documentary.

If we were ever in doubt about the authenticity of cinematic representations, "the original" and "the copy" challenge us to question the notion of the real in these two films. Together they certainly undo our sense of temporality and spatiality, but, more importantly, they go a long way in destabilizing *any* notion of a real, sustained, unified, or authentic identity which we are somehow more willing to attribute to a peasant than to an educated city dweller. This play on the original/copy, and the tensions between reality and fiction as well as the fictional realism within the two film fictions, produces a self-reflexivity that radicalizes our reliance on the visual and underscores the importance of attending to cinematic enunciation. The concomitant effect of this self-reflexivity in the trilogy filmed in Rostamabad is to raise questions about class and power relations within the limits of the local. These are questions that ultimately become central to *Through the Olive Trees*' unfolding heterosexual drama, and that are heightened in Kiarostami's 1999 film *The Wind Will Carry Us.*

Through the Olive Trees takes up issues of class and power by pursuing the sartorial in the second scene. Upon her arrival at Tahirih's house, Shiva finds Tahirih missing and chats instead with the girl's grandmother. When Tahirih finally arrives, she refuses to do as she is instructed. Although she has been selected to play the role of a peasant in *Life and Nothing More*, she refuses to wear a peasant's dress. Tahirih firmly declares that all she needs to do to prepare for her role as Husayn's new bride is tailor her friend's black skirt to fit. She insists that no one wears a dress like the one she's being asked to wear *anymore* and that those who once did wear them were peasants and illiterate—unlike her. Her status is obviously above the rest. An educated woman cannot also be a peasant in dress and custom. Since this scene is an instance of staged realism in a Kiarostami fiction, it is certain that such women, the "real" peasants of whom Tahirih speaks, will appear on the narrative screen. She ultimately appears as one of them. In fact women speaking in dialects appear in Kurdish and Gilaki outfits in *The Wind Will Carry Us* and throughout the early trilogy. In doing so fictively, they too cast a spell of realism and authenticity on the stretches of field captured by Kiarostami's patient camera. In Kiarostami's films, these "authentic" and "inauthentic" women become associated with the very apparatus that constructs the new language of Iranian cinema.

VEILING AND THE LANGUAGE OF CINEMA

Cinema is more than a framed visual image. So, rather than simply assert that Kiarostami is disinterested in creating a cinema of realism when it comes to the representation of urban and rural women, this essay will focus on Kiarostami's use of the restrictions placed on the representation of women and heterosocial relations to develop a cinematic dialect. Kiarostami's new cinematic language situates the framed figure of the post-revolutionary Iranian woman and the perpetual movement and transformation of fabulous ethnic subjects as the very impetus capable of unframing the established codes of cinema globally. Though Kiarostami himself admits that he avoids themes that demand close interaction between men and women in order to evade the issue of censorship, his latest films, the most popularly acclaimed in the West, seem to pay significant attention to the ways in which the demands placed on the representation of women in the Iranian context affect the formal components of representation in cinema. This gesture is taken to the extreme in his latest film *10* (2002), where he radically absents himself, the director, from the set, in order to foreground the representation of the life and preoccupations of urban Iranian women. In this way, he exposes the logic of his film production after the Iranian revolution, associating its processes and the technologies of cinematic representation as intimately linked to the veiled female body.

Though Kiarostami may have ignored the visual representation of women within his narrative screen for many years, his signature has been to cede the very texture of his films to the figure of the veiled Iranian woman and to grant this framed body the power to affect every syllable of his cinematic language, just as an accent affects every part of speech. The veiled figure of the woman is imprinted in the film as a productive principle appearing as a hidden figure within Kiarostami's film frames. "Her" ability to construe a new cinematic language is emphasized through the association of the veiled body with the technologies of filmic production at moments of enunciative rupture within the film itself. The technology of filmmaking is, in other words, gendered feminine through the association of the veiled body with the clapper and the camera. The first scene in *Through the Olive Trees* provides a provocative example.

SELF-REFLEXIVITY AND THE ENUNCIATIVE RUPTURE
Scene one, following the prologue in *Through the Olive Trees* opens in typical Kiarostami fashion (Figure 1, shot 1). We know we have entered his auteurial world as the long take/long shot from the interior of the truck captures the scenes and settings for the film that came before it in the Koker trilogy, namely the film *Life and Nothing More*. The shot is presumed to be from the perspective of the driver, who until about a minute into the scene (shot 2) remains unidentified (whether visually or aurally) and

Figure 1

shot 1

shot 2

shot 3

shot 4

shot 6

shot 7

shot 8

receives her first reverse point-of-view shot a long three and a half minutes into the opening sequence (shot 8). This shot sequence is the first of many instances in Kiarostami's post-revolutionary films that refuses to identify the point-of-view shot with a viewing subject, thus disorienting the film spectator's positioning in relation to what is seen. The shot exposes the frame and prohibits, for more than the conventional length of time, any identification with the gaze of a character on screen. The presence of the car-framed-window within the camera frame reminds us that our view is framed too. What we see is mediated and limited by the camera's framing. As such this scene reflects on the production of the visual image before us, a shot sequence, in other words, that alerts us self-reflexively to the film's enunciation. "Who is seeing this," we ask? The camera is. This is because the visual image cannot for the moment be identified with a character in the plot.

Countering classical conventions in cinema, the technology of production exposes itself (shot 3) and then becomes the topic of conversation when the camera's gaze becomes identified with the voice of a crewmember (Shiva's voice in shot 2) who, though outside the frame, is assumed to be driving the truck. She picks up a local schoolteacher who played the role of a schoolteacher in *Where is the Friend's Home?* on the way. He delivers the chalk, which she explains she will use to write on the clapboard (shot 4). Recognizing the instrument from the film he played in previously, he reminds her of his part in the film and encourages her to find a role for him in this film, too (shots 6 and 7).

The point-of-view shot from behind the car window is first linked to Shiva's voice, though she remains outside the frame in this interaction. Her point of view is later associated with the clapboard and chalk, the filmic apparatus, that marks the beginning of subsequent scenes. Shiva's veiled body (and principally, her speech and vision) becomes associated with the apparatus that produces the images on the screen.

Such moments of enunciation are moments of rupture in the film narrative and as such they alert us to the labour involved in the production of the images we see on screen. These moments of self-reflexivity occur time and again in Kiarostami's work. The processes of production and hence the technology of the film itself become associated, at such moments, with the otherwise unframed figure of the Iranian woman. It is as if Kiarostami's films link the very techniques and technologies of filmmaking in the Iranian context with the figure of the veiled woman, while excluding her image from the narrative screen. A brief example follows.

LIFE AND NOTHING MORE

In *Life and Nothing More*, the second film in the Koker trilogy, the fictive director of the film *Where Is the Friend's Home?* drives to Rostamabad after a massive earthquake that has destroyed the homes of many residents, and left them destitute. In his quest to find those who played parts in his film among the survivors, the director runs into an old man carrying a bathroom fixture up a steep hill. The old man is the character in *Where Is the Friend's Home?* who guided the young hero of that film through the streets of Koker. Following the old man to his home in *Life and Nothing More*, the director expresses surprise and says that he had expected to see the artisan and door maker in his old home in *Where Is the Friend's Home?* This comment inaugurates a long discussion between the two regarding the nature of reality in film. The old man replies that the home in *Where Is the Friend's Home?* was his "film" home and that in fact this home, too, is not really his home. His real home was destroyed in the earthquake.

As this peerless carpenter from *Where Is the Friend's Home?* starts talking about the fakeness of his ornate home in that film as well as the one we are watching, he abruptly breaks the fourth wall of the narrative. He looks directly at the camera from the upstairs veranda and addresses the film crew. When he does this, a female crewmember runs into the frame to help the old man find a cup for his water and then quickly runs out again. While this is the only instance in which the crew and the technology of filmmaking (though not film distribution) are exposed in this film, the scene blurs the boundaries between the fictional and the real and makes the constructedness of the fictional world tactile and immediate. That the veiled body of a crewmember appears at this moment of enunciative rupture is significant. Her presence becomes amplified in the next film in the trilogy (*Through the Olive Trees*) when every retake of the scene of exchange between Tahirih and Husayn is associated with the clapper and chalk that enter the screen in tandem with the veiled body of the assistant director, Shiva.

This is one of many examples that illustrate how the veiled body becomes signified along side the apparatus which makes our visual access to the film narratives possible.

While it would seem as if Kiarostami's films abide by the early restrictions placed on the industry with respect to the representation of women, that is, by barring them from central roles, the production, indeed the very language of cinema articulated by the codes and conventions of Kiarostami's work, is formulated in relation to the restrictions that have informed the industry since the 1980s. Watching Kiarostami's post-revolutionary films chronologically may give us some insight into the pattern by which this filmic language has developed and the ways in which this dialect has been rooted in the association of the filmic apparatus with an embodied modesty and an averted gaze.

THE AVERTED GAZE

We return now to the third scene of *Through the Olive Trees* to follow an averted gaze, informed by the regulations prescribing visual modesty in Iranian films. For, in my reading, the association between the veiled female body and the filmic apparatus is developed in Kiarostami's work alongside a subtle undoing of the quest for the authentic and the exotic in ethnographic projects. This undoing is informed by the adoption by the camera of a modest and averted gaze.

Hamid Naficy explains that when the direct gaze of desire was prohibited in cinema after the Islamic revolution the averted and unfocused gaze, signaling modest relations between men and women, began to predominate the screen (131–50). Cinematic grammar shifted henceforth as shot-reverse shots between men and women (signaling close heterosexual communication between non-relatives) became less frequent and as women appeared instead in long, static shots that translated the desexualization of cinema into cinematic language. Though some filmmakers have satisfied these de(hetero)sexualizing demands by merely following the rule of the law in their shot constructions and editing patterns, Kiarostami has taken the modest and averted gaze literally.

In scene three of *Through the Olive Trees*, Shiva drives off from Tahirih's home to find a suitable "peasant outfit" for the educated girl. The camera, which has entered the truck with Shiva, does not shift, however. It acts as if it has come in the driver's-side door, lens forward, and remained there facing the passenger-side window. Once the car moves, it resists the conventional camera association with the gaze of the driver. Rather than look ahead with Shiva as she drives forward, the camera looks out the side window at the greenery along the roadside (Figure 2, shot 1). It captures a pair of

Figure 2

shot 1

shot 2

shot 3

shot 4

children in the side window as we hear them calling Shiva's name. She backs up and Ahmad Ahmadi from *Where Is the Friend's Home?* appears in the frame followed by his friend. The entire conversation between Shiva and the village children occurs as the camera continues to look out of the window on the passenger's side. The camera does not provide the conventional reverse point-of-view shot from the perspective of the school children at Shiva. And as the car continues to move to its destination, the camera proceeds to capture the fields of green, the children, and the villagers' new school tent in the side-view mirror (Figure 2, shots 2–3).

Scene three not only dissociates the camera from the gaze with which the narrative has identified since scene one, in it the camera also assumes an independence that it also seeks to grant to the film viewer. It does so by extension. In this scene, the viewer whose primary identification is with the camera, is no longer positioned as an invisible mediator on whom the closure of the narrative will depend. Released in this way, the viewer is detached from the film's ideological and discursive constructions. The viewer, in essence, becomes an autonomous being in relation to the images and sounds unfolding on screen.

The camera thus averts its gaze from the linear gaze that moves forward with the car and that looks ahead. It only rises to the alert as the cut to the next scene moves Shiva's body into the frame, clapper in hand. Her clapper and voice identify the shot and take of the first scene of exchange between the newlyweds of *Life and Nothing More* (Figure 2, shot 4). Typically, Kiarostami plays a trick on us, identifying the scene that is being recorded as Scene 4, Shot 1, Take 1 of *Through the Olive Trees*—the film we are watching.

The averted gaze assumed by Kiarostami's camera in 1994 brings him closer to what he coins "the half-made film," in 1999. This is a type of film that demands the audience to be an equal participant in the making of the narrative. The averted gaze suggests, more importantly, how the viewer is positioned within the artificially simple narratives Kiarostami's films layout especially in *The Wind Will Carry Us*.

THE WIND WILL CARRY US (1999)

Like many of Kiarostami's films, the narrative thread in *The Wind Will Carry Us* is worn very thin. Behzad, the film's lead, travels with his crew to the remote village of Siah Darreh to record a ritual performed by village women after the death of an ailing hundred-year-old village elder. The death fails to take place. In fact little happens on the level of the narrative. Behzad and his young guide, Farzad, become the visual locus of "what goes on." The conversations between the two repeat and revolve around Behzad's inquiry into the old villager's vital signs. The obsessive return to this issue leaves no doubt about the film's morbid narrative reality: the hero of our film wants this woman to die so that he and his crew can return to their worn urban lives having amassed some great ethnographic footage.

As for our film footage, it would seem that what is outside the frame and, indeed, what is centrally in it, is of no significance whatsoever. There is no story per se. There is no reason for the viewer to follow Behzad's quest. And though the central question of the film is the hushed: "When will she die?" the old villager doesn't die and the crew doesn't leave. Neither the villager's death nor the ethnographic project is able to provide the film with narrative closure. In fact, narrative closure is uninteresting, even morbid.

HOW IS SHE?

With these scenes, the narrative elements that progress the film are forced into a cyclical repetition of questions and responses: "How is she?" Behzad asks the Farzad. "Who?" the boy responds. "You ask 'who?' again. . . . Our patient, of course." The scenes of Behzad and Farzad walking through the village, discussing Mrs. Malek's health, repeat over and over again. We know the flow of the conversation. We know the sites in which they take place, we know their pattern of movement through the streets. What is there to follow in these scenes? And who?

Like the drive uphill to the graveyard that provides Behzad the altitude he needs to make the cellular phone connection, the discussions between Behzad and his crew become excruciatingly predictable. The crewmembers want to return home. They want to know when the villager will die. They want to know how Behzad knows that her death is imminent. They will sleep long hours, eat strawberries, and long for fresh milk. And though the exchanges between Behzad and his crew become rote, the crewmembers only appear in an establishing long shot within the frame *once*.

We learn to recognize their voices and their complaints, but their faces remain unknown to us. Behzad speaks to his fellow travellers through the doorway of their bedroom. When he peers in, the camera holds back. Indeed, as is the case with Shiva's gaze in scene three of *Through the Olive Trees*, the camera refuses to respond to Behzad's point of view when the crewmembers appear outside his passenger-side window on a strawberry-picking adventure. Going against all that is standard convention in dominant cinemas, the camera again and again dissociates its gaze from that of the character's. It even fails to associate itself with the crucial reverse point-of-view shot from the groggy vantage-point of the crews' bedroom. While Behzad is ostensibly obsessed with death, we are visually confronted with a dead end.

What are we to look at when our vision is proscribed? What are we to follow when the narrative stubbornly resists closure? What is the film saying to us?

A turn to the cellar scene, which has been the subject of much fascination and debate amongst film critics, may provide some clues in that it provides one of the most evocative moments of enunciation inscribed in the visual track of the film.

THE CELLAR SCENE

The sequence opens with the lead character's (Behzad's) descent into the cellar where the heard-but-never-seen ditch-digger's female lover milks her cow. Behzad goes to her to get milk for his crew. We should note immediately that though the ditch-digger, and ten other characters are outside our frame throughout the film, in the cellar scene, the ditch-digger's lover, Zeynab, is not. Rather, she is lit in such a way that her face, though presumably in the cinematic frame, is never seen by the lead character nor by the spectator before the theatre screen. She is, typically, unframed by the apparatus.

In the darkness of the cellar, Zeynab appears carrying a gas lamp that lights up her long red skirt and slippers (Figure 3, shot 1). She makes her way past the camera to a corner of the cellar where her lamp illuminates the hind legs and teats of the cow. As she milks her cow, Behzad recites memorized fragments of poems to her. These fragments are stanzas from the poetry of Forough Farrokhzad, the modernist poet and filmmaker whose untimely death has imbued her life and work with revolutionary potential, and hence infamy. After speaking to Zeynab about Forough, Behzad asks her to lift up the lamp so that he can see her face.[1] He claims to have not seen her lover's (i.e. Joseph's) face and that he would like to be a witness to his taste (shot 2). Without

1. For a discussion of Forough Farrokhzad and her work see Farzaneh Milani.

Figure 3

shot 1   shot 2   shot 3   shot 4

exchanging a single word, Zeynab denies Behzad this visual access to her body and falls silent when he asks her name (shot 3). Instead, she asks about the poet and Forough's schooling. When Behzad recites the lines that motivate the film's title, Zeynab cuts him short and tells him that his milk pail is full (shot 4).

The title sequence should be recognized, in its self-reflexivity, as a moment of enunciation where our inability to see Zeynab, is reflected upon in the exchange between the characters. He wants to see her face, but, like the viewer, he is visually blocked by the technology of film production. While the ban against the close-up on females has, it would seem, been lifted on the industry, the ditchdigger's lover is never represented in a close-up. We realize indeed, that more than merely citing the early restrictions on the representation of women, Kiarostami *quotes* and then applies the regulation *differently*. That is, he does so as a *technique* which is not only reflected upon in the film narrative, but which is also actively used to absent and unframe *other* characters (i.e. not only women) critical to the continuity and closure of the narrative itself.

Behzad's extensive conversations in medium shot and close-up with other female characters reassures us that Kiarostami is not about bowing to censorship or turning it into his own form of orthodoxy. Rather he seems to be interested in developing a language and a filmic technique in relation to those demands in an attempt to make Iranian cinema principally national; a cinema that speaks with a dialect in the global context. Recognizing the impossibility of closure in a desexualized cinema, the cinematic language he develops ignores closure by averting its gaze. This gesture destabilizes the quest for the authentic and the exotic in ethnography, while halting a notion of progress that, in film, is embedded in framing and editing conventions that militate the always forward march of the narrative plot.

WHAT IS "THE HALF-MADE FILM"?

Cheshire explains: "In talking about *The Wind Will Carry Us* as well as his work in general, [Kiarostami] has referred to his notion of the half-made film in which the elements that are erased or left incomplete invite the viewer's imaginative participation" (8–15).

What we see when we don't see in Kiarostami's *The Wind Will Carry Us*, is what we see with a modest and an averted gaze. And it is perhaps this averted gaze that brings what is most central into stronger focus. In Kiarostami, this gaze, linked to the camera's framing, captures movement. The shifting movements of everyday life occur on the conspicuous peripheries of repeating scenes. They alert us to what is important to the film itself. Here bodies cast shadows as they drape clothes on lines to dry (Figure 4), herds of sheep fill the unpaved roads (Figure 5), and baby chick litter stairwells. The modest look of the camera frames a world where balls appear followed by running children, where apples roll in the dirt and get brushed off and passed on to rest next to an elbow in a coffee shop (Figure 6). In this fabulated world, green hay moves as if on its own, on the back of a disembodied voice of an "ethnic" subject (Figure 7). Time passes here like yesterday was a month ago and an old villager lives to be one hundred and fifty or a hundred with a discount.

This fabulated world shows technology's capacity to dream and its own wonderment in capturing motion. Unlike the direct voyeurism of narrative film, this is an exhibitionist cinema, the kind discussed by Tom Gunning, as a cinema enraptured by the magical possibilities of cinematic technology itself (Gunning 1986).

In our mystified craving for narrative closure, we tend to forget that movement was the fascination of primitive cinema. And it is this primitive fascination that Kiarostami turns to in order to capture the fictive primitive with a newly gendered lens. It is as if the new

Figure 4

Figure 5

Figure 6

Figure 7

form of cinematic language, the new dialect of Iranian cinema, must retrieve an ur-form lodged in the ur-history of contemporary technologies of film, in order to take shape. The fictive primitive appearing alongside the productive technologies of cinema, represented in the figure of the female coffee shop owner who briefly confiscates Behzad's camera, reminds us of the primitivism of the camera's obsessions and the redemptive turn of Kiarostami's camera itself. Lodged in this way, his camera frames and fabulates peripheral movement as the object of its fascination, ignoring its contemporary audience's naturalized quest for the forward push of the narrative, even in the face of a narrative that deems closure morbid, even impossible.

As Gunning argues, the viewer of primitive cinema, was "positioned less as a spectator-in-the-text, absorbed into a fictional world," by the relay of gazes that presumably suture her into the narrative. Like the viewers of the first films, Kiarostami's camera positions us rather as "gawker[s] who [stand] alongside, held for the moment by curiosity and amazement" (Gunning 1994, 189–201). In Kiarostami's "half-made film" the narrative is our artisan craft, for the most part. What we make of the scraps of everyday life and the peripheral movement of objects and subjects framed by the veiled body and directed by that of the fictive primitive, is our part in the film's making. In its own self-absorbed wonderment at its technology's magical capabilities, the camera cuts the cord and permits us to reflect on what we bring into the darkened theatre. Like the conditioned homophobic reflex that might have some wondering if Mr. Badii is trying to turn a trick on the dirt road in the opening sequence of *Taste of Cherry*, the "half-made film" allows us to self reflexively ponder the unconscious dreams we knot around the scraps of a fabulated everyday life, conditioned as we have become by the standardization of a particular cinematic language to weave ourselves into a narrative that we may *think* is progressing on screen.

CODA

10 (2002) screens ten conversations between an urban female visual artist and photographer, Mania Akbari, and the passengers she picks up as she drives around Tehran. Many critics, including Roger Ebert, have expressed frustration with Kiarostami's *10*, and have performed surprising exoduses long before the penultimate segment, in which one of Akabari's female passengers unveils her shaved head. Understandably, the film appears as nothing worth watching. A series of often repeating dialogues that sustain a long and averted camera gaze in the closed quarters of a mini-SUV, the film becomes tedious even if taken, as many have, as an ethnography of urban life for Iranian women. But as I have tried emphasize throughout the essay, the decisive underlay of Kiarostami's oeuvre is a critique of the morbid effects of ethnography, a critique that is foregrounded especially in *The Wind Will Carry Us*.

Precluding the possibility of ethnographic realism, as the narrative thread of the film, *10* appears as a coda to Kiarostami's oeuvre, the filmmaker's reflection on his own filmmaking culture exposing the logic of his film language and the productive link between the body of the veiled women and his cinematic apparatus.

Each sequence of Akbari's conversations with her passengers is cut in between a numbered countdown reel. Wedged in this way, the ninety-four minute film fiction plays as a scrap of film that screenings generally edit out. One can't help but hear that trickster whisper, "Here is a film about women that the projectionist should have wound into the receiver reel minutes before you entered the theatre."

Jonathan Rosenbaum has described *10* as a "daring enterprise," not because of this formal intimation about the nature of the project, but because of the film's attempt to eliminate the directorial role altogether (100). Kiarostami's obvious absence from the set in a film he has coined the "non-made film" points up the impossibilities of hetero-social relations between female actors and their male director. Women have been edited out of the screen in the era of post-revolutionary modesty. To show women as central characters, in this logic, means absenting the male director altogether.

In the opening sequence of *10*, a small DV camera, fitted on the dashboard, turns on to a close-up of a young boy in conversation with his divorcée mother, Akbari. Fifteen long minutes later, as if to relieve viewers of the patriarchal rant of a young boy acting like a puny version of Akbari's suffocating ex-husband, the camera cuts to a medium close-up of Akbari, fully made-up and in Islamic garb—a contradiction in bearing that has taken media-focused Western audiences by surprise. From this point on, the camera associates its view with the photographer's veiled body, gives itself to the claustrophobic environment she has long tried to escape, and attends to her tempered frustration with the erasure of women within Iranian societal laws.

As feature length coda to Kiarostami's post-revolutionary oeuvre, the film is not about merely exposing the frame to show the reality behind the fiction, which admittedly is part of the function of the controversial coda to *Taste of Cherry*. Instead, it reads as the exposure of the now de-auteured auteur's literal quotation of modesty laws in his post-revolutionary work. His films are only movies, and though imbued with an air of realism they are *also* movies, as Rosenbaum once said. But as Kiarostami's films *Close-up* and *Through the Olive Trees* have amply demonstrated, his films are also about the processes of *making* movies in Iran. As such, what *10* reflexively reveals in formal terms, is his oeuvre's attempt to allegorize the restraints and the possibilities of cinematic enunciation under the stringent laws of dictating modesty in the Islamic Republic.

10, the film that should have been reeled forward past the countdown to the overture of an actual film, shows not outtakes but the veiled female bodies that are constitutive of the language and the grammar of his cinema. As formative technologies the bodies are consumed with the contradictions of a Republic that is outwardly Shiite and inwardly secular. These bodies, structured by and projections of Islamic laws, are forces that have become constitutive of a cinema of contradictions—a cinema in which life on screen must appear somewhere in the wedge between presence and absence, between realism and fiction, between the original and the copy, between a narrative and the magical signature of peripheral movements, articulating itself as the deferred allegory of the condition of film production itself. It is perhaps this, Kiarostami's allegorization of the structuring conditions of the language of the Iranian narrative screen, that has produced the bewildering association between Iranian cinema and a European modernist inheritance in the work of many reviewers.[2]

2. I would like to formally thank Michelle Lach and the graduate students in my Contemporary Iranian Cinema class in the Literature Program at Duke University (Spring 2003), Arnal Dilantha Dayaratna, Abigail Lauren Salerno, Shilyh Warren, for their insights on the film industry and for giving shape to this reading of allegory.

Godfrey Cheshire (2000)
How to Read Kiarostami
Cineaste 25:4

Tom Gunning (1986)
The Cinema of Attractions:
Early Film, Its Spectator and the Avant-Garde
Wide Angle 8

——(1994)
The Whole Town's Gawking:
Early Cinema and the Visual Experience of Modernity
The Yale Journal of Criticism 7.2

Farzaneh Milani (1992)
Veils and Words:
The Emerging Voices of Iranian Women Writers
New York: Syracuse University Press

Hamid Naficy (1994)
Veiled Vision / Powerful Presences:
Women in Post-Revolutionary Iranian Cinema
In the Eye of the Storm: Women in Post-revolutionary Iran
Mahnaz Afkhami and Erika Friedl, ed.
Syracuse: Syracuse University Press

Mehrnaz Saeed-Vafa and Jonathan Rosenbaum (2003)
Abbas Kiarostami
Urbana: University of Illinois Press

THE GREAT DANCE: TRANSLATING THE FOREIGN IN ETHNOGRAPHIC FILM
Brenda Longfellow

Ethnographic film would not exist without a deep and foundational relation to the foreign but while foreignness in the realm of art cinema conjures up the cultural capital of connoisseurship, a cinema of old countries, dark pasts and heady, existential sexualities, the foreign in ethnographic film is linked to discourses of sobriety, truth, and authenticity. In the disembodied discourse of this discipline, desire goes underground, banished to the margins, as in the case of Bronislaw Malinowski's intimate journal (published in 1967, forty years after *Argonauts of the Western Pacific* was enshrined as a classic of ethnographic method) in which anguished confessions of sexual fantasy, identity dissolution, and visceral anger at his subjects created, as James Clifford discretely observes, "a minor scandal" (97). The best writing on ethnography today, the work of Trinh T. Minh-ha, David MacDougall, Michael Taussig, Bill Nichols, George Marcus, and James Clifford, sets out to expose the implication of desire, to deconstruct the epistemological strategies of the discipline for whom the institutions of the museum and gallery, the university and the social sciences, provide the alibi of objectivity and dispassion.

Historically, "foreignness" in ethnography was constructed through a concept of epic time in which the ethnographic subject was considered along the scale of evolution as an earlier, primitive (if rather imperfect) incarnation of European man, the implicit standard by which difference was measured and embalmed. Cast as noble savage by the romanticism which has always pervaded the discipline, the ethnographic subject came to act as the symbolic repository for all that modernity had torn from the West: innocence, animal sensuality, a spiritual oneness with nature. This romanticism, moreover, was supported by a melancholic assumption that the primitive was facing imminent extinction by the relentless progress of modernity. The liberal mission of the ethnographer, as such, was to salvage representations of the "vanishing race" as a visual archive of humanity. That the West's own culpability for cultural genocide remained largely unacknowledged did nothing to prevent the flourishing of ethnography's mission, from Edward Sheriff Curtis's mammoth documentation of North American Indians in the early twentieth century to today's television ethnographies of the "Vanishing World" genre. If one of the strategies by which ethnography has constructed the foreign is the denial, as Johannes Fabian phrases it, of coeval temporalities between the ethnographic subject and the observing European eye, a central strategy in visual ethnographies has been the indexicality of the image itself, in which difference is embodied in signifiers of epidermal schemes, body types, dress, habitat, rituals, and customs, the ensemble of visual cultural practices which constitute the "raw" data of ethnographic experience.

The troubling immediacy of the image has always proven to be a crucial dilemma for visual ethnography. Written anthropology constructs meaning through a process of secondary revision, narrativization, and elimination. "In a sense," as David MacDougall writes, "translation is always to anthropology's advantage, for it channels data through the keyhole of language, producing a condensation of meaning and leaving most of the data behind" (68). It is precisely through this process, MacDougall insists, that the raw data—the experiential encounter between two cultures, the ethnographer's and the culture the ethnographer is observing—is stripped of the idiosyncratic, the excessive, the opaque, the difference that is immanent and not translatable. Such stripping, however, cannot be definitively accomplished in visual ethnographies because the image, ontologically, has a fluid and unstable semiosis. On the sound track to her anti-ethnographic film *Reassemblage*, Trinh T. Minh-ha narrates the following apocryphal story. "A man attending a slide show on Africa turns to his wife and says with guilt in his voice: "I have seen some pornography tonight" (1992, 101). The visual is always threatened by misconstrual as Trinh T. Minh-ha suggests, when images of naked breasts can be pulled effortlessly from *National Geographic* into inappropriate generic contexts.

In early silent ethnographies, the central issue of cultural translation, of delivering stable meanings about the other, was accomplished primarily through the use of intertitles or in the case of Curtis's *In the Land of the War Canoes* or Flaherty's *Nanook of the North*, by the use of dramatization in which re-enactments of traditional rituals or everyday life are embedded in generic narrative themes of man versus nature or good versus evil. With the coming of sound in the 1930s, ethnographic film was provided with a technology that allowed for the direct application of language to the recalcitrant material of visual imagery in the form of voice-over narration. The separation of image and voice in ethnographic films from 1930 to 1970, where voice is ascribed to the white European investigator and image to the bodies of colonial others, reiterates, morphologically, the political binarisms of colonialism: mind versus body, subject versus object, us versus them. Here, to be sure, descriptive narration forces the data of the foreign encounter through the keyhole of language, generalizing, explaining, leaving nothing exempt, as Trinh T. Minh-ha notes, from the "totalizing quest for meaning" (1991, 29). But this forcing frequently occurs in ways which utterly foreground the limitations of translation. In Mead and Bateson's classic *Trance and Dance in Bali* (1952), Mead's voice drones on describing the actions presented in the image with an astonishing redundancy and superfluity. Equally in Jean Rouch's *Les Maître fous* (1954) and Maya Deren's *Divine Horsemen* (1947–85), both of which record possession rituals, the voice of the narrator takes on an uncanny supplementary quality.

The exaggerated distance of the voice from the images is the most extreme in *Divine Horseman* where Deren's raw footage is reconstructed posthumously and a male voice-over added, reading extracts from Deren's voluminous and dense book on voodoo rituals, also titled *Divine Horsemen* (1953). That Deren, an accomplished film-maker, struggled for ten years to complete the editing on this project and eventually abandoned it, says a great deal about her perspicacity in recognizing the deeply complex and politically-charged challenge of harnessing explanatory language to documented experiences (of possession, trance, and ritual) which defy the logic of explanation. Perhaps too, her failure—and it is clearly only a failure when measured against the classical ethnographic text in which the authority and presumed omniscience of the voice are secured by the voice's detachment from the image—has to do with the way in which Deren was incapable of elaborating a necessary distance from the images she had filmed. A voodoo initiate herself (with documented episodes of possession in which she threw a refrigerator across a room, held her hands in burning fire, and cursed fellow filmmaker Stan Brakhage), her images of ritual possession in Haiti might have presented an immediacy too close, a psychic reminder too palpable, a lure too dangerously seductive. While personal implication could be contained in the dispassionate act of writing *Divine Horsemen* (the book), as obsessively "thick" with description as it is, the magical and potentially suggestive properties of the image perhaps presented too grave a threat of personal dissolution.

The personal troubling and subversion of ethnographic authority is also apparent in *Les Maîtres fous*, in Jean Rouch's stuttering, hesitant, improvisational voice-over narration which endeavours, but ultimately fails, to provide a secure context for understanding the frothing mouths, spirit possession, and dog-eating rituals which transport his subjects out of the everyday world of poverty and disenfranchisement. Rouch's failure no doubt accounts for the fact that *Les Maîtres fous* has been subject to diametrically opposed readings from Teshome H. Gabriel's denunciation of the film as racist to Michael Taussig's reading of the film as a performance of radical colonial parody (Gabriel 75–7; Taussig 240–3).

Catherine Russell, in her work on ethnographic possession films, notes how these films are structured by a central and irresolvable paradox: "Absorption into the pulsating rhythm of the dance may be a threat to ethnographic distance and objectivity, and yet this is precisely what attracts filmmakers in search of a subjective entry into the ethnographic scene" (194). At issue here is not simply a desire for the exotic other, but a desire to abandon the distance of the observer/outsider through an act of transcendence that lands the Western subject in the place of the foreign other. But, as Russell argues, the "actual experience of possession remains outside the limits of visual knowledge and constitutes a subtle form of ethnographic resistance: films of possession cannot, in the end, represent the 'other reality' of the other's subjectivity" (194).

The desire to be in the place of the other certainly represents the limit position of liberal ethnography. Sympathetic to the cause of anti-colonial struggles, bound in relations of deep affection and affinity to their subjects, the liberal ethnographic tradition (of which Rouch is no doubt the most prominent exemplar) had always laboured under an acute reflexivity concerning its own practices. Advocating cultural relativism against the racist hierarchies of the metropolitan countries, ethnographic filmmakers like Rouch proved time and again his willingness to re-negotiate relations of representation under colonialism, inviting direct participation in his films, converting erstwhile ethnographic subjects into colleagues, collaborators, and friends. In films like *Jaguar* (1954–67), where the improvisational dialogue is collectively created and post-dubbed, ethnographic detachment is eclipsed by a form of participatory fiction and creative synergy. Certainly the genius of a film like *Jaguar* stems from the way in which it upsets the subject/object, self/other, Westerner/native dichotomy so central to the epistemological infrastructure of colonialism through its fictional attribution of point of view to the central characters themselves who journey to Mali in search of work and adventure, in search of a story that will be taken home to the village. Encountering other tribes, foreign customs, and rituals, they tenuously occupy the place of the ethnographic subject, looking at the other not with the clinical eye of ethnographic discipline but with a sense of wonderment, curiosity, and play.

Rouch's formalist challenge pales, however, next to the political challenges mounted by the wave of anti-colonial struggles initiated in the 1950s and 1960s. For anti-colonial leaders and intellectuals like Frantz Fanon, the struggle for self-representation was as essential for emerging nations in the process of decolonization as the gaining of political independence. Western ethnography's moral authority, its presumption to represent the "other," was called severely into question, as ethnography itself became a source of parody for the postcolonial imagination. Confronted with this political and postcolonial epistemological crisis, Western ethnographers, rarely electing to actually halt the production of the vast institutional manufacture of representations of the other, sought alternative formal and technical strategies as a way of alleviating the hierarchical relations of representation bequeathed by colonialism.

David MacDougall tells an apocryphal story of the "invention" of subtitles in ethnographic films when, in 1961, Timothy Asch and John Marshall were editing *A Joking Relationship*, a film largely structured as a conversation between N!ai and her great-uncle. After viewing Godard's *À bout de souffle* at Harvard one night, Asch returned to the editing room with a brilliant idea. By the 1970s both Asch (*The Feast*, 1970) and MacDougall (*To Live With Herds*, 1972; *Under the Men's Tree*, 1974) were producing subtitled ethnographic films in which the actual speech of their subjects was reproduced. Along with the technological development of portable sound recording devices like the *nagra*, the soon to be standardized use of subtitles in ethnographic films meant that the authority and interpretative monopoly of voice-over was ceded to the synchronous voice of the ethnographic subject. Synchronized sound obviously had the enormous advantage of bringing the inflection, cadence, and rhythm of the speaking voice into representation, shot through with intentions and accents—the performative elements of meaning production. Phenomenologically closer to the experience of ethnographic observation, *synch sound* allowed for the representation of the ethnographic subject, not simply as a category type or mute cipher in a kinship/tribal structure, but as an individuated personality with a rich inner life, humour, and intelligence. Suddenly cultures could be represented, not simply as homogenized collective entitites—"The Nuer," "The Balinese," etc.—but as sites of internal diversity, dialogical encounters, and competing interpretations.

The enrichment of semiotic possibilities that synch sound enabled, however, was largely overdetermined by the ideology of documentary verisimilitude that claimed the synchronous voice as a mode of presence and authenticity, truth and interiority, no matter that meaning for the Western spectator was always mediated by the process of subtitling, a prior act of condensation and exclusion which Abé Markus Nornes refers to as the "violent reduction demanded by the apparatus" (18). Given that the speaking voice is always faster than the time required for a spectator to read titles,[1]

1. Trinh T. Minh-ha has perceptively argued that: "The duration of the subtitles, for example, is very ideological. I think that if, in most translated films, the subtitles usually stay on as long as they technically can—often much longer than the time needed even for a slow reader—it's because translation is conceived here as part of the operation of suture that defines the classical cinematic apparatus and the technological effort it deploys to naturalize a dominant, hierarchically unified worldview" (1992, 207).

translation in film, apart from all philosophical concerns, is always and already techni-cally bound by the necessities of condensation by "the physical space of the frame and the temporal space of the utterance" (Nornes 20). The mechanics of translating the raw material of the subject's voice into the graphic form of titles is never a word-to-word homologous rendering of meaning, but an act of semiotic transformation. As MacDougall observes, all subtitles imply a certain violence: "they are like a stamp of possession on a film, projecting a particular interpretation. Although the people in the film are speaking to each other, subtitles are one of the ways in which the filmmaker speaks to us" (174).

The erasure of this act of violent transformation from the scene of representation, however, has serious consequences. While some authors argue that the graphic inscription of titles offers a visual reminder of linguistic difference, this unintentional reflexivity operates mainly under erasure in the majority of mainstream ethnographic films. "Subtitles," MacDougall points out, "may induce in viewers a false sense of cultural affinity, since they so unobtrusively and efficiently overcome the difficulties of transla-tion. They may reinforce the impression that it is possible to know others without effort—that the whole world is inherently knowable and accessible" (175). Subtitles can only allow for a facsimile of intimacy, a disguise and distortion of the actual work of cultural mediation. Filmmakers like Trinh T. Minh-ha are committed to exposing this illusion of unmediated translation, using discrepant text and voice against each other, introducing a temporal lag separating the activities of reading and hearing, adding the redundancy of a title over a speaking voice, deploying the heavily accented voices of her "actors" in *Surname Viêt Given Name Nam* as sites where meaning struggles, audibly, from one linguistic context to another.

The Great Dance: a Hunter's Story, a recent ethnographic film shot by two white South African brothers, Craig and Damon Foster, has been garnering prizes and critical acclaim in the festival circuits of Europe and North America. Its use of subtitles is sparse, barely noticeable in the weave of visual pyrotechnics and writerly narration which immediately distinguishes the film from the banality of contemporary ethnographic practice. Shot in the Central Kalahari, a scant four years after the historic universal suffrage election in South Africa in 1994 where the African National Congress took power from a brutally violent regime of apartheid, the film poses a rather extraordinary response to the challenge of representing "the foreign" within a postcolonial context.

In many ways *The Great Dance* cannot be understood apart from the very precise factors governing the historic moment in which it was produced: the lived actuality of decolonization in an allegedly desegregated South Africa, a new state-mandated interest in indigenous culture and traditions coupled with the enormously complicated emotional and political responses of white progressives to the apartheid system which had guaranteed their privilege by the brutal oppression of the black majority. All are a part of the complex context in which the film is made.

Ostensibly a film about tracking, *The Great Dance*, follows three San "bushmen"[2] as they travel through the great open plains, reading its signs and signals. The land is transformed into a vast semiotic field in which the texture of a springbok's spoor, paw prints in the sand, a scorpion's journey, or a vulture's flight are redolent with meaning. The San have been frequent objects of the ethnographic gaze in films like John Marshall's *The Hunters* (1958) and more infamously in *The Gods Must Be Crazy* (1980). As African critic Keyan Tomaselli notes, "contemporary academic interest in the San has been sustained partly because of their accessibility to observation even while

2. The use of the term Bushmen is highly controversial. At a screening of *The Great Dance* at the Toronto Environmental Film Festival, a representative of the South African embassy took strong exception to the use of the word in the film. The filmmaker claimed that the word was a production of the self-assignation of his subjects. Keyan G. Tomaselli explicates some of the controversy surrounding the use of the term in "Myths, racism and opportunism: film and TV representations of the San."

'disappearing'" (213). Produced within the paradoxical political economy of postcolonial cinema, the film was brought into being by a Dutch producer, with the financial backing of broadcasters and distributors in Germany, Holland, and South Africa.

> This is an intimate film about their own experiences as expressed by them—in their words and through their eyes; what hunting and tracking mean to them from an experiential (emotional and intellectual), a physical (survival) and a historical (the old days versus the present reality) perspective.[3]

Like much ethnographic film, *The Great Dance* is rationalized as an unmediated translation of inaccessible realities; like most postcolonial ethnography it subverts its own authority in the gesture of handing over, giving voice, allowing *their* perspective (emotional and intellectual) to frame the representation of experience. While the film may well be unalterably bound by the structure and power dynamics of its production (white filmmakers, black subjects), what it does endeavour to do, in an extraordinary act of racial ventriloquism, is to enunciate itself from the place of the other, long the dream and fantasy of the ethnographic imagination. Certainly it was this possibility which both tantalized and eluded Deren and Rouch in their recording of possession rituals: a subjective entry into the ethnographic scene, an impossible crossing into the actual experience of the voodoo and Hauka initiates which left them stuttering, hesitating, and immobilized on the other side of representation.

The Great Dance manages its feat of enunciation through an act of fictional appropriation. "We are San bushmen. The sons and daughters of the first people. We are the chosen ones, the ones Kisabala gave fire to," intones the baritone narrator of the film. Spoken in English in the first person, the narrator (South African actor, Selo Maake ka-Ncubo) assumes the composite character of !Nqate, one of the hunters. It is his

3. http://www.senseafrica.com/greatdance/greatdance.html

subjective voice which functions as interior monologue, articulating the collective myths and traditional ecological knowledge of the San. According to the film's website, the narration was based on extensive field interviews with the !Gwi and !Xo San in the Central Kalahari. Traces of this original raw material are evident in the synch sequences with !Nqate, Xlhoase, and Karoha as they gather around their fire at night to tell stories, make jokes, and relive the hunt of the day. In these synchronized, subtitled sequences, the hunters address each other in language that is resonantly embedded in the traditions of oral culture. As Walter Ong has pointed out, expression and the structure of knowledge in oral cultures is dependent on enormously skillful mnemonic retrieval systems which shape the particular usage of language. While writing externalizes memory, in oral culture memory is assisted through the use of mnemonic patterns such as rhythm, alliteration, repetition, assonances, and antitheses, as well as epithets and clichés. For oral cultures, language, he writes, "is basically formulaic, structured in proverbs and other set expressions. It is aggregative rather than analytic, participatory rather than distanced, situational rather than abstract" (Ong, Preface).

The filmmakers acknowledge this form of language usage and structure the narration accordingly. Avoiding the meta-language of explanation, the narration uses the "parole" of San oral culture as its performative medium. Composed by writer, Jeremy Evans, self-described as a "typical British viewer [with] scant experience of Africa, little knowledge of animals or hunting; none at all of tracking," the narration was distilled from a "mass of transcripts, books, poems, and academic sources." As Evans notes: "The film's structure (three main hunts) and repeated speech ('women like meat,' 'taking without asking,' 'tracking is like dancing') mimic patterns in which the San explain or tell a story. The layers build up so that new meanings of the same phrase become possible." Dialogic, rather than monologic, the narration bears the logic of poetry and the traces of the many voices which embody San tradition.

Not unlike the participatory ethnography of Inuit director Zacharias Kunuk, whose series *Nunuvat, Our Land* involved the entire Igloolik community in recreations of traditional practices, *The Great Dance* sets out to collaboratively recover an extraordinary San custom—the running hunt—from cultural oblivion. Because of the construction of new game reserves, the enactment of legislation restricting San hunting grounds, as well as the enormous changes wrought on San traditional life by the incursion of a cash economy and by increasing immizeration, the hunt (in which the hunters chase their prey across the savanna for hours on end, in temperatures approaching 120 degrees Fahrenheit) had not been practiced for many years and, in fact, existed only as hearsay.

Recreation is perhaps the wrong word to use to describe the activities recorded in the film because it implies a definitive break with the past and because it casts tribal customs as archaic relics of a vanishing race. On the contrary, the running hunt is part of the living memory of !Nqate, Karoha, and Xlhoase, as is their consummate skill in the intricate art of tracking. Here tradition is not coded as something exterior to the contemporary culture, as it is in cultures where writing and the book are the chief technologies of memory, but remains immanent in the performance of the hunt itself. Foregrounding the performative aspect of tradition marks the film's radical departure from nostalgic recreations, such as Flaherty's, where all indications of modernity are framed out of the image or rendered, as in the famous gramophone scene in *Nanook*, in incongruous juxtaposition with the "primitive" mind. The representation of time in *The Great Dance* is far more complex. Here history is not represented as a present recoding of past events, for the past, as it is experienced in San culture, is understood as the time of the ancestors, a living present where the "now" encompasses 30,000 years of continuous San life in the central Kalahari. This "now," furthermore, is inextricably tied to the specific geographic space of ancestral land and is referenced in the film through the shots of cave paintings and through the uncanny, virtually timeless spectacular images of the land itself. As is the case in oral cultures, it is the performance of tradition itself which reciprocally binds and recreates communal meaning through the generations. Performing the hunt, according to !Nqate, means to walk in the footsteps of the ancestors, to act according to the embodied memories carried through thousands of generations.

The Great Dance, however, is clearly framed by an awareness of the precariousness of cultural survival as the San are confronted with the contemporary realities of political change, economic hardship, and environmental degradation. This knowledge is reflected in sequences of the scripted narration as !Nqate reflects, "In the old days we could speak to the rain and ask the sky to send soft rain. The sky used to listen to us but now lightning is very dangerous. It brings no rain, it kills, because our ways are being changed." The pressure on their traditional ways of life is not only indicated by the last title of the film where an immediate political reality is referenced, "Since the scenes were filmed, the !Xo people's individual hunting licences have been revoked. Their hope is to regain rights to ancestral land where their forefathers hunted and gathered for over 30,000 years," but is there in the particular signifiers of village life: the cut-off jeans and t-shirts, the boom box and running shoes, the detritus of a capitalist world market. These signifiers eloquently speak to the contemporary economic and historic position of the San, caught, like so many indigenous peoples, on the margins of a cash economy when traditional subsistence modes are imperiled by the advance of so-called modernity. While the film does not dwell on these political aspects, their traces ensure that the hunt, as it is depicted, can never be collapsed into an idealized version of a vanished nomadic past.

Walter Ong makes a distinction between primary orality—the condition of cultures which have never been exposed and transformed by the technology of writing—and a secondary orality of the electronic age, where the technologies of video, radio, and the telephone provide for a certain orality that is, nonetheless, completely dependent on writing and print for its existence. In two principal ways *The Great Dance* produces and inscribes secondary orality via the mediation of digital technologies. The first has to do with the manner in which digital post-production facilitates the use—and cost—of visual effects such as overlays, superimposition, black and white, time-lapse, and slow and fast motion, all of which proliferate in the film, transforming photographic realism into artful and clearly processed signs of semiotic density and texture. The digital processing of visual material is also connected to the extensive use of new lightweight mini DV cameras and DV night vision cameras. Strapped to the back of a cheetah, to the underside of a steenbok, to the rotting carcass of a hyena as it is devoured by vultures, the visual perspective presented by these mini DV cameras takes us out of the realm of ordinary ways of seeing. Moving low to the ground, following the sinuous muscles on the back of a cheetah, or staring into the opaque eye of an antelope, we confront an absolute subversion of the conventional visual cues and coordinates which naturalize visual perspective and tie vision to the fixed perspective of the humanist subject. Here, on the contrary, is something prior and atavistic, a mode of vision that challenges Western perspectival space.

Within the diegesis of the film, these extreme shots are connected to the inner psychic life of the hunters. As !Nqate observes, the penultimate skill in hunting is to be able to psychically project oneself into the mind and body of the animal: "When you follow the prints, you see in your mind how Porcupine thinks. Every animal is like this—you jump when the track shows it jumps. . . . When you track an animal, you must become the animal. . . ." In the uncanny perspective of these digital cameras, the boundary between the human and the non human world is eclipsed. Seeing through the eyes of a kudo, the digital takes us into the realm of magic, the supernatural, and into traditional cosmological beliefs of San culture.

At the same time, these uncanny shots are only intermittent and are woven into extended documentary footage of the hunt itself. !Nqate often remarks that "hunting is like dancing" and the film foregrounds the extraordinary grace and astounding physical stamina of the hunters as they run barefoot for miles across grass plains and burning sand. Indeed, the filmmakers hired an Olympic athlete to run behind the hunters with a small camera, but even he could not keep up with them across the rough terrain and in the burning sun. Throughout these sequences, the camera is always close to the bodies of the hunters, gliding below their hands as they signal to each other in the silent semaphore of tracking, observing the smooth and lithe muscles of Karoha, the blood flowing down the legs of !Nqate as he is marked before the hunt. This footage testifies to an almost haptic state of filmmaking in which the bounded limitations of the two-dimensional medium of film are transcended by an incredible phenomenological "feel" of both the hunters' and the animals bodies in extreme motion. There constant mobility of these shots, the visceral quality evoked by the extreme close ups of hands, feet, fur, and eyes, explodes the subject/object dichotomy of classical ethnography where the "other" is habitually held at a distance and pinned in fetishistic contemplation. Here the contemplative gaze is prohibited by our virtual immersion in the experience of the hunt itself.

David MacDougall argued that, in the postcolonial moment of ethnographic practice, "new concepts of anthropological knowledge are being broached in which meaning is not merely the outcome of reflection upon experience but necessarily includes the experience. In part, then, the experience is the knowledge. Such knowledge cannot survive the translation process: it is relational rather than an object in itself" (79). In many ways the performative aspects of *The Great Dance*, its enunciation as a first person narrative, its inscription of extreme subjective points of view, its visceral evocation of the physicality of bodies in motion (animal and human), more than meets the call of theorists like MacDougall, Nichols and Stephen Tyler for an ethnographic poesis in which evocation rather than representation is the norm. Displacing the production of ethnographic knowledge from the classic forms of voice-over narration, the synchronized interview, or observational camera—forms that have historically prioritized the production of interpretation, data extraction, and explanation—*The Great Dance* poses a new model of empathetic understanding. In this model, the foreign is never constituted as an object susceptible to seamless translation. Like poetry, its meaning is figurative and associative, grounded in the representation of an experience which retains those qualities which define, according to Walter Benjamin, the intractability of poetry to translation: "the unfathomable, the mysterious" (70).

Walter Benjamin (1969)
The Task of the Translator
Illuminations
New York: Schocken Books

James Clifford (1988)
The Predicament of Culture:
Twentieth-Century Ethnography, Literature, and Art
Cambridge: Harvard University Press

Maya Deren (1970)
Divine Horsemen: Voodoo Gods of Haiti
New York: Chelsea House

Jeremy Evans (n.d.)
Notes from the Writer
http://www.senseafrica.com/greatdance/greatdance.html

Johannes Fabian (1991)
Time and the Work of Anthropology
Chur, Switzerland: Harwood Academic Publishers

Teshome H. Gabriel (1982)
Third Cinema in the Third World:
The Aesthetics of Liberation
Ann Arbor: UMI Research Press

Walter J. Ong (1982)
Orality and Literacy:
The Technologizing of the Word
London: Methuen

David MacDougall (1998)
Transcultural Cinema
Princeton: Princeton University Press

Bill Nichols (1994)
Blurred Boundaries:
Questions of Meaning in Contemporary Culture
Bloomington: Indiana University Press

Abé Markus Nornes (1999)
For an Abusive Subtitling
Film Quarterly 53.3

Catherine Russell (1999)
Experimental Ethnography:
The Work of Film in the Age of Video
Durham: Duke University Press

http://www.senseafrica.com/greatdance/greatdance.html

Michael Taussig (1993)
Mimesis and Alterity:
A Particular History of the Senses
London: Routledge

Keyan G. Tomaselli (1992)
Myths, Racism and Opportunism:
Film and TV Representations of the San
Film as Ethnography
Peter Ian Crawford and David Turton, eds.
Manchester: Manchester University Press

Trinh T. Minh-ha (1992)
Reassemblage (The Script)
Framer Framed
New York: Routledge

——(1991)
When the Moon Waxes Red:
Representation, Gender and Cultural Politics
New York: Routledge

IN LIMBO: CREOLISATION AND UNTRANSLATABILITY
Isaac Julien interviewed by Kass Banning

The following conversation began in New York City, July 19, 2003.[1]

Kass Banning: Could you speak to that particular moment in the eighties—the filmmakers, the rupture of independent black culture—as it traverses a range of formative factors? On the one hand you have those reified aesthetic heady days of Screen *theory and then the visceral lived race politics, the uprising against policing. On the other hand you have the critiquing of image culture. The politics of representation, the chant of the moment, and the institutional determinants like the formation of Channel 4, were operating. The conjoining of aesthetics and politics that surpassed Third Cinema determinacy, beyond the realist constraints of your black Brit documentary precursors, signalled something new. But at the same time, elements learned from political modernism were added to the mix.*

Isaac Julien: In a way, what you summarize brilliantly encapsulates a generation of paradigmatic shifts. Theory was more pronounced and developed in photography than in visual arts at the time. Obviously, structuralism and psychoanalysis were important—Mary Kelly and Laura Mulvey are good examples—and certainly for most of the members of the collective Sankofa that I helped co-found. We read Kristeva and Colin McCabe, but also Bhabha and Hall as well. It was very difficult not to come to deconstructionist thinking about representation and language. Those ideas very much permeated the work. In that sense we saw ourselves being close to a number of what I want to call deconstructivist photographers, such as Mitra Tabrizian or Victor Burgin. There weren't many black people making that kind of work in the British independent film movement at that moment.

Did the paradigm shift away from structuralism influence you?

*Baltimore Series
(Martin/Still Life)*, 2003
framed digital print
100.01 cm × 123.51 cm

Previous page:
Baltimore, 2003
installation view
three-screen DVD
projection with sound
20 minutes

1. Thanks to Nina Øverli of
the Victoria Miro Gallery
and Blaire Dessent of the
Bohen Foundation for their
assistance.

We're the stepchildren of it, you could say, and so have an ambivalent relationship to it. *But didn't critical dialogue with Stuart Hall, Paul Gilroy, Homi Bhabha, and others, both enrich and lessen obstacles? Or the lack of translation between more formidable film/art discourse and communities?*

Well, of course, they guided us and it was also our lifeblood. We were in dialogue with a lot of work happening ten years before. Homi Bhabha's essay "The Other Question" appeared in *Screen* in 1982. Something has now appeared called visual culture or visual studies, which is part of the *raison d'etre* of a number of colleagues who we worked with. Now, mutations continue to grow in their own directions.

I think it's a fine line in visual studies as well. Your moment was decidedly interstitial, a specific conjecture.

Yes I think it's gone. Other versions of visual studies are manifestations of these questions now, but unfortunately have become over-institutionalized. While cinema was the catalyst during the mid-eighties and early-nineties, the fervency of these debates has shifted the visual arts now.

While the art world might be all aflutter with the novelty of the cinema/gallery convergence, I see your shift to the gallery context not as a break with your earlier work, but as a continuity, partially enhanced by new technologies. The cinema of ideas or independent interrogative filmmaking is relatively scarce these days. Shifting these modes of inquiry into a gallery space makes sense given the seismic alterations in global film production in the last decade. Your 1992 film The Attendant *anticipates the cinema/art convergence, where both desire and capital activate a range of museum subject positions. While François-Auguste Biard's* The Slave Trade *(1840) might offer the ur-text, the iconography gives way to a sadomasochistic translation. These staged dialogic encounters, between*

*Baltimore Series
(Ida B. Wells/Still Life)*, 2003
framed digital print
100.01 cm × 100.01 cm

*shifting personas, the attendant, the conservator, the museum walkers, reconfigure chromatics and sexuality. Recent multi-screen installations—*Vagabondia *(2001),* Paradise Omeros *(2002) and* Baltimore *(2003)—extend the archaeological and archival impulse to reframe and reposition blackness within specific, and indeed latent, locales. Throughout your work, the trace, the palimpsest, multi-layered archival footage,* Black Skin, White Mask's *(1996) mobilization of* The Battle of Algiers, *as just one example, is constant.* Looking For Langston *(1988) similarly ignites the archive, a meditation on Langston Hughes that rubs photographer James VanDerZee's* Harlem Book of the Dead *against Robert Mapplethorpe's contentious hyper-sexualized imagery of black male models. This consistent cross-hatching, these dialogues between genres and communities and across geo-political territories, within a past-present temporality, under-girds your practice, as well as the reconstruction era we spoke of earlier. John Akomfrah's work at Black Audio, from the early* Handsworth Songs *(1986) to* Seven Songs for Malcolm X *(1993) to* Martin Luther King: Days of Hope *(1999) and beyond, also comes to mind.*

Paradise Omeros *offers your third visitation to the Caribbean.* The Darker Side of Black *(1994) plumbs the machinations of homophobia in diasporic black communities and the interview with Shaba Ranks in Jamaica remains with me. The Fanon film utilizes Martinique, Fanon's brother is interviewed, and 1950s archival photographs of a boy in drag deftly challenges Fanon's elision of homosexuality with reference to Antilles. Why St. Lucia?*

A return to a primal scene I guess! *Paradise Omeros* is an installation that's set in my family's "home space" so to speak. It's absolutely correct to talk about the relationship between cinema and what I call visual studies, but a different formation of art history prevails as well. *Looking For Langston* was somewhat motored by the burdened relationship between black artists and the white patron, one of the film's motifs. Whether it

*Baltimore Series
(Déja-Vu),* 2003
detail, centre panel
framed digital print
124.78 cm × 100.01 cm

was looking at "Beauty" (a character from Nugent's poem constructed into a character in the film) or looking at James Baldwin or Langston Hughes or even the archive itself, which is set in a gallery *en passant*, or gallery of moving images.

Looking For Langston *anticipates the museum walk that is so integral to* Vagabondia *and* Baltimore, *both multi-screen installations.* Vagabondia *is set in the historic Soane museum in London, home of the architect Sir John Soane (1753–1837). A treasure trove of grand tour colonial artefacts plays host to a cast that includes a dandy dancer, Javier De Frutos the vagabond, Cleo Sylvestre (again) a black conservator who oversees the collection, two ghostly elegantly dressed nineteenth-century black women and Sir John who steals in and out.* Baltimore *was shot on location at three museums in Baltimore: the Walters Art Museum, the Peabody Museum, and the Great Blacks in Wax Museum.*

Yes. Invoking the museum can be traced back to a number of other artists as well. There's always been a relationship to the plastic arts, with visual artists in my works. And this points to a particular formation, coming from an art school background. I think that you're absolutely right that making work in a museum context does not constitute a radical shift in the way that some critics describe it. The vagabond character is more of a trickster figure or shaman, reinvented in the postcolonial space of the Soane Musuem. The early films have these traces, and in a way *The Attendant* is the most prophetic film because it's almost entirely based in the museum, for better or worse.

To return to this notion of visualizing ideas, in the Fanon film concepts such as the fracturing and mirroring of identity were suggested through formal means.

The film was a kind of finale in relationship to those questions around postcoloniality that we had began working on the early 1980s. I was trying to translate Fanon's ideas for a younger generation and was also spurred on by a conference at the Institute of

Contemporary Arts on Frantz Fanon and visual culture. It was the high point of Fanon mania, and we were all deeply involved in redefining what Fanon could mean for us today.

But "translating" a reconfigured Fanon to a North American context proved fascinating: witness the Critical Genealogies conference that you organized in New York at NYU in 1996.

It seemed to us that the Americans never understood the link to visual culture, which had been made in Europe. It was really interesting because the investments were purely institutionalized, resulting in competing versions of Fanon.

Stuart Hall's insistence that Fanon the perpetrator of revolution and Fanon the psycho-analyst cannot be separated remains integral to your film. These two strands conjoin without contradiction or panic.

We didn't want to construct a hagiographic portrait and we were criticized for this approach. The idea that you could simultaneously support Fanon yet criticize some of the shortcomings of his work was anathema to some. Many people had been working on the translation of Fanon's ideas for several years. Homi Bhabha, Stuart Hall, and Françoise Vergès for instance, and I think this came together with psychoanalysis. We were interested in a conversation, visually reframing Fanon in those terms.

Could you speak further to your consistent use of tableau vivant, *from* Looking For Langston *to* The Attendant *to* Black Skin, White Mask *to its most recent all-out deployment of the waxed figures of Baltimore, and indeed their repositioning in a high culture/ art context? Why place existing works, wax ready-mades, into new contexts? Why the static embodiment of paintings by human actors? Or why interchange actors with figures in paintings or pose figures, wax or living, in front of paintings?*

Following page:
*Baltimore Series
(Angela in Blue No. 2),* 2003
framed digital print
125.5 cm × 102 cm

A waxwork, unlike a real person, doesn't move, they stay where they're told.

This embalming-like practice references Bazin, pointing to cinema's precursors, as well as the death trope that resounds throughout your work.

Yes, That's in *Looking For Langston*, but the attraction to Baltimore's Great Blacks in Wax Museum should be obvious—the question of necrophilia, without being too dramatic about it, and its relation to both trauma and the diaspora, drew me. In a fine art sense you can view the waxwork as a precursor to the *tableau vivant*, but the relationship to the death of the spectator is also relevant. In a sense, waxworks epitomize black viewers within the arcane space of the museum. Archiving is one gesture, but I'm also performing a sly social commentary. One of the questions being posed is: "Who's your audience?" With *Baltimore*, demonstrably black figures inhabit a museum space. Obviously they are not alive. There might be something to be said here about the relationship between museums and artists who are black. I'm not saying they are black artists but artists who are black, who are making works related to the question of the spectator…and there is an ambivalence about the museum's history and the kinds of figures that were showcased in these spaces. A crude ethnography of black bodies on display in museums informs the historical legacy of museological practice, and perhaps versions of it still persist in different forms.

Which you nod to in the basement with the Egyptian inscriptions.

Yes. But there's rift from such gesturing as well…suggesting that now we can take some of these questions for granted. If artists are black and they participate in or take for granted avant-garde techniques, then boring questions are asked concerning audience that I find returns to the essentialist and ethnographic. The refrain is deeply rooted and will never disappear. It implies black people are not really meant to make

Previous page:
*Baltimore Series
(Street Life)*, 2003
framed digital print, 3 panels
each 100.01 cm × 123.51 cm

art. Obviously art works exist...they're just there. The truth is that when installation pieces are shown most of the time there isn't an audience.... You have to say to yourself, why would one want to lavish iconic figures in this particular manner? In a way it's a desperate attempt to memorialize. The real question that I wanted to pose about this wax museum phenomenon is perhaps these wax figures are works of art, like going to see a Thomas Hirschhorn installation. It's fantastic. The Great Blacks in Wax Museum is a scary museum. I was speaking to an intelligent contemporary art collector the other day. He said the museum was "pretty spooky...." Apropos of his comment, the black wax figures literally transform the museum space.

Yes, removing these waxed icons from their "low art" popular culture context and placing them within a "high art" space, the Walters Museum, blocking sight-line access to the Italian masters, points to perspective in all its possible permutations and invites a sardonic comparison between contemporary Baltimore with della Francesca's Ideal City. *At the same time,* Baltimore *archives your recent documentary on the legacy of Blaxploitation movies,* Baadasssss Cinema (2002). *Melvin Van Peebles is both museum walker and our guide; his visitations to these three museums and subsequent encounters within, including a face-to-face meeting with his own wax effigy, drives the work.*

But does the particularity of the wax leader figures feed into the "only one" father syndrome? One Martin, one Malcolm, one Melvin, etc.?

Yes, it's an idea at the heart of black politics about black leaders, which is always gendered unfortunately. So the question of mourning, of melancholia, and black masculinity is imbued in the space. It's funny how all the names begin with the letter "m"!

Is not Blaxploitation mourned as well? The iconography, the genre-specific period car, the Pam Grier/Lara Croft morphed cyber character, even the final words, riff on lines from

COLIN POWELL

Former Chairman
Joint Chiefs of Staff
1937-

The son of struggling Jamaican immigrants,
Colin Powell has throughout his career in the
military possessed the qualities of valor, courage,
and leadership that characterize a good soldier.
He has come to epitomize the legions of African
American soldiers who have defended this nation
in every major war it has engaged in.

The Mack *(1973), and of course, our museum walker, Melvin Van Peebles, who enacts a circular cat and mouse game with the cyber character.*

Certain moments of Blaxploitation film history are privileged because obviously one strain became valorized, and transmuted into the language of computer games. Of course Lara Croft is an incarnation of Cleopatra Jones. It just became de-raced and depoliticized in CGI.

Why couple Blaxploitation with waxed effigies of Civil Rights leaders and other accomplished folks? A comment on black masculinity? One sanctioned, the other not, or both illusory?

It was, but I think the question I want to pose is: "Where is the artist in this?"

While Van Peebles might constitute the father, was he not displaced? Blaxploitation evolved in a different direction after his film, a decidedly avant-garde text. Certain iconic aspects remained...I guess one can't say the wrong things...nevertheless the experimental impetus petered out as the genre devolved.

The experimentation was important but *Sweet Sweetback's Baadasssss Song* (1971) was the most popular film of its era, not just a black film, but an independent film, and Van Peebles also initiated the marketing of music in films. These aspects are not fully acknowledged, but the other lack of acknowledgement is the question of why there is little space for those interested in participating in an avant-garde. Interest in our works falls outside this sphere, harking back to "two kinds of otherness," what you would call a black avant-garde. This positionality is allowed in jazz, but it's not necessarily championed by black intellectuals.

Same old, same old. Regarding financing, the Bohen Foundation sponsored Paradise Omeros. *How did this source of financing affect the project?*

*Baltimore Series
(Colin/Still Life),* 2003
framed digital print, diptych
each panel 100 cm × 100 cm

The Bohen Foundation allows you to make a film like *Paradise Omeros* without market concerns. The artist doesn't have to compromise in terms of creativity.

Which brings me to the one-off performance at the Bohen Foundation. One particular sequence where the Achilles figure speaks on one edge of the frame and Derek Walcott speaks across to Achilles on the other, both inaudible, is looped continuously as Derek Walcott read sections from his opus. Paul Gladstone Reid, the composer of the film's sound track, performed a new piano piece for this specific loop and Hansil Jules, who plays Achilles, sang. I think the "liveness" added a further mnemonic aspect to the installation's extant approximation of territorial traversing and hybrid psychic states.

It was very performance orientated, with the improvized aspects intended to show the simplicity of thinking through the project. And there's a way in which their performance can't be commodified in the same way as an installed artwork.

Are you referring to improvisation?

Sort of, yes. The performance attempted to show the different thoughts at work and the preparation that goes into making a piece, because so much work goes into making a piece of work of which you only see 10 percent. It's just an invitation to an audience to experience these different aspects on a deep level.

Vagabondia is phantasmagoric and the Brixton house party section of Paradise *approximates a ghostly masquerade, anticipating the waxy fauxness of Baltimore. While not an orthodox museum space, the mise en scene of the house party, while minimal, is almost uncanny in its perspicuity, from Kennedy's portrait, to the 1960s period furniture and adornments, to the record player, to the dance moves, and of course, the perfect song, John Holt's "The Tide Is High."*

In this sense I think the aesthetic figures in your work more correctly approximate Deleuzian conceptual personae. For instance, Achilles is revisited through Omeros *so new concepts materialize. And, as you insist, movement is crucial and a figure implies a stationary position, and conceptual personas maintain a sense of movement. Difference here isn't swallowed up by identity, perhaps referring back to the idea of non-translatability.*

I like this idea of the Deleuzian time image. In *Paradise Omeros* it is the oscillation effect which is created in the movement back and forth, both in its geographical translations—the Achilles character travels back and forth from St. Lucia to England—and the time between past and present which is transgressed, and the fact that the film itself is looped in the gallery context, which makes for repeated viewings, hopefully if the spectator who goes to the gallery space can bear to sit through the piece twice, which I've found usually they can.

The word translation is etymologically close to the word treason. When you think about the word...translation-treason. Glissant insistently claimed that there's no adequate linguistic equivalence, that translation is ahistorical. Translation isn't merely linguistic or hermeneutic but it's cultural. There's this blockage, what he calls the opacity of culture.

Would you agree that this idea of non-translation recognizes difference?

I like the idea of non-translation because I'm attracted to the idea of certain knowledges not always being mastered or known. In Glissant's idea, I'm attracted to the idea of treason, because the notion of creolizing vision in my own practice is very concerned with the idea of contamination. But I think one of the problems with some of the visual culture approaches is an idea that new differences, like the development around creolization and créolité can always be knowable and framed, and thus fixed in a new discourse. The enigma of arrival in a new location, of developing new languages or artistic practices, is a far more complex a phenomenon. It suggests that in art or in my

film installations one isn't always able to know what it is one's doing. Paradoxically perhaps, I think the unknowingness about what you're doing, not mastering the actual practice of making, creates a space for improvisation which is close I think to ideas around the development of creole practices.

What does Derrida say about truth and painting? Something to the effect that art always outruns any discourse around it, with museums and criticism functioning as what he would call the apparatus of capture. Perhaps this points to a shift from representational thinking to this concept of the trace.

Maybe it has to do with unknowability and that's the flux that we find ourselves in.

But less strident cultural criticism seems to be the order of day. There's a return of the aesthetic, don't you agree?

Yes, there's a return of the aesthetic, but it's not exactly aesthetic formalism.

In a way we're back to affect, not a return to transcendence and the sublime but affect, that's what I implied earlier, that it's now okay for art to impart emotion, the renewed interest in the haptic, etc. Do you see an accompanying shift in the critical vocabulary as well?

I think that in a way that the question of identification has become part of the vocabulary around trying to articulate a newness. For me it's really how this newness can come about in relationship to age-old questions to projects which started in the early 1980s that need to forge a new position. That's why the recourse to earlier paradigms, thinking about what one's trying to develop. Perhaps one doesn't have the language exactly, and that's the thing that's important. We're in a kind of limbo.

It's now a commonplace to note how new horizons of experience have opened up; the local/global interface has become almost obligatory. The approximation of memory and

Previous spread:
*Baltimore Series
(Fin de Siècle)*, 2003
framed digital print, 7 panels
each 100.01 cm × 99.85 cm

the triggering of affect are heightened in the installation works, evoking an ontology that reaches beyond the gaze. God, we never would have used these terms. Sounds too phenomenological. Regardless, digitalization does convey new forms of consciousness in the case of Paradise Omeros, *the residual traumatic effects of colonial relations, for one. Could you comment upon the film image's potential in a gallery context to problematize cinematic spectatorial regimes?*

I'm not sure if there's some sort of epistemological break. Cinema in an art context in my practice could be seen as a continuation of some of the black independent cinema concerns of an earlier decade. It's basically just reconfiguring itself, but of course this mutation from one technology to another, from celluloid to digital, makes new interventions possible. Changes in subjectivity can be linked to these processes in which spectatorship is reconfigured. Deterritorialization of the cinema into the gallery means that spectators who come to these spaces may have a different set of priorities, beyond the normative expectations of a general cinema audience. Okwui Enwezor's *Documenta 11* could be another citing for the re-emergence of the political in art. In *Paradise Omeros* the three screen format allows the spectator to enter into a cinemascopic arena, one where they can enter the film at any point. It is the looping of the film, and being able to view the story several times, that makes for a more in-depth experience of the haptic. The choreography of the editing of the multi-screen geometries of the triptych also lends itself to a more open-ended relationship to narrative. The formal pictorial and compositional arrangements of the screens are also as important as the film's content. The spectator is not in a black box but rather a white cube. The notion of expanded cinema comes to mind, but there's a re-emergence of some of the detritus of unfinished debates of *Third Cinema* in a piece like *Paradise Omeros*.

While Paradise Omeros *doesn't utilize museum space, it does archive and reconfigure Derek Walcott's original poem* Omeros*. How does the original function?*

In a way the piece is a meditation on *Omeros*. Derek Walcott did actually write a poem for the film. He collaborated on the narration of the main protagonist, in the post-scripting of the work, suturing and stitching parts of the film's montage.

Isaac, the work is so organically realized. An incorrect term I know, but repetition is so central, not just visually. St. Lucia's landscape is used to great effect, mixing the sublime and geo-poetics...yet the picture-postcard effect is interrupted.

Oh completely. In terms of the West Indian island, the fictional landscape, the tragic West Indian...all of these things are evoked, for example, in Jamaica Kincaid's *A Small Place*...where the pictorial exotic landscape is interrupted. And in a way, I wanted to evoke that elegiac, postcolonial melancholia in relation to certain haunting questions that just won't go away.

I find it perplexing that celebrated West Indian literature, mostly from Martinique, Conde, et al, but also Kincaid, Braithwaite, or Walcott, hasn't been visualized as you say.

But I do think there could be a problem with the translation from the literary to the visual in these discourses.

There's a paucity of images nonetheless. Creole and translation, between French and English is evident here. But terminology differs. Braithwaite, for example uses the term demotic, not creole.

Creole in the film is purposely not translated....There have been so many debates about créolité...always spoken in the Anglophone world of course. The Achilles character in *Paradise Omeros* moves between these spaces in the film, but his journey is different from that of his artisan ex-patriots. Of course there's a class difference.

Before Paradise, 2002
pigment ink print, 3 panels
each 100 cm × 100 cm

Morphing the soccer ball into the globe helped to bring that movement home. The other side of Bend It Like Beckham *(2002).*

That's right, *Bend It Like Beckham* proved to be very popular with certain audiences. Of course it's a cinema that everybody understands, a cinema where difference is made understandable and translatable. I think it's very astute to think about the globe and the ball, cinema, nationalism, and sports. It's difficult to talk about the globalization of visual culture without resorting to clichés.

Paradise Omeros, 2002
installation view
three-screen DVD
projection with sound
20 minutes

THE HOLLYWOOD SOUND TRACT
John Mowitt

Perusing the "Entries by Country" list of foreign language films entered into competition with the Academy of Motion Pictures, Arts, and Sciences (AMPAS) one finds notes justifying the designation "ineligible" of the following sort: *Ways of Love* (1950), "it is a composite of the production ability of three different production units who worked in three different countries"; *A World of Strangers* (1962), "original sound track was made in English and no Danish-language version existed"; *The Harder they Come* (1972), "Calypso (Jamaican) determined to be an English dialect, not a foreign language"; *Scenes from a Marriage* (1974), "film released in the Los Angeles area, disqualifying it for Foreign Language Film Award consideration."[1] Of course, many entries were deemed eligible (indeed many were nominated), and it would be a mistake to infer that my interest here is in detecting some conspiracy at work in the disqualification of these particular films (though, truth be told, Perry Henzell's film raises some provocative issues). Instead, what this list calls attention to is the discourse of regulation, the rules that were invoked by the review committee in determining the eligibility of foreign language film entries.

This paper will tease out the genealogy of this regulatory discourse and go some considerable distance toward tracing the official production of the links between film, language, and foreignness. In this exploration I will examine the role played by the Academy of Motion Pictures, Arts, and Sciences (AMPAS) in institutionalizing a distinctly cinematic concept of the foreign, one that must be interrogated whenever film scholars or, for that matter, consumers avail themselves of the term. Although several issues need to be examined here—how foreign language films have come to be so designated within the West, how foreign languages (notably the speech of "natives," "Indians," and even "aliens") have been represented within

1. This information derives from materials held in the archives of the Academy of Motion Picture Arts and Sciences. As such it is not organized in a manner that conforms to the standards of bibliographic discourse. Nevertheless, the notebook "Entries by Country" can be consulted at the Margaret Herrick Library in Beverly Hills, California. I am most grateful to Linda Mehr and Libby Wertin for providing me with access to the Academy's files and for giving me permission to publish the materials cited in the text.
2. "International" was dropped from the name almost immediately, indeed even before it was announced to the public and this despite the fact that at its inaugural dinner none other than Cecil B. deMille toasted the formation of AMPAS by characterizing its power to, "influence[s] the mental processes of mankind" (Sands 39). Moreover, in order to regulate the

Western cinemas, and how the two preceding issues converge to render language itself "foreign" to the cinema—I will restrict myself to tracing some of the relevant institutional history, tracking how foreignness belongs to the very process of institutionalization.

Though formed in 1927, and originally conceived as an international organization, AMPAS did not begin to officially acknowledge what came to be known as "foreign language films" until Vittorio de Sica's *Shoe Shine* (1946) was brought to its attention in 1948.[2] The space for such acknowledgement was opened within the "Special Awards" category of the Academy Awards Rules when, in 1944, sub-section I was introduced. It read:

> It being the intention that motion pictures from all countries shall be eligible for consideration for the Awards, the rules shall be construed literally to include such motion pictures, except that they must be shown in Los Angeles within the awards year, must be in English or with English subtitles, and the producers or distributors shall provide prints when necessary for review showing. (AMPAS archive)

When, in 1949, sub-section D was introduced to define a then-emerging Foreign Language Film Award, sub-section I was revised to read:

> Exception to this rule shall be made for the foreign language film award for which pictures need not be in English or have English subtitles and need not to have been shown in the United States. (AMPAS archive)

Sub-section D reads:

> This award is intended to honour films first made in a language other than English and first released in a commercial theatre in the United States during the Award Year. (AMPAS archive)

submission process for foreign language film entries, rules were developed that required the formation of "organizations whose aims and purposes" mirrored that of AMPAS, and this only after an effort to involve the United Nations—through the good offices of M. Jean-Benoit Levy—were deemed inadequate. Thus, one might reasonably argue that—intentionally or not—"international" was dropped because it threatened to make the obvious explicit, namely, that in establishing an organization designed to police the film industry in the US, AMPAS was also shouldering the burden of "policing" the international scene, at least at the cultural level.

Obviously, sub-section D was developed to ratify the review committee's decision to recognize *Shoe Shine* with a special award, and, already, one sees an important configuration emerging, a configuration in which films are characterized as being made "in" certain languages (English serves as the "unmarked" term) and destined for a specific form of exhibition (in a commercial theatre, in a certain country, during a particular business cycle). However, the process which culminates in the shift whereby Foreign Language Films are recognized under their own rubric as opposed to the "special awards" rubric has a beginning worth reconstructing precisely because of the light it projects onto the significance of this configuration.

In March of 1992, Barbara Hall (an oral historian at AMPAS) interviewed Robert Vogel, who came to MGM in 1930 to oversee international publicity for the studio and joined AMPAS in 1942, where he organized the foreign language film special award and came to serve on its standing review committee. Here, from Hall's oral history, is Vogel's account of the process that led to the creation of the category of the foreign language film.

> We had a producer on the lot named Walter Wanger, who happened also to be the Academy president. He came into my office one day and told me that…he used the personal pronoun throughout. Whether any or all of this was done with the knowledge of the board, I really don't know, because he talked *I*. He had found out during the war there had developed overseas some very, very fine young directors who had begun to turn out some very, very fine pictures. He named three of them: Clair of France, Kurosawa of Japan, and Rossellini in Italy. And he said, "The day must come, and soon, when these pictures come to be recognized around the world and the Academy will be in the terrible position of appearing provincial if it ignores pictures that are produced outside of Hollywood. So

> I want to set up a special honorary award for the foreign pictures so that the foreign world will see that we are honoring the great picture-makers of other countries. So I want you to join the Academy..." I'm quoting Wanger. "I want you to join the Academy, keep your ears to the ground, look for any pictures that you hear are outstanding, and we'll arrange to get a print for you, long enough for you just to look at. If you hear of any such. And at the end of the year, if you have any picture or pictures to recommend for a foreign special award Oscar, let me know. Will you do that? (Hall and Vogel 298)

Vogel goes on to protest the exclusivity of his proposed authority and Wanger concedes that other studio people (Luigi Luraschi at Paramount and Bill Gordon at RKO) will have to be involved.

Although Walter Wanger is a very interesting character (for example, his intervention as a producer re-framed Don Seigel's *The Invasion of the Body Snatchers* [1956] so as to rescue the US from full-tilt paranoia), it is the words that Vogel puts in his mouth that are decisive, beginning with Vogel's own insistence on Wanger's enunciation. Several points need to be made.

First, as a scholar like Richard Jewel might insist, Wanger/Vogel (a contrivance the preceding observation requires) approaches the cinema as an *auteurist*, his deep relation to studio culture notwithstanding. Films are the expressions of their directors (Clair of France, Kurosawa of Japan, etc.), an assertion that ultimately works to link the foreignness in the cinema, to the foreignness of the filmmaker. Language here goes without saying.

Second, perhaps for this very reason, foreign (as an adjective) is put to work grammatically in telling ways. In the passage it modifies "pictures," "world," and "special award Oscar." Pictures are, of course, films (conceived, as has long been the custom, as silent).

Thus, a foreign picture is a film made by a foreigner, though grammatically nothing prevents it from denoting a picture coded within conventions of visual literacy unknown to Wanger/Vogel. "World," which oscillates between earth and the quintessential apocalyptic object ("worldview"), locates the foreign "outside of Hollywood." Thus, "foreign world," as used by Wanger/Vogel, refers in a rather straightforwardly Lacanian way to the Other within whose gaze "our" activities fall. The vaguely ethical tone of Wanger/Vogel's concern about the US either being or becoming "provincial" virtually solicits such a reading. Here the grammatical ambiguity of "foreign pictures" is restated as an expression of something like a guilty conscience where a world (largely Western) ravaged by war—indeed a war from which the US emerged as victor—is recast, not as an object, but as a subject. It is not just that Wanger/Vogel has come to learn of foreign directors, but that these directors are in a certain sense *owed* our recognition. Something like "obligation" is here converted into, not the assumption, but the presumption of responsibility. In a final twist, foreign is used to modify "special" which is in turn used to modify "award." Thus, the award is not for something foreign, it is something foreign. This matter is highlighted in a report from Geoffrey Shurlock (a member of the Foreign Language Film Award review board) dated January 1, 1956 to George Seaton in which Shurlock recommends *Wages of Fear* and *Samurai*, but goes on to warn of the "political overtones" of the films, proposing that their "anti-Americanism" be edited out (AMPAS archive). Clearly, the foreignness that the "foreign special award Oscar" introduces within the award category risks becoming an officially sanctioned anti-Americanism.

Third and lastly, though language, as I have said, goes without saying, its absent presence is manifest throughout the citation, nowhere more assertively than when

Wanger is charging Vogel with the task of scouting for prospects. Note the shifting character of the filmic signifier: "I want you to join the Academy, keep your ears to the ground, look for any pictures you hear are outstanding, and we'll arrange to get a print for you, long enough for you just to look at. If you hear of any such." First, Vogel, through the rigours of a colloquial expression, is counselled to listen for suitable foreign pictures. Then, in the same sentence, he is counselled, this time through the rigours of an idiomatic locution (look for, as opposed to, look at) to look for foreign pictures that, as the sentence continues, his listening has turned up. In the concluding clause of this sentence, foreign pictures are again reduced to sights when Wanger promises to arrange things so that Vogel will have prints "just to look at." Then, as if to retrace his own footsteps, Wanger/Vogel concludes by saying, "If you hear of any such."

So what might one conclude? Are foreign pictures things one encounters through the eyes or through the ears? Or both? In sub-section D (cited above) the foreign language film is defined as a film "made in a language other than English." I, of course, am inclined to take such formulations literally, but even if one does not, it is clear that, sticking to the letter of the rule, a foreign picture will exhibit its foreignness not by virtue of what it *looks* like, but by virtue of what it *sounds* like. In this sense, the ear is the proper organ for discerning the foreign filmic signifier, and Wanger/Vogel's indecisiveness may have to do with the clash between American speech patterns (whether colloquial or idiomatic) and their subject matter, in this case, films made in languages other than English. Which is to say that perhaps, when speaking of foreign pictures, "keeping one's ear to the ground" is not a colloquial expression after all. Or, in the same vein, that "to look for" or "to hear of" are not merely idiomatic.

But surely I am "over-reading" Wanger/Vogel. When he counsels keeping one's "ears to the ground," he could just mean that one should be attentive to what is now called "buzz." When he promises to arrange screenings, "just to look at" prospective nominees, he is simply reassuring his interlocutor that careful, exhaustive study of prospective nominees will not be required. But, just the same, one might argue that it is precisely this sort of unstudied, indeed "spontaneous," discourse that speaks most clearly about the institutional culture from which it is derived. Thus, while I am not proposing that Wanger/Vogel is *really* talking about the relation between foreignness and language, I am proposing that his speech derives from a discourse, a frame of intelligibility, in which more than what he means to say is at work. Describing this discourse and the relations it has constructed among film, language, and foreignness obviously requires that one be sensitive to what Wanger/Vogel means, but also to what he says and how he says it, let alone what is done in the act of saying it.

There is more than a methodological or theoretical warrant for such claims, and this can be clarified by looking carefully at the history of the "Rules for the Foreign Language Film Award." When, in 1956, the Foreign Language Film Award became recurrent (that is, no longer honorary and therefore subject to the "Special Awards" provisions) the following characterization of the award appeared:

> (1) This award shall be given for the best feature-length motion picture [in 1958 this was specified to mean 3,000 feet] produced by a foreign company with a non-English sound track, first release from January 1, 1956 to November 30, 1956 and shown in a commercial theatre for the profit of the producer and the exhibitor. The picture need not have been released in the United States and English sub-titles are not required. A story synopsis of the picture written in English must be sent to the Academy when the film is submitted for award consideration.

(2) Every country shall be invited to submit its best film and the selection in each country shall be made, wherever possible, by organizations whose aims and purposes compare with those of the Academy of Motion Picture Arts and Sciences. (AMPAS archive)

Also, in 1958, one of the more extraordinary features of this characterization of the foreign language film was revised. I am thinking, perhaps predictably, of the formulation "non-English sound track," a formulation which, when its brutal conflation of sound and voice is set aside, either evokes, for example, Spanish "barking" (*jau-jau* as opposed to "ruff-ruff"), or an insight into the linguistic organization of sound perception that the very concept of the foreign language film seems determined to interdict. The revised material reads (between the second and third sentences in (1): "However, if a print is available with titles in English the Academy will be glad to have that print submitted for voting. Prints will not be accepted with a dialogue track other than in the original language." Perhaps uncomfortable with this solution (where the sound track simply becomes the dialogue track), a much later revision of the rules (from 1981) restored the decisive status of the sound track with the phrase, "basically non-English sound track," where the adverb compresses concerns that arose in the 1970s over whether dialogue had to be entirely in a language other than English, a matter of special significance in the postcolonial context.

Needless to say, the unmarked status of English only complicates matters. On the one hand, AMPAS certainly did not mean the foreign language film rubric to exclude from consideration films from the "Anglophone" world, say, the UK, Australia, Canada, or the West Indies. On the other hand, however, given the regulatory stipulation that foreign language films had to have been made in languages other than English, films from such countries or regions were excluded *de jure*. This matter was discussed within AMPAS as early as 1949, and it comes up in Hall's interview with Vogel, who insists that AMPAS intended to treat Anglophone films as US films, a claim that suggests that AMPAS was prepared to violate the stricture routinely (Hall 305). Again, though this dilemma openly thematizes the very concept of language (is it, in fact, synonymous with a so-called natural language, or is there something distinctly foreign about "the language" in which, say, *The Piano*, was *made*?), the conception of language rationalized by a certain enunciative monolingualism, the very monolingualism protecting the unmarked status of English, does not permit the possibilities latent within this dilemma to flourish.

This is precisely what makes AMPAS's exclusion from consideration of Henzell's *The Harder They Come* (1972) so interesting. Officially, as already noted, the film was deemed ineligible because "Calypso" (what might also be called Creole) was determined to be an "English dialect," and thus it was not made in a language other than English. Nevertheless, as Michael Thelwell (the writer approached to "novelize" the film) makes clear, copies of the film that circulated in the US—indeed the print submitted to AMPAS review committee—were actually subtitled in English because the "English spoken" sounded foreign enough to surpass the competence of most US audiences (Cham 178).

Because foreign pictures present themselves, as such, to the ear, AMPAS had to both accept the submission from Jamaica, and withhold recognition, taking the opportunity represented by the film to tighten the link between language and speech. In other words, beyond making the openly linguistic judgement that dialects fall within languages, the review committee also implicitly specified that the "language" referred to in the phrase "foreign language film" was indeed to be modeled on speech, that is, on the vocal sounds to be found on the dialogue track, not the codes of audiovisual literacy organizing the messages of the film. The implicit character of this more theoretical point derives not from its status as theory, but from the fact that AMPAS remains conflicted about precisely where it wants to locate foreignness within the cinematic field, and while it is true that any frame of intelligibility (whether institutionally localized or not) stumbles when thematizing its enabling conditions, the problems posed by recognition of the foreign language film are, in a certain sense, distinctive to AMPAS, and, one might assume, any institution involved in adjudicating competitions among cultural commodities. The force of law at work in converting the power to judge into the right to judge must be disavowed.

Further confirmation of the contention that Wanger/Vogel's indecisiveness is due to the conflicted status of foreign language films within the discourse of AMPAS is exemplified in the following two exchanges between Vogel and Hall. At one point Hall asks: "Were you looking for films that were just generally excellent artistically or were you interested in films about certain subject matters?" To which Vogel responds: "Oh no. Subject matter never entered into it. I mean, it was never any consideration. . . . After all, we were looking at motion pictures. I don't think the Academy ever looks at subject matter specifically. I don't think it should" (Hall 300). The salient phrase is, of course, "after all, we were looking at motion pictures." True, at one level it simply reproduces the tired distinction between form and content, but considered in light of the language problem, what Vogel's response suggests is that he recognizes the degree to which dialogue—as rooted in the subject matter (characters in a particular situation talking about it)—is not as important to the film *qua* film as would be the fluency with which it is placed within a sound track and joined, via the sound track, to the image track. Here, Vogel gives voice to the elided concept of language that AMPAS's construction of the foreign language film depends upon.

Intriguingly, the second example appears to contradict the principle invoked in the first. Responding to Hall's repeated suggestion that AMPAS has tended—in the name of the foreign language film—to recognize, nominate, and award "Western-style" films (that is, films from Western Europe), Vogel proceeds from a defense of the review committee members (they are called "A-1"), to an articulation of the following concession: "The one category of pictures which suffers in my estimation is the Oriental picture, from Japan or China, whose code of living and code of morals are so very different from ours that we can't understand them. A picture having to do with social problems in Japan won't be understood by Yankees. I don't see how it can win an Oscar" (Hall 310). It is difficult not to read this as an insistence upon the importance, indeed the centrality, of subject matter. After all, what would "social problems in Japan" be, if not subject matter? But is it not possible to discern in this formulation, through its thick Eurocentric haze, Vogel's recognition that even if a US citizen fluent in Japanese (say, a student in international banking) were to see a film organized in accord with a "code of living" he or she was unfamiliar with, it is possible, even likely, that such a person would fail to understand the film? In other words, are we sure that in the first sentence of the cited passage "them" has "code of living and code of morals" as its antecedent? Or, to reiterate an earlier point, is this an instance of US speech patterns colliding with the foreignness in foreign language films? If so, then perhaps Vogel is not literally contradicting himself. Instead, he is positing that precisely because "Oriental" films are coded differently, that is, expressed in what might better be called a foreign film language, "we" are not likely to understand them, nor is AMPAS likely to give them any awards. How far into the cultural domain does a "code of life" reach? I would say far enough to shape the way images, sounds, and events get assembled in the medium of film.

I am not here trying to make a case for the subtlety of Vogel's views. Instead, my aim is to suggest how they emerged within a frame of intelligibility shaken, and therefore exposed, by the necessity of accommodating "the foreign," that is, the outside that is inside. True, the importance of Vogel's "witnessing" derives from the fact that he, rather than a discourse, was given the task of establishing the mechanism whereby foreign language films could be officially recognized by AMPAS. But just as the language he speaks precedes him, so to does a certain way of thinking the relation between language and film. When, through him, his speech and this way of thinking converge on the foreign language film, a certain symptomatic ambiguity results. This is what has been charted above. However, the larger insight at stake here, namely, the significance of the link forged by AMPAS between film language and foreignness, still remains to articulate. To proceed two points need to be established: first, the influence of AMPAS within the US. In other words, what general status might be claimed for AMPAS construction of the link between foreignness and film language given that other institutions in the Anglophone world (AFI, MoMA, BFI, etc.) might also be said to be involved in forging it? Second—and this is really the crucial matter—what is the significance of the fact that foreignness becomes the conceptual means by which language is separated from the filmic medium? In ways yet to be determined, these points converge.

Of course, it is one thing to acknowledge that AMPAS perceived itself as having global significance (recall de Mille's inaugural remarks) and quite another to establish that, whether on its own terms or not, it has indeed had such significance. In Hall's oral history Vogel relates a relevant anecdote about Kurosawa whose *Rashomon* (1950) was the first "Oriental" picture to win an Oscar. Hall provokes the anecdote by asking Vogel about why, at the time of their interview, no other Japanese films had won the foreign language film award. Instead of resorting to his "codes of living" argument, Vogel recounts the efforts of Jim Gordon who worked with the government in Tokyo to set up, as the rules stipulated, an organization with aims comparable to those of AMPAS. Predictably, his efforts culminated in the development of an organization that sought, after a point, to award Japanese films internally, to in effect, develop a Japanese Oscar (the French "César" is probably the most widely recognized example of this phenomenon). Vogel's anecdote then centres on Kurosawa's reaction to the invitation extended to him to accept an "Oscar" from this comparable institution. He says that Kurosawa responded by saying—and the following material is presented as a citation in Hall's text—"Yours is a second-rate Academy. The only Academy that really amounts to a row of beans is the one in Hollywood and I am not going to bother to come to your ceremony" (Hall 301). Vogel then concludes by suggesting that once slighted in this way, the Japanese film industry refused to promote its own best talent, hence no more American Oscars. Why Hall does not remind Vogel of Kinugasa's Oscar winning *Gate of Hell* (1953) escapes me, but what is crucial here is that this rich anecdote (what, for example, is "row of beans" a translation of?) speaks volumes about the way AMPAS perceives its own, as we say, global reach. Even more important, at least for my purposes, is the fact that even if Vogel is misquoting Kurosawa, Vogel and AMPAS are not entirely wrong about why "Oriental" pictures have so frequently been overlooked at Oscar time.

The study of AMPAS by Pierre Norman Sands establishes the crucial link between it and Hollywood, the link that allows one to recognize the scope of AMPAS's influence on global film cultures. Written as a dissertation at the University of Southern California, this study explicitly attempts to answer the question "why did the founders [of AMPAS] conceive of the need for a professional society composed of members of the motion picture industry?" The response Sands elaborates is worthy of sustained reflection.

At the risk of parading out another "myth of origins," it is nevertheless worth citing the invitation sent to prospective members in the wake of the dinner attended by Fred Niblo (a director), Conrad Nagel (an actor), and Louis Mayer (a producer) where, as legend has it, the concept of the academy was hatched. It read:

> If we producing workers, actors, directors, technicians, cinematographers and producing executives, who have the future progress of this great universal entertainment at heart, will now join unselfishly into one big concerted movement, we will be able to effectually [sic] accomplish those essential things we have hitherto neglected. We can take aggressive action in meeting outside attacks that are unjust. We can promote harmony and solidarity among out membership and among our different branches. We can reconcile our internal differences that may exist or arise.... We can encourage the improvement and advancement of the arts and sciences of our profession by the interchange of constructive ideas and by awards of merit for distinctive achievements. We can take steps to develop the greater power and influence of the screen. (Sands 38–9)

Evident here, as Sands's research shows, are allusions to emerging labour conflicts (AMPAS has long been regarded as a producers' union), the unrelenting public attacks on the industry (the agitation that culminated in the Hays Office production code of 1930 actually began in 1922), and the soft-pedaled imperial ambitions of the industry; in short, all the concerns one would expect to find in a cultural industry of the sort so meticulously described by Bordwell, Janet Staiger, and Kristen Thompson (Bordwell et al., 1985). Perhaps less conspicuous is the call for "the improvement and advancement of the arts and sciences of our profession," a patently modernist gesture that culminated in the Oscar, but also in the standardization of practices that came to define the so-called Hollywood style. Specifically, as Sands notes (though without further comment), AMPAS produced a manual in 1931 titled *Recording Sound for Motion Pictures*, a topic—as I have argued—that, through the concept of the sound track, touches on the very frame of intelligibility in relation to which AMPAS operated. In many respects, of course, AMPAS was simply legitimating the practices that had emerged within the five major studies as they positioned themselves in relation to the Vitaphone breakthrough, an episode much analyzed within film scholarship, but nowhere more thoroughly and cogently than in the work of Douglas Gomery. Recognizing that sound confronted US studios with both the problem of translation (here the foreign language issue arises directly) and the problem of standardization, Gomery, in "Economic Struggle and Hollywood Imperialism: Europe Converts to Sound," makes explicit what Sands does not, namely that sound served as a decisive locus for the coordination of domestic and "foreign" industrial strategies. This coordination, vital in certain respects to the capitalist aim of vertical integration, did not simply standardize a certain technological system; it also displaced the infancy, the pre-linguistic era, of the cinema. In other words, with the exportation of standardized sound practices, the cinema entered language, or, as Fitzhugh Green famously put it, film found "its tongue." Hollywood presided over this phylogenesis, a posture reflected in *Recording Sound for Motion Pictures* and thus clarifying in what sense AMPAS participated in a material transfiguration of the cinema with global consequence. Indeed, this is a transfiguration with immediate implications for the links among language, film, and foreignness.

Two aspects of the preceding point need to be drawn out. First, by stressing that AMPAS's investment in "improvements in arts and sciences" finds expression in displacing the infancy of the cinema, I wish explicitly to propose that this material transfiguration reaches, as does the structure of the commodity itself, into the cultural practices of filmmakers world wide. Resistance is not exactly "futile," but it is constrained to a degree that projects glaring light on "modernity at large," that is, on the social, economic, and cultural constellation that re-frames "indigenous" practices even as quite unevenly developed realities adjust this constellation's focus. This is not a dynamic to be resisted or countered by simply recording indigenous sounds, whether these assume the form of dialogue or not, and here I am sympathetic to the doubts cast upon the very viability of the concept of resistance in the recent work of Pierre Bourdieu. Or, seen from a slightly different angle, if "indigenism" is indeed what is meant by resistance, then the latter concept desperately needs revisiting. In a certain sense, making a film (even one likely to be screened at Sundance) now means making a commodity that exhibits among its other features, a sound track. Indeed, a sound track recorded in a manner designed for a certain kind of post-production manipulation and eventual playback. Though often regarded as a "tempest in a teapot," the controversy of digitalization is precisely a struggle over the cultural politics of standardization. Second, if such claims are restated in the context established by the rules regulating the submission of foreign language films to AMPAS, not only do they acquire additional substance, they illuminate rather acutely the link forged therein between film and language. After 1956, the rules contain the following language: "This Award shall be given for the best feature length motion picture produced by a foreign company with a non-English sound track, first released from January 1, 1956 to November 30, 1956 and shown in a commercial theatre for the profit of the producer and the exhibitor." In requiring that foreign language films be 3,000 feet in length, made by companies, shown in commercial theatres, and produced for profit, AMPAS was explicitly intervening in the domain of indigenous cultural practices not only to impose the capitalist logic of standardization, but also, in effect, to eliminate foreignness from the cinema, or, to put it less polemically, to situate foreignness on the sound track and in the speech of those "foreigners" recorded there.

It is useful here to invoke Bordwell's figure of the "straight corridor," to clarify what is at stake in such an assertion. Introduced in his brief summation of *Narration in the Fiction Film*, "Classical Hollywood Cinema: Narrational Principles and Procedures," this vaguely architectural figure describes the relation between the narrative and the spectator sought by practitioners of "classical Hollywood cinema." The "straight corridor"—though characterized with rigour and subtlety—boils down to the insight that for films seeking to make a profit for their producers through commercial exhibition in the US, access to the product—in this case the narrative (or the film reduced to its narrative)—must be as direct and immediate as possible. What Bordwell calls narration, the delivery or transmission of the narrative, must be subordinated to this end, and all traces of "film work" must be effaced, that is, integrated into the comprehensive task of producing the affective charge (whether "cerebral" or not) of the spectacle. Now, if foreign language films, precisely in order to be recognized by the centre of the cinema ("the only Academy that amounts to a row of beans"), must be conceived with potential US commercial exhibition in mind, then their makers are obliged, indeed compelled, to deliver their narratives by way of the straight corridor. This means that virtually without regard to their narrative content, foreign language films must look and sound like the sorts of films perceived to be appropriate for commercial distribution and exhibition in the US. I would go further. Precisely because of this central constraint on the organization of narration—or, as I prefer, enunciation—"foreignness" is compelled, indeed required, to gravitate toward the speech audible on the sound track. If we accept the notion that what is specific to the cinema is not the narratives it delivers—narratives which, after all, often derive from or convert into extra-cinematic forms—but the codes that have developed to link film delivery techniques to the apparatal constraints of the medium, then perhaps the polemical version of my point is closer to the truth: the straight corridor operates to expel foreignness (in the sense of "other" codes of audiovisual literacy) from the cinema.

The point can be taken further. Once expelled from the cinema, foreignness echoes, that is, it returns as sound and is subordinated to subtitling, the very optical distraction that, from a different angle, underscores and reinforces the centrality of the image. Already in 1944, when foreign language films were recognized within the "special wards" rubric, English subtitling was included among the traits of foreignness. Indeed, when, in 1978, the Egyptian film, *The Assent into the Abyss*, was deemed ineligible it was because the print submitted had French subtitles. Although I have no evidence for this, Henzell may well have been hedging his bets by subtitling his film in English. Even if this is untrue, it draws attention to an important issue. If, as I have argued, foreign pictures present themselves to the ear, what is interesting about the insistence on subtitling is the way it shifts foreignness back toward the eye. In other words, and this would be especially true of a film like *The Harder they Come*, the questions raised by the dialogue (is this English, or not?) are settled, as it were, in the image, that is, at the foot of the image where one sees not merely the graphic traces of bad translation, but "foreignness." This is an effect consummated in *Star Trek: the Next Generation* where, precisely through subtitling, an entirely concocted language, Klingon, is made simultaneously foreign (alien) and real language. Consider though, the symptomatic importance of the fact that in the year following the submission of Henzell's film, the rules defining the foreign language film award were revised so that the phrase "must have English subtitles" appeared in bold caps.

As if passing through an inverted Ellis Island where, instead of names being made to sound less foreign their sounds become the predominant site of their foreignness, the concept of the foreign language film functions, in effect, to drive a wedge between film and language. In other words (here more than a turn of phrase), once foreignness is reduced to the speech of foreigners—the vocal sounds delivered as dialogue on the sound track and translated in the subtitles—language is, as it were, spoken for.

David Bordwell (1988)
Ozu and the Poetics of Cinema
New Jersey: Princeton University Press

David Bordwell, Janet Staiger,
and Kristen Thompson (1985)
The Classical Hollywood Cinema:
Film Style and Mode of Production to 1960
New York: Columbia University Press

Mbye Cham (1992)
Ex-Iles: Essays on Caribbean Cinema
Trenton: Africa World Press

Douglas Gomery (1980)
Economic Struggle and Hollywood Imperialism:
Europe Converts to Sound
Yale French Studies 60

Barbara Hall (1991)
An Oral History with Robert M. W. Vogel,
Interviewed by Barbara Hall
Beverly Hills: AMPAS Oral History Program Archives

Pierre Norman Sands (1973)
A Historical Study of the Academy of Motion
Picture Arts and Sciences, 1927–1947
New York: Arno Press

A NEW LINE IN THE GEOMETRY
Eric Cazdyn

1.

The media representations of 9/11 and the previous War in Iraq call to mind the same question we might ask when reading the seemingly endless string of credits following a big-budget Hollywood film: how could so much money, so much talent, so many human and technological resources produce so much mind-numbing mediocrity? But if we can agree with Fredric Jameson that in every dystopian configuration (from the cultural to the political) there is a utopian dimension (a genuinely radical quality that the dystopian requires in order to conduct its ideological work), then we might want to look again at all of the CNN footage, at all of the interviews and updates, at all of the garden-variety montages and exclusive video-phone footage and ask: what, alongside the mainstream media's Disney-lensed, flattened-out production of History, might persist, might flash a new critical spectatorship that can imagine (however unconsciously) a properly historicized detour from today's prevailing parade route?[1]

It is here that a review of the subtitle is in order. In this case the running subtitle, that termite text gnawing right to left on the bottom of the screen. Beginning with the first Gulf War and finding its home following 9/11, this new line in television's geometry is nothing less than one of cinema's classic tropes. It is indeed ironic, however, that in a country like the US whose audience is so averse to foreign films, and whose mainstream core so vehemently detests the subtitle, there would develop such a dependence on the subtitle itself. It is true that the running subtitle has gained ground ever since the stock market has made its way into the middle-class home, requiring that hypnotized half-eyed optic on the cable channel's running ticker—an activity that has replaced the soap opera and detective novel as the dominant mainstream distraction. What is going on with the running subtitle? How is it related to the cinematic subtitle, to foreign film,

1. See in particular Fredric Jameson's "Conclusion: The Dialectic of Utopia and Ideology" and his 1978 article "Reification and Utopia in Mass Culture."

and the foreignness of film? And how might it hint at a different form of representation, one that not only represents news and events differently but, in its most allegorical and utopian form, one that also opens up the possibility for a different shape of political representation?

2.

At moments of crisis, formal limitations become exposed. This is just as true for aesthetic systems as it is for financial and political ones. For example, when the bottom drops out of a currency the arbitrary nature of value is exposed. Likewise, when social uprisings hit a critical mass the limitation of political representation is clear to see. The same general structure is true for the aesthetic system of television. Television's running title comes into being precisely around a crisis, around an unmanageable surplus of meaning impossible to contain within its usual form: the running subtitle is not a transcription of the broadcaster's words, but either provides more detail on the item in question or on a different but nonetheless related item. Such a form is particularly useful when commenting on real-time events. Take for example, the events of September 11: too much was happening at once, thus opening up the formal possibility of running subtitles—an aesthetic strategy that could better provide multiple, real-time news updates. As with any eruption danger is involved; the danger that the thing/being as presently configured can no longer manage itself, but must endanger its own existence to remain in existence. The running subtitle flashes (however momentarily and before it is recuperated) television's essential lack: what is presumably full and self-sufficient is essentially lacking and in need; what appears as full presence is in fact organized around an absence that cannot be filled or even acknowledged, only camouflaged and repressed. Dan Rather no longer runs the show. The "white elephant" quality of broadcast news, that quality that asks you to stare at it and be satisfied by it and only it, has vanished, laying bare all of the props and pulleys, all of the magician's hardware.

In terms of composition, the running subtitle is located on the bottom of the screen. Already this marks a crucial departure from television's compositional dominant, a dominant that I have named the pornographic aesthetic.[2] The pornographic aesthetic is one in which the active content monopolizes the absolute centrality of the frame to the marginalization of everything else; the body that exists in the centre of the frame (the talking head of the broadcaster, the implosion of buildings, the copulating couple, the advertised product) pushes-out, crowds-out, snuffs-out significant relational elements of the shot. Relations to other elements inside and outside of the frame, relations to history, relations to that abstraction called the relation itself (all of which might be called the negative space of the shot) are out of sight leaving only the phatic positivity of the look-at-me content. The pornographic content relates to what is called positivism in philosophy, that method whereby speculation is shunned and any resort to the negative (in the name of a bad metaphysics) is eschewed in favour of the here-and-now fact.

But the running subtitle challenges the compositional fact of television; it returns the relation to the equation—the relation between text and image, between the margins of the frame and the centre, between the different speeds of information delivery, and between multiple narrative lines. One can now watch and hear the news about causalities at Manhattan's Ground Zero and at the same time read about preparations for an ensuing war. But before moving to what quickly has become the most notorious

2. See *The Flash of Capital: Film and Geopolitics in Japan*.

act of subtitling (the US Defense Department's titling of a fifty-minute video of Osama bin Laden speaking to associates in an Afghanistan cave) and then to the unlikely relation between the running subtitle and current globalization processes, I first want to establish the link between the most recent trend in television subtitling and the already established history of film subtitling. Which, as usual, comes by way of an excursion into literary translation.

3.

The debate over literary translation usually centres on the issues of fidelity and freedom. The former designates a strategy that sticks as closely as possible to the text being translated while the latter departs from it as the translator sees fit. The objective of both is to transmit the meaning of the original text into a different language. In "The Task of the Translator" Walter Benjamin dismantles this debate and questions the priority placed on the transmission of meaning as the *sine qua non* of all translation. By focusing on syntax and a word-for-word translation that is not concerned with comprehensibility, fluency, or "saying the same thing" in a different language, Benjamin envisions the task of the translator as something completely different, as representing the hidden kinship among languages. The task of the translator is not to get as close as possible to the original text but to release or liberate the pre-Babelian "pure language" (*reine Sprache*) that is imprisoned in the original as well as in the language of the translation. This pure language is not the pristine original that is then defiled by the translation, rather it is a negative category that cannot be attained by any single language but only hinted at by the totality of intentions (of both the original and the translation) supplementing each other. The act of translating then, for Benjamin, is a longing, a promise, a messianic hope for linguistic complementarity. Or, to put this another way: the deadly serious task of the translator lies in the importance placed on the concept of utopia as such—utopia as a critical category in its most tactically disabused and reflexive form.

To speak of utopia in such terms is thus not to suggest the actual possibility of achieving it, but rather to underscore the significance of the strategy, no matter how doomed, of working toward it.[3] The promise of touching the untouchable pure language is what marks the thoroughly dialectical character of Benjamin's preface: to be fully aware of the limitations of translation (Derrida), of the structural impossibilities of language and necessary failure of translation (de Man), while at the same time aware that these limitations are not static and thus occupy within their very logic the possibility of transformation.[4] This pure language is not a destination or even an ultimate beginning, but it is what inspires the task of the translator. By strategically sacralizing such a notion as pure language, Benjamin is effectively able to de-sacralize the original text.

4.

Our move from literature to film comes by way of Japan. During the same years in which Benjamin wrote about translation, an exemplary performance of his theory was being worked out in Japan, however different the cultural context. In early Japanese cinemas, from the 1890s to the early 1930s, an in-house commentator named the *benshi* (or *katsuben*) was present.[5] Standing underneath and to the left of the screen, the benshi commented on the images as they were being projected. From explanations of the projection process (film stock, the workings of the projector) to sharing

3. As Derrida writes in his comments on the Benjamin preface, "the promise is not nothing, it is not simply marked by what it lacks to be fulfilled. As a promise, translation is already an event, and the decisive signature of a contract. Whether or not it be honoured does not prevent the commitment from taking place and from bequeathing its record. A translation that manages to promise reconciliation, to talk about it, to desire it or make it desirable—such a translation is a rare and notable event" (191).

4. See Jacques Derrida, "Des Tours de Babel," and Paul de Man, "'Conclusions': Walter Benjamin's 'The Task of the Translator.'" Also, for an interesting analysis of both of these pieces within the context of anthropology, see Rey Chow.

5. For more on the *benshi* in English see Aaron Gerow. In Japanese, see Yoshida Chieo.

gossip about the actors, from providing historical background to translating a Griffith inter-title into Japanese, the *benshi*'s role did not come after the film in some epiphenomenal way but was dynamically included from the outset so that Japanese cinema equaled the sum total of the film plus the *benshi*. The *benshi*, at their best and before subsequent systemic constraints, approached the type of translation dreamt of by Benjamin in which the film (original) and *benshi* (translation) were dynamically related so that every new *benshi* performance would necessarily transform the film itself—producing that something in excess of both, pure language or Cinema. By 1931, however, the possibilities of the *benshi* were snuffed-out by (1) the political right: the military government that enforced a rigid *benshi* licensing system and a terribly unimaginative template for how *benshi* should go about their work, (2) the new cultural left: those who argued that the *benshi* blocked the growth of cinematic art and thus the critical possibilities of the form (such as writer Tanizaki Junichiro and dramatist Osanai Kaoru), and (3) Marlene Dietrich: the Hollywood talkie, with which the *benshi* simply could not compete.

With the end of the *benshi* system came the beginning of subtitles in Japan, in fact Joseph von Sternberg's *Morocco* was one of the very first films subtitled in Japan (Tanaka, Nornes). At this early stage of Japanese subtitling, the effects were quite different than twenty, fifty, or even seventy years later. With the *benshi* no longer in the theatre and no longer factored into the film during the production process itself, the spectator now had a less mediated relation to the film. Despite the addition of the new subtitles, spectators could still focus on the lighting, composition, narrative development, and acting in ways that had become hard to do after the *benshi* became more heavy-handed by the early thirties. As the subtitle became dominant and the memory of the *benshi* faded by the late thirties and early forties, however, the possibility of something more abstract (what I am calling Cinema, an analogy to Benjamin's pure language) was closed.

It is true, however, that some of the original *benshi* spirit (and some of the original subtitling spirit) persists in current Japanese subtitling. For example, one title of Quentin Tarantino's *Pulp Fiction* explains that the diner is located in a dangerous neighborhood of the US. Still, the dominant discourse on subtitling has gone the way of literary translation—avoiding criticism of the presumed ontological status of the original while remaining eager to enter into the fidelity versus freedom debate. In this context the debate either tiredly turns on (1) the infidelity of dubbing over the faithfulness of titling, (2) how the subtitles are either carefully faithful or flexibly free in relation to the original dialogue, or (3) how ridiculously inexact the story-distorting subtitles are. What dominates this debate is the idea of the static title at the bottom of the frame (not running on the bottom or popping up throughout the frame), or the subtitle that only translates dialogue (not, say, a prop or, as in *Pulp Fiction*'s case, one that comments, documentary-like on the setting). This old saw of proper subtitling emerged most powerfully in relation to the heated controversy over the bin Laden videotape.

5.

Just over two months after the terrorist attacks in the United States (on December 13, 2001), the Bush administration released a video tape of Osama bin Laden speaking about the September 11th bombings, a smoking gun so damning and undeniable, the administration argued, that those still in doubt are clearly questionable themselves—possible collaborators.[6] The video consisted of two scenes: the first a meeting in which

6. "It is preposterous for anybody to think that this tape is doctored," said Donald Rumsfield, adding, "That's just a feeble excuse to provide weak support for an incredibly evil man" (Sales).

bin Laden (surrounded by a group of buoyant comrades) relaxes on pillows and talks to a Saudi sheik in what appears to be a Kandahar safe-house; the second, approximately twelve minutes of downed US helicopter footage. With a low-end video camera mounted on a tripod about waist-high, the camera operator often shifts the length of the lens and can be heard whispering to someone off-camera. No one ever looks directly into the camera and yet everyone seems aware that it is there. The version released by the Pentagon (with subtitles running up almost half of the frame) divided the two scenes into three parts, leading with the second part of bin Laden's conversation, followed by the helicopter footage, and ending with the beginning of the meeting. Two questions: (1) why did Pentagon officials cut-up the footage, and (2) why did they wait over one month to release the video to the major networks?

The video was re-cut so that the most incontrovertible evidence would be front and centre, such as bin Laden's admission that the hijackers knew that they were on a martyrdom operation. But why not provide only the most relevant scenes? Because then the tape would appear more mediated (edited and cut-up): the Pentagon, in other words, wanted to provide a context, but not one that would obscure the key moments that it wanted to highlight. (And we must remember that the release of the video came on the heels of the Bush Administration's request that broadcasters not air any unauthorized images of bin Laden for fear that he might surreptitiously transmit possible directives to his North American supporters.[7])

The decision to wait to release the video is connected to this same desire to emphasize the video's authenticity. Bush officials, who explained that they found the video in a private Jalalabad residence, believed that it was shot in Kandahar on November 9. When asked about the elapsed time of over one month from the day they found the video to

7. With major networks buying footage from Al Jazeera TV in Kuwait, the Administration made a public request for all news organizations to consider the public safety issues involved with such transmissions. All major US networks fell in line as well as the Canadian Broadcast Corporation (CBC).

the day they released it to the major networks, the administration pointed to the bad audio quality and their desire to employ four outside translators to double-check their own Arabic-to-English subtitles, a precaution needed to answer possible claims that the White House had doctored or provided an inaccurate translation of the video.[8]

Of course these skeptical claims are precisely what followed. On the more conspiratorial level are those who believe the video was "Forest Gumped"—totally fabricated from stock footage and basic digital video manipulation. Others did not question the authenticity of the footage but argued that the subtlety of the language was reduced, thus assuring bin Laden's culpability. As one skeptic put it,

> The intention was to satisfy the public that it was not biased—Arabic being a language notoriously vague to translate, with concepts rather than one-for-one equivalencies often being the closest that can be attained. It has no future tense at all, which makes conversations about planning something perhaps less distinguishable from discussions about current events and descriptions of things that have already happened. (Irving)

Then there is the running parenthetical commentary that the Pentagon inserted into the dialogue. Revisionist historian David Irving writes, "The Pentagon transcript subtitles had over-useful interpolations in round brackets, making direct reference to the World Trade Center, the Pentagon, and civilian deaths, and in one instance identifying an Egyptian member of this Islamic mafia referred to in conversation only as Mohammed, as 'Mohammed (Atta)'—which might seem a bold step, given the likely number of other Egyptians called Mohammed."

More specifically, here are the subtitles for one of the most incriminating segments:

> *Osama bin Laden*: (...Inaudible...) we calculated in advance the number of casualties from the enemy, who would be killed based on the position of the tower. We calculated

8. CNN <http://www.cnn.com/2001/US/12/13/ret.bin.laden.videotape>.

> that the floors that would be hit would be three or four floors. I was the most optimistic of them all. (...Inaudible...) due to my experience in this field, I was thinking that the fire from the gas in the plane would melt the iron structure of the building and collapse the area where the plane hit and all the floors above it only. This is all that we had hoped for.
> *Sheik*: Allah be praised.

David Irving skeptically analyzed the subtitles this way: "Suppose Osama's opening remarks were inaudibilized, an audiotape technique that US presidents have long mastered? Suppose the missing phrases were something like, 'According to CNN thousands died in the upper floors. Well, that may be so. I'm a trained engineer and we've done the calculations and....'"

So here, as in the debates over literary translation and film subtitling, is the question of fidelity, of how accurately the content of the original is caught by the government-employed subtitlers. But here, too, what gets lost in this debate is the very form of subtitling itself. The Pentagon chose subtitling over dubbing in order to lend greater authenticity to the original. But with so many viewers familiar with the basic concepts of video production, the status of the original itself is called into question. (This skepticism was no doubt heightened when the US considered authorizing a new government department—The Office of Strategic Influence—whose misinformation mandate would include employing such new media morphing techniques.[9])

There was a similar obsession with content in the video of the Rodney King beating by Los Angeles police officers in 1991. The repetitive viewing and analysis of George Holliday's amateur video footage led to juror confusion over precisely who was assaulting whom. When defense lawyers for the LAPD performed a frame-by-frame analysis for the jury (with the help of noted cinema studies professors), the larger issue

9. In late February, the office was proposed only to be quickly dumped by Defense Secretary Donald Rumsfield. President Bush proclaimed zero tolerance for lies from US officials.

of how the very form of the portable video camcorder—that made it possible for the surveyed to turn the technology back on the surveyors—was lost in the minutiae of whether the exact position of Rodney King's arm indicated that he was getting up or stumbling down. The lesson of the Holliday tape is not that a picture (or a frame of a videotape) tells a thousand words, but that it tells a thousand (conflicting) stories. Part of the disappointment over the not-guilty verdict of the trial stemmed from a sense that the new democratic and libratory dimension of video was done for, that it was no longer a tool for the oppressed. One cannot be caught red-handed on video when those hands could very well be someone else's. And we are now living with the consequences of this with the present dominance of reality TV, a genre in which the political potential of the amateur videographer has been replaced by the value of the free labour he or she gives to the networks by shooting freak footage of baby and pet accidents.[10]

If the King footage flashed the simultaneous radical possibility of the video camera and its ideological recuperation, then the bin Laden footage does the same with video editing and subtitling. The Pentagon's subtitles are understood as coming after the event of the original video, thus burying what is most significant about the subtitles— that they (in a Benjaminian and *benshi*-like fashion) do not follow the original but are in dynamic relation with it. This now prepares us for the allegorical move, one that relates this more de-privileged understanding of the original (in terms of film and video) to the way the original (in this case nation-states) functions during the most recent transformations of the world-system.

6.

All subtitles invariably transform the original text. This concept of transformative subtitling

10. I write about reality culture in my article "Representation, Reality Culture, and Global Capitalism in Japan" in *South Atlantic Quarterly.*

seeks to de-link and de-territorialize the subtitled version from the original. At stake is a disruption of the usual temporalization ascribed to the original subtitle trajectory. Transformative subtitling implies that the original is not only what it is, but that it also exceeds itself. The original is part of a dialectical process in which it is at once part of the past, present, and future. If we view the original and the subtitled version as both belonging to the present tense—every subtitling of the original as changing the meaning of the original itself—then we will be right in the thick of a method that stresses the through-and-through dynamic and political nature of subtitling.

At stake here is quite a lot since the present state of the world is one in which the inequality of wealth and power is a result of centuries of past events. And for many of us, the way we justify our concerns and make daily life-choices depends upon how we explain this past to ourselves. To say that the past has not ended (and for our present purposes to say this about a pre-titled film or video) is to set this past (film or video) in a space of real vulnerability, perhaps on the order of those conspiracy theorists who deny the original video itself. But this vulnerability is marked not only with danger and doubt, but possibility. To pull up the anchor of the past is not only to risk obscuring a historical explanation of the present moment, but also to enliven the past and stress how the past is not only past but also part of the present and thus integral to shaping the future. Transformative subtitling draws attention to this process. Although this process is always in motion, it becomes dominant when discourses regarding "origins" are most immediate, such as during the re-fetishization of national origins in Benjamin's Germany and the return to nativist origins in 1930s Japan. It is for this reason that the emerging force of transformative subtitling is manifesting itself at the precise moment when the nation-state is experiencing another important transformation.

We know that since the early 1970s the global economy has been turning into a different moment of capitalist development, symbolized by the flexible accumulation of capital, cybernetic technologies, a global division of labour, transnationalization of business practices, new times and scales, and the weakened decision-making power of the nation-state. To be sure, the nation-state and various nationalisms (on both the discursive and operational levels) are still strong due to the different speeds at which the various levels within the social formation move. In other words, the cultural dimension of nationalism is stronger than the economic dimension. The North American Free Trade Agreement's (NAFTA) controversial Chapter 11 process, whereby companies who feel their investments are in jeopardy by the intervention of foreign governments can sue these governments for compensation, grants a certain transnational—or more specifically non-national—personhood to corporations of which real persons, who must still obey older rules of national subjecthood, can only dream. This relates to one of the common confusions in globalization discourse: the assumption that the global system's political-economic and cultural-ideological dimensions move at the same speed. For this reason, many political and cultural theorists expect to find the rise of global cultural movements and global working-class movements on par with the rise of global corporations. Whereas no one is surprised to learn that a CEO of a transnational corporation may have more power than local or national politicians in the congresses and parliaments around the world, when it comes to national identities and ideologies—the primary unit by which people locate themselves in the world—the nation's stock is still sky high. We still root for our own teams in the Olympics and our own armies in war while the political-economic stakeholders—without any nostalgia—focus on the bottom line.

The unevenness of the different levels of the social formation produces one of the great contradictions of our time: between the persistent power of residual national forms and the emerging influence of transnational ones. The force of this contradiction paralyzes our capacity to exist squarely in either dimension. Rather, we exist dead-centre in the contradiction and must wait for the movement of history (which is based on both our individual acts and its own structural logic) to transform the situation. This contradiction also explains why there are such odd bedfellows in the current political landscape: anarchists and neo-nationalists, Luddites and cybernauts all participating in the counter-globalization movements. Yet socio-political limits and contradictions always presuppose aesthetic possibilities and solutions. The aesthetic, in other words, offers a realm within which formal escapes are posed—however much these experiments might never directly engage the problem at hand. And it is here that the unevenness of the new running subtitle can be read allegorically: as a formal attempt (however unconscious) to square the circle of the national/transnational paradox.

There is a disconnection between the running subtitle and the central broadcast content. The subtitle is running ahead of the main content. It is running at a different speed. At the moment of crisis, we found ourselves focusing (with a double-optic that provided lucid insight rather than vertigo) on both the subtitle and the main content. For a brief moment we were flowing at both speeds, the slower speed of the main broadcast and the faster speed of the running titles: the slower speed of the national and the faster speed of the global. The subtitle is to the global as the main content is to the national. What could not be grasped on the social level (this utopian double-optic) was effortlessly experienced on the aesthetic one.

With the bin Laden video, even though the subtitles directly connected to the main content, due to the new realities of video editing and the re-valuation of original texts in the name of transformative subtitling, the two realms remain discrete. The running subtitle, this new line in the geometry of the visual, flashes for us hitherto impossible ways of seeing and living the new global realities—ways of seeing and living that are not yet possible at the present moment.

Walter Benjamin (1968)
The Task of the Translator: An Introduction to the Translation of Baudelaire's *Tableaux Parisiens*
Illuminations
Hannah Arendt, ed.
New York: Schocken Books

CNN
bin Laden on tape: Attacks "benefited Islam greatly"
http://www.cnn.com/2001/US/12/13/ret.bin.laden.videotape

Eric Cazdyn (2001)
Representation, Reality Culture, and Global Capitalism in Japan
South Atlantic Quarterly 99.4

——(2002)
The Flash of Capital: Film and Geopolitics in Japan
Durham: Duke University Press

Yoshida Chieo (1978)
Mo hitotsu no eiga-shi: katsuben no jidai
Tokyo: Jiji Tsushin-sha

Rey Chow (1995)
Film as Ethnography; or, Translation Between Cultures in the Postcolonial World
Primitive Passions: Visuality, Sexuality, Ethnography and Contemporary Chinese Cinema
New York: Columbia University Press

Paul de Man (1986)
"Conclusions": Walter Benjamin's The Task of the Translator
The Resistance to Theory
Minneapolis: University of Minnesota Press

Jacques Derrida (1985)
Des Tours de Babel
Difference in Translation
Joseph F. Graham, ed.
Ithaca: Cornell University Press

Aaron Gerow (1994)
The Benshi's New Face: Defining Cinema in Taisho Japan
Iconics 3

David Irving (2001)
Controversial Historian David Irving on the bin Laden Tape
http://www.rense.com/general18/ckk.htm

Fredric Jameson (1981)
The Political Unconscious:
Narrative as a Socially Symbolic Act
Ithaca: Cornell University Press

——(1992)
Signatures of the Visible
New York: Routledge

Abé Markus Nornes (1999)
For an Abusive Subtitling
Film Quarterly 52.3

Leigh Sales (2001)
White House defends authenticity
of latest Osama video tape
http://www.abc.net.au/am/s441284.htm

Tanaka Junichiro (1980)
Nihon eiga hattatsu-shi II
Tokyo: Chuokoron-sha

MY LAST INTERVIEW WITH ULRIKE OTTINGER: ON *SOUTHEAST PASSAGE* AND BEYOND[1]
Laurence A. Rickels

The last time I interviewed Ulrike Ottinger (in 1992), the receiving area of her films was pressing to divide into a "Before" and "After," Ottinger's dual—and in every film moment double—investment in fictional art cinema and documentary film. A series of films that could be identified as documentary led (1) to a sense of changed direction in Ottinger's work in progress, (2) to massive repression of her recent art-cinema past, and (3) to projection of Ottinger's exclusively documentary filmmaking in place of the other cinema that had been lost. But back then, as the interview underscored, the movie Ottinger was looking forward to making was a new film, *Diamond Dance*. That project spent the interim in the Hollywood from "development hell." In the 1990s Hollywood set a spell with so-called Independent films, inoculated itself with a shot of what was "new," and doubled and contained all "other worlds." As the protracted near-miss of the *Diamond Dance* project "documented," European art cinema was over and out with Hollywood's declaration of Independents. Consequently, in 2000, Ottinger went on relocation in the international art world. Her photographic work began to be shown in prominent art scenes and venues—rather than, for example, in ethnological museums. In 2002, when the Goetz collection was selectively presented in Munich, Ottinger's photographs "in the context of Freak Orlando"—only recently acquired—nevertheless made the cut and were prominently displayed alongside works by Matthew Barney, Robert Gober, Yayoi Kusama, Tony Oursler, and Cindy Sherman, among others. Her film *Southeast Passage*, while identifiably documentary in nature and budget, was at the same time commissioned for the 2002 Documenta in Kassel, the international art extravaganza where the film premiered.

The document of a trip along historical trade routes through the forgotten half of Europe, *Southeast Passage* is Ottinger's most highly edited film to date. In fact it is her

1. Conducted September 2002.

first film that can be said to have originally taken shape only in the course of editing. In particular, the inclusion or installation of her photographs within the film is a striking feature of her editing process. Her photographic work—until 2002 a parallel universal in her artistic production, hovering mainly "in the context of" her films—entered her film work as montage element with *Southeast Passage*.

I saw the rough cut of *Southeast Passage* in Winter 2001 and the final cut in late Summer 2002. While the structure of the film and of each part had already been in place in the rough cut, the final version reveals a highly encrusted and intrawoven product. In addition to photographs, *Southeast Passage* also incorporates black-and-white sequences, including one extended insert based on Valentine Kataev's short story of 1926, "The Exemplar," in which actors perform with a silent-film mannerism that draws from both Eastern European traditions of the grotesque and German Expressionist film. While the actors mime speech, Hans Zischler narrates the text about an Odessa official who falls asleep in 1905 and wakes up years later in the Soviet Union. When the official understands the new situation, he withdraws from his series of comic encounters with the new order into the anonymous crowd. The story thus glosses another reversal in the fortunes of Odessa that is not part of its own plot but which we witness (by turning up the contrast) in the film document. Now the people wake up to find themselves no longer within collectivism: they struggle to make the new crowd of individuals in which they in turn must disappear. But the film (as film, as a projective medium that, both historically and technically, is at the peak of its development and refinement) also admits continuity shots lifted from its own history. At one point in the Odessa portion of *Southeast Passage*, the pressure is on—it's ready-made—to include a more direct citation of one of cinema's most memorable scenes. Raymond Wolff comments on this self-reflexive moment: "This viewer's favorite scene in the film concerns a child. All film buffs will recall the famous baby carriage scene in Sergei Eisenstein's 1925 classic *Battleship Potemkin*. The steps shown were in Odessa and are still there. They lead down to the harbour and are known as 'The Potemkin Steps.' In the Eisenstein version a mother with a baby carriage is shot, and there is great drama as the carriage heads down the steps on its own. In the Ottinger film, a four-year-old boy and his father are seen heading down the steps hand-in-hand. Because of the differences in their gait, the child seems to trip more than walk. The viewer has that Potemkin feeling all over again."[2]

Before her journey, Ottinger was acquainted with the places of her documentary trip mainly through books. In *Southeast Passage* she selects quotations from Isaak Babel, Walter Benjamin, Elias Canetti, and Joseph Roth, among others. These run by the document of contemporary settings—which everywhere admit historical remnants and fragments—as a now audible, now legible commentary from a past that only the dead know as more or less whole. As is typical for Ottinger's approach to filmmaking, the musical score represents a profoundly archival montage that meets the visuals more than halfway. But it is photography that makes the grand entry at the art of her film work with a layering effect that at the same time stages and staggers the motion within or passage through the picture titled *Southeast Passage*.

In English, "subtitles" designates the words of translation printed along the bottom of the screened film image of audible words from a foreign language. But subtitles are also the upward displacement of captions associated with printed still images which still have a border in which to accommodate them. In film, therefore, subtitles represent a symptomatic, foreign-body disturbance (especially in their white-on-white effacement

2. "Ulrike Ottinger Takes On Europe's 'Blank Spaces.' Her New Documentary Premieres at Documenta," *Aufbau*, No. 13, Thursday, June 27, 2002.

they are such a strain). But, according to the *OED*, the first English-language meaning of "subtitle," still as new as the late-nineteenth century, referred to the second (often explanatory) title of books, linked to but separated from the principal title by a punctuation mark, frequently a colon—the mark Heidegger singled out for its technologizing effect on language. The subtitle that follows the colon indeed puts the main title in the ready position—to be identified, applied, consumed, reproduced as reproducible.

Southeast Passage has a subtitle: *A Journey to the New Blank Spaces on the Map of Europe*. In German they are literally "the white spots" on the map which, cartographically speaking, is how empty or undescribed (or uncathected) spaces appear. In its form and content Ottinger's film explores the dislocation of Eastern and Oriental Europe. This dislocation and this missingness circumscribe the (white) spot of projection. Everyone's talking about Europe. But how could we have overlooked it? Half of it is missing.

A sign advertising the services and address of an insurance firm named VERITAS opens the relay and delay of still images (including a photograph of the director herself on location). The first part of *Southeast Passage* concludes in Varna, a turning point in a journey or quest that is legend to the map of Ottinger's project. It was in Varna, in Stoker's novel, that Western European and American vampire hunters (and gadget lovers) began to double and contain Count Dracula's Oriental challenge to systems of circulation and orientation as new and improved: our mass-media culture of long distance connections—or, in relation to Freud's second system, we might term it the security or insurance drive—thus emerges over the doubly dead embodiment of this challenge from the east of Europe. The uncanny zone can now be mapped and tourist trapped, registered or identified, and forgotten.

An absence right next door is the place setting of what Adorno identified (in a letter to Benjamin dated August 25, 1935) as the recent past, conceived, that is, as the most remote or primal past, a past that can be received only as catastrophe or return. The "white spot" of the recent past and the culture next door is thus—in VERITAS—a "reality" effect (beyond the media of projection) of our TV era of "liveness" in which, for security reasons, the present tense (and ongoing tension)—the seeing I of our media sensorium—is dislocated within the fantasy arc of past (perfect) and a future of wish fulfillment.

Accompanied by stirring music of the lost era, the titles also rise with the photographs in the opening moments of *Southeast Passage*. Then text from Ilya Ilf and Yevgeni Petrov's *The 12 Chairs* commands the frame. With the commencement of "Part 1 (Wroclaw to Varna)" the motion pictures for the first time let roll. But photographs continue to punctuate the movement.

By and large photographs are pressed into the service of ironic self-reflexivity at the blended boundary between documentary real-time travel and the advent of the other. For example, in filmed images we watch three girls shyly resist being portrayed. The sequence ends with a photo portrait of the beaming threesome proudly looking at the camera (and ultimately at themselves). In passing, a Hungarian mimics Ottinger's camera with a bottle. Then two old women are caught in the act of commenting on being filmed. One says: "It is not permitted." But the second assuages her friend's anxious sense of decorum: "But it doesn't really matter." Someone asks: "Will you send me a photo?" Another subject comments: "I am being filmed now." We are told that the goats she helps herd are often used as extras for Italian TV movies. Then we see the shepherdess's photo portrait. Ottinger also films the goat herds. Then we see the still photo images of the animals. Halfway to Varna the camera looks out from the driving minibus giving the digital gadget the frame of automobilic, analogic technology and apparatus—thus another twist of self-reflection or self-historicization in this affirmation of the medium of film. A digital camera is not (yet) a movie camera. But it synthetically gets around the former divide between video and film that Ottinger would otherwise never have crossed.

Laurence Rickels: I understand you are working on two new projects, a short here in Berlin to premiere this fall, and a feature-length film, between documentary and fiction, that will take you back to the former Soviet Union.
Ulrike Ottinger: In Berlin we have "Jewish Culture Weeks" and the organizers had the idea to commission several short films for the November 2002 celebrations. Since the budget is very small it will cover only a digital production. They were thinking mainly of documentary films. The guidelines were left open. But they were looking for a Berlin theme that, however freely or flexibly, would stand in some relation to Judaism. The Esther story plays a very big role in *Diamond Dance* and in the course of my research I became more and more interested in the Esther story and in the Purim games and plays. The Esther story is so interesting because there are so many of them, there are Babylonian and Jewish variants, for example, and simply the most diverse interpretations, and in addition there are so many local versions. In recent years the Jewish community in Berlin has grown unbelievably, more than doubled. For the most part, the newcomers are Russian Jews. Many of them had very little contact with Judaism but then perhaps because their immigration here was made possible by their being "Jewish," since otherwise they never would have gained entry into the European fortress, a form of contact was renewed. What interests me about this group are the many new fascinating faces. I

thought it would be lovely to perform an Esther story with these older people, who speak in altogether different languages: some still speak Yiddish, others a heavily-accented German, yet others only Russian, and are just starting to learn German. I would like to keep it simple. They will wear their everyday clothes (I would probably still help make the selections). Then, as it was in former times in the Purim plays of the children (as one knows from photographs or oral histories from the turn-of-the-century through the 1920s), I will have them put on hats, crowns, the diadem of Esther painted on paper maché or made with gold lamé. They can play the different roles, possibly argue about the competing versions. I have to wait a bit and see what will happen. In any event, that is my plan, a sort of Esther story performed and followed through with these people. They have been through so much already. I expect they will bring a new relationship to, or experience of, the Esther story through their memories, or that through the Esther story they will be able once more to face certain fundamental threats. For the Esther story is associated in particular with the overcoming of threatening events.

And the larger Russian project?

In the course of my research for *Southeast Passage* I became enchanted by the literary works of several Odessa authors. The novel which I would like to use as the basis for the new film is a kind of travelogue that traverses the entirety of the former Soviet Empire, and at every way-station one encounters the madness of bureaucratic administration. The narrative is written with an unbelievable joy in fabulation and yet at the same time discloses a certain Russian reality that one can only convey with the formal means of the grotesque. There is, in Central and Eastern Europe, and also in Russia, an ancient tradition of the grotesque. I would like to take up and follow out this travel route again with a troupe of actors, encountering this time realities of today that are no less grotesque than those of the past.

Will you write a screenplay?

Yes I will, and then one can change and adapt it. I will start by building a scaffold in the manner of Mongolian dramaturgy, which allows me the freedom to insert and build up all manner of details inside it. I love travelling. I love the form of travel and the cinema of way-stations that corresponds to it.

Russia played a role in your earlier film work as backdrop, as part of the background of certain characters, as part of history. But a documentary encounter seems to have been reserved for the new millennium. How did this newer documentary interest come into focus?

It was already very interesting in Mongolia to see the differences arising from the two competing administrations, the Chinese and the Russian. You can recognize the different influences right away. I was interested to see these different influences on Mongolian culture. In *Taiga* [1992] I showed settlements in the north that look like Siberian villages. The Chinese part, in the south, looks different. And you can follow the history of these influences by the comparison of a current setting with old photographs and even fiction films from the 1920s and 1930s.

But in the year 2000 you travelled through Eastern Europe with a digital camera. How had this region come closer? You no longer had to take the detour via Mongolia.

The fall of the Berlin Wall introduced rapid changes that were immediately perceptible. Suddenly you could hear so many Eastern European languages in Berlin. I'm always fascinated when places that were off-limits for so long are opened up for travel. Odessa was always a magical place for me, like Samarkand or Timbuktu, places that extend into our fantasies.

I have good friends here who speak excellent Russian, Ada and Boris. Boris is Bulgarian and speaks several Balkan languages, or at least understands them well. He studied in Moscow. As did his wife Ada, who is a scholar of the 1920s, an unusual topic of study back then in the Soviet Union. It was surely considered inappropriate to specialize in that period. And so I would ask them how one goes about travelling there. And one day they said, "Why don't we go together?" And so we began to plan the trip. The most difficult thing we faced was the car rental, because we were apparently going to be driving beyond the Europcar universe. The rental agency is called Europcar and it is significant that one cannot travel to Eastern Europe with one of their cars. We travelled together for two months. Yugoslavia, of course, was not an option.

Did that block a historical route you had wanted to take?

No. There are many routes, and they're all historical. Up until World War II there was one Europe, it all belonged to Europe. The opera house in Odessa is up to the standards of Vienna or Paris. Beautiful old hotels, arcades, and streetcars, everything you would expect to find in a major European city. That is one thing I tried to show. Old Europe is still entirely there in the cities, intact, right down to the clothes of the people who, no matter how poor they are, and even if they have to piece together their outfits out of rags, are clearly determined to look fantastic. The same old European atmosphere pervades the arcades of Istanbul. In this spirit I explored and used the music of the 1920s, tangos from Odessa and Istanbul, music that counted as modern back then, elegant and chic, and the music in turn bore a unique local stamp. Bucharest was famous for its tango bars with famous female tango singers. Ataturk was involved with a famous tango singer who stood by him at political gatherings especially when he was promoting change in the social standing of women. The relics of old Europe, which are still manifest in these cities, I showed them, in the architecture, music, streetcars, in the arcades, in the countless details, even in the cuisine, but always with a focus fixed on the local variation and alteration.

It seems that while Berlin changed from being an allegorical site in its divided and split-off state and started functionalizing, these Eastern European cities, among other things, took on the allegorical format of memorial relics.

Yes. They are relics, memory fragments, but at the same time I have the feeling that they are parts of something, parts that in some form, perhaps psychically, save the people in all their poverty. Certainly that is true for the older people. Then I documented all the new developments that can also be seen on the street. I think that what distinguishes my films is that I look around the streets to see what is different, what has remained.

I also used a great many literary quotations from different eras in the film. For example, I quoted from Joseph Roth, who travelled a great deal through the Soviet Union. Back then all the utopians visited the Soviet Union and invariably published glowing reports of their travels in the West. They were themselves so enthusiastic about their utopian ideals that they were often too uncritical. Joseph Roth was an exception. He travelled in the countryside too, through the villages, and he documented his travels in a mode that was thoughtfully and critically observant. I also quoted Walter Benjamin, Issak Babel, and Elias Canetti. Canetti writes about his place of birth, a small town in Moldova, almost at the mouth of the Danube, and he relates how when one travelled up the Danube toward Vienna, one would then say that one was going to Europe. He comes from a Sephardic family that had lived a long time in Turkey. When the Spanish Jews were cast out many landed in the Balkans and in what later became the Ottoman Empire, especially in Istanbul where they were prized for their skills.

I structured the film in a differentiated way. The part dedicated to Istanbul is structured according to the story of the seven princesses, which I transposed to the seven hills of Istanbul and the seven days of the week. The first part passes through Poland, Chechnya, Hungary, Romania, Bulgaria, and stops in Varna. The second part is dedicated to Odessa but includes an outing into the countryside, and in this section I reflected on the past with literary citations. The film as a whole is a permanent exchange among old Europe, the Ottoman Empire, and the new Europe—including all the desolate conditions of life in Eastern Europe. In Ukraine the only remaining export, the country's only saleable raw materials, are the women.

It seems that with Johanna d'Arc of Mongolia *you created a work that, even in the title, invites a mix of languages that proves difficult to translate into one language, that resists such globalization. Untranslatability is among the phenomena you "document" in* Taiga.

First off, everything that can be translated is translated in my films, that is, in their different versions. There is an international version of *Johanna d'Arc of Mongolia* that doesn't translate the journey on the Trans-Siberian Express, during which the passengers converse in different languages—in French, English, German, Russian—often at the same time. This was common practice around 1900 or so, in the old Europe, and seems to be happening once again. When people who speak three or four languages converse with one another, it is at any given moment possible to switch to another, as a way of being considerate. That is something I enjoy very much. But there is a German version that translates all foreign languages into German, and there is an English version that translates whatever is spoken, whether Mongolian or Russian or Chinese. Still, the original languages are very important to me. They are an inseparable part of the given culture.

They have their own music and their own rhythm. For example, I find it unbearable to watch Japanese films that have been dubbed. It is such a different way of speaking. The rhythm, the breathing is so different, and to familiarize all that strikes me as absurd. But perhaps that fulfills a wish to assimilate whatever is foreign. Or it reflects a human need or drive to react to what is foreign with anxiety. Probably not, or I should say, it all depends.

Regarding *Taiga*, I was filming in an area in which both Mongolian and Tuvin were spoken, and the Mongolian was a specific dialect that drew on different lexica including, in part, that of ancient Turkish. And since the people live so close together there, one language crossed over into the other. For a historian of languages it is interesting to contemplate which words were adopted. The whole translation process in the course of making *Taiga* was certainly fascinating. For example, I was allowed to film, to record, two complete shamanic séances, which were not staged for me, but which were simply happening because the time was right. In one instance a certain constellation was in place, in the other the occasion was illness. I had a sound engineer with me and everything was recorded. And afterwards I asked the shamaness if she would like to hear what she said during those six hours. Customarily the utterances during a séance are interpreted by the community, as with the oracles of Delphi; the discourse is often so cryptic that it calls for interpretation, though some of what is said is clear, unequivocal for listeners in a certain situation. And she said she would like very much to hear the recording. Because she was listening I was able to ask questions with regard to translation that I would otherwise never have asked because I do not conduct Inquisition-like interviews; if people feel like telling me something I'm very pleased. Her resulting narration flows into the film. But the interview is not in the foreground. In *Taiga* there were passages that were incomprehensible to us and which were not translated. Some words or cries exchanged in greeting were not translated. But there is not a whole lot that was left untranslated.

I don't introduce myself into the film like many documentary filmmakers do, showing us how they cross the desert in the jeep or how it gets stuck in the river. I don't show that sort of thing because it doesn't interest me. Just the same, I am present in the reactions of the people I encounter. And that does interest me. I never edit out the moments in which people address me. For example, I was with tribesmen living together with reindeer. These animals have two small bones at their heels that click like castanets when they walk. And when a herd arrives or the people are bringing a caravan—they ride the reindeer there—one hears the clicking, and they of course hear it more acutely and know the sounds better and hear them before we would. And so they said, "Watch out now, get the camera ready, soon you can take pictures, soon the reindeer will be here." Moments like that I leave in my films. And I translate them. I don't want to keep anything from the viewer. But there are a few small things that I left untranslated, two or three things that just couldn't be translated, despite all the assistance to which I had access. There were certain Mongols who were formerly Tuvin and had Mongolized themselves in the meantime; others lived more in the wilderness, the steppes, and spoke a more mixed language, including both adopted words and ancient words that had been retained. But as far as possible I translated all that I heard and included in the film.

But it is of course a false conception to believe that one can experience a culture by translating language word-for-word. One must also know the significance of the word, its context—it is all so much more complicated. We, too, have our own social codes and know when something is said in one way that has additional meanings. What was said in a polite way can also imply criticism. All of these codes must be taken into consideration. One can't just imagine that one has grasped something completely by translating it word-for-word. This is a misunderstanding or perhaps a widespread fantasy that one can immediately and completely comprehend anything at all that comes from another culture. It is a long process. Even with cultures that one has studied and with which one has concerned oneself intensively there are always surprises, and that is a good thing.

I read the précis for *Subtitles* which raises several questions about what is foreign in or as film. I find it interesting to consider what is foreign, what is other, in particular in film. To give an example, while I was making *Exil Shanghai* [1997] I occupied myself intensively with the programs of Chinese films in Shanghai in the 1920s and 1930s. American, British, and French movements in cinema were all represented. But it was primarily American movies that influenced Shanghai cinema, and there was a development—just as there was with photography in the United States—to document what was happening in the streets. I don't know if this is the case, but I ask myself if this isn't an influence, I mean those American films that were made outside, no longer in the studio, already on the streets, whether these films didn't have a certain influence on Chinese filmmakers who also began to make films in the streets. Much of what is foreign is reworked in the new setting and interpreted so that it can be understood. This process tended usually to stimulate the development of interesting new forms, including the adaptation of other things, also of foreign things from other cultures. Something very interesting in culture is the adaptation, which can indeed be a matter of misunderstanding, but one that takes on a brand new meaning in a new cultural setting. Adaptation, perhaps assimilation, certainly alteration, describe the creative process. But while I have always affirmed this, it seems today under the conditions of film business, the conditions of monopoly—strictly economically speaking—the conditions of the so-called global, something quite other than adaptation is happening, namely a certain production of sameness is what is promoted or allowed. The last time I was in Beijing I had a hotel room with a television set and I watched American shows with recognizable stars speaking perfect Chinese. They could speak Armenian too, I'm sure. And I wonder what this could lead to.

A Korean artist who lives and works in New York told me that when he first came to the United States as a young man he expected everyone to speak Korean because that's what the Americans always spoke on Korean television.

Of course. It seems to me that this no longer has anything in common with the creative alteration, the adaptation, the encounter with the foreign or with the other.

But maybe after the fact, through this shock of recognition that the world is not peopled by Americans who speak Korean. That changes everything.

Yes, that changes everything. But really only for the weaker partner in the exchange.

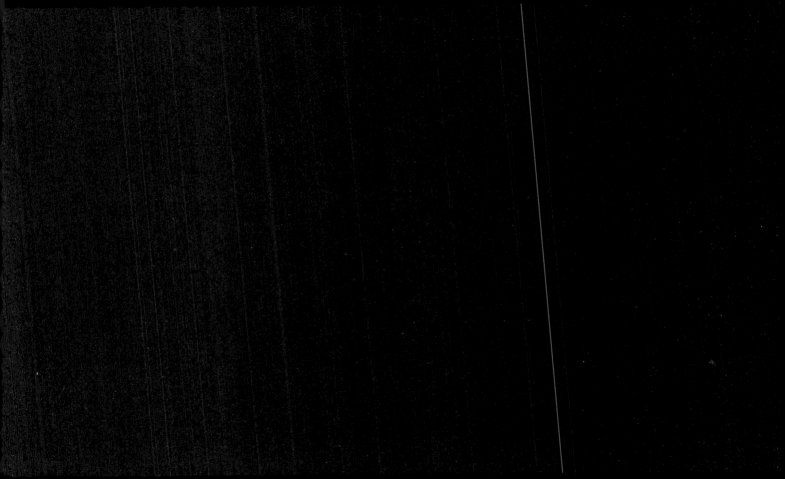

THE FOREIGNNESS OF THE INTIMATE, OR THE VIOLENCE AND CHARITY OF PERCEPTION
R. Bruce Elder

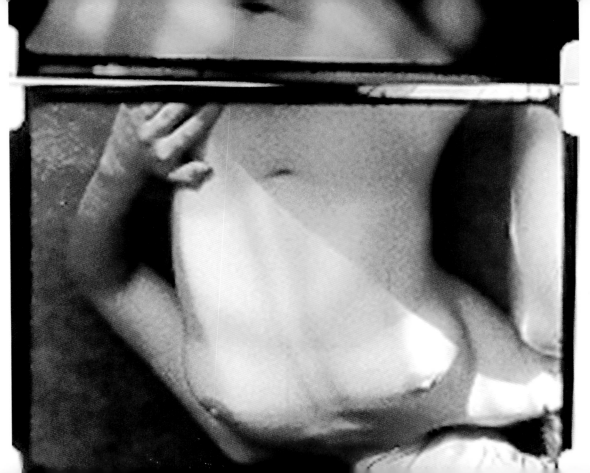

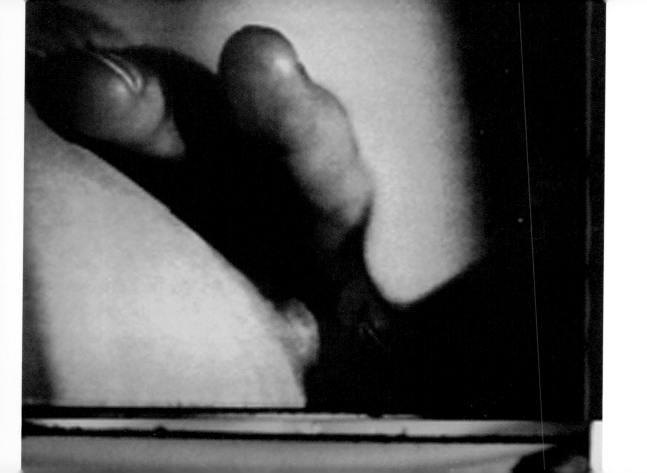

Imagine everything beyond one's self turned into nothing. What would then be left? Not a pure negativity, but an indeterminateness that retains a measure of positivity, an absence we experience as something present. Would this absence, this nothing, be an imaginative projection? An external absolute? Be-ing itself, anterior to all beings? It is not possible to determine. We know only this much: though this idea would be of a universal nothing, it would not be of a nothing that is without be-ing. What it would concern, though indefinite, nonetheless is. It is not thought. It summons no words; indeed it deranges discourse. For it disturbs, like a miscreant that threatens to return, particularized, anywhere and everywhere. This nothing is not weightless; to the contrary, as a fluidity of forces, as an atmospheric pressure, it exerts pressure everywhere, and always differently.

Awareness which is not of anything definite, of anything concrete, of anything that definitely is, then, is the awareness that nothing also is, the awareness that nothing is not without being. As it is on the side of object, so it is on the side of the subject—the subject is no more a definite entity that the object is. Each is nothing other than flux—a flux of such indefinite character that we might as well call it a nothing. It is a simply a presence, a force, an atmosphere, that has no definite being. There is, in fact, only the universality of an epistemic process anterior not just to the formation of a definite subject but even to the division between subject and object.

In order to acknowledge its primacy, let us call that awareness which is anterior not just to the formation of a definite subject but even to the division between subject and object, "thinking." All thinking is a revelation of a transcendent be-ing, and is, in its ownmost be-ing, itself a transcendence of the given (as an object of awareness).

This nothing is the underworld of things, an underworld anterior to anything definite. But if this realm is the primal, what possibly could be the appeal of cinematography, for cinematography is a means for reproducing definite things? Because an image's ontology bears evidence, through a sort of inversion, of be-ing's ontogenetic capacity (its capacity to create beings). For an image comes into evidence as the double of an object in the very act of the object's withdrawing—this is the very meaning of representation. An image is not a transparency that our mind passes through on the way to apprehending the object to which it refers. An image is actually the double of the object, the appearance that an actual being leaves behind as it departs—the ghost of a departed object one might say. In creating its own double, which it highlights through the emptying—the *kenosis*—that appears as it withdraws, an object indicates the ontogenesis of its own existence.

Every image, then, speaks of origins, of beginnings. Every image is an evidence of fecundity. For every image belongs to another order entirely different than that to which ordinary existents belong. Hence, the dimension of transcendence pertains to all images. Because an image belongs to a transcendent order, it can seem so terrible. But there is more to its *terribilità* than just the transcendence of its referent: because the image reveals the substantiality, the weightiness of nothing, it reminds us that the other side of be-ing is not non-existence. It terrifies us with the prospect that seems to have haunted the vast majority of pre-modern people (and which Dante's *Commedia* allegorizes), that our passing out of existence will not be an utter annihilation. Images, as the leavings of beings, testify that to pass beyond being is not really to go out of existence, that everything that is really is forever, that for be-ing there is no endgame. Film's character as midden speaks to this condition.

An image, in revealing the presence of the past and the future in the here-and-now, also reveals the temporalizing that is the origin of time. For a particular existent reveals itself only in the mode of immediacy, while an image always speaks of what has departed and what is yet to come—it speaks of the departed because its appearance is the result of that which has been left behind after the object has departed, and it speaks of the future because every image summons what it might become: the tablets are forever about to slip from the pressure of Moses's right elbow (or not to slip—we do not know which, for the future is unknowable). The ontology of the future, like the ontology of the image, is that of pressure, a force, an atmosphere, exerted by something that has no be-ing; it is that of absent presence.

Images shatter the consolidated presence of focal awareness and, by animating thinking, introduce what is foreign to reality, what belongs to the realms of the "has been" and the "yet to be" into our spiritual life. Images, by their association with thinking, introduce the Otherness of what has been and what is yet to be into consciousness; but they do so not as something that is, but as pressure emanating from that which has no existence.

All artmaking begins with an intimation of the uncanny, with the intrusion of something foreign, something that is close to non-being, into the everyday realm. It begins with a particular form of thinking, one that begins in a scene of violence that wrenches us from presuppositions concerning what is. These presuppositions are—despite the complacency they engender—really the ultimate of will's violent imposition upon reality, for these presuppositions violently hold at bay reality's (Be-ing's) eruptive disposition. I call that thinking which opens itself towards what is foreign, uncanny, Wholly Other, and the process of being disturbed and disordered by it, "genuine thinking," because it is creative and because as a form of thinking it lies closer to the origins of thinking than any other. This form of thinking breaches the monotony of time which presuppositions engender. Genuine thinking emerges from a power that prevents what it receives from ever being closed, from a power that disrupts all finality, and that renders self-identity impossible. From the power of genuine thinking emerges something that is more like an electric sensation-in-and-of-flux than it is like an idea. I call this electric sensation "perception." Rendering the strangeness of perception is the goal of artmaking. Perception, the source of all genuine thinking, is attentive. Through this act of attention, what hides is able to impose itself upon us with the force of a shock.

Yet, despite their violence, these shocks are charitable. Without them, we would have to surrender to our fear that the world, in its sheer givenness, is without novel possibilities. We would succumb to the lethargy of believing that everything is determined in advance—would succumb, that is, to the mechanistic worldview that made early modern philosophers shudder. We would inhabit a too-familiar world of mechanistic necessity, a world bereft of good and evil, a world where the "being there (*Dasein*) of human be-ing" made no difference. The convulsions induced by genuine thinking produce wonderment—a wonderment that soon enough devolves into a more rationalized, instrumental form of thinking. But before that occurs, this wonderment give one over to something primal.

These shocks also encourage us to be aware of the act of perception itself. They lift one out of what Edmund Husserl called the "naive standpoint," where consciousness, because it is absorbed by its object, avoids the question of what human beings—what the fact that the human be-ing is there, as an opening for disclosure—contribute to the object perceived, the objects that make up the world we inhabit. The opening towards disclosure that characterizes the "be-ing there" of human beings, is at one with that openness, that emptiness, that nothingness that is the scene of beings' coming-to-be. This essential unity allows us to sense, however vaguely, the being-together of human be-ing and what there was even before all creation. We discover thereby the primordiality of Be-ing, that which makes human be-ing, in its openness, the image of the Divine.

The shock induced by a sensation creates an opening through which that which is strange, foreign, unexpected, novel, disrupts the complacent surface of everyday experience that is constituted when our perceptions are filtered through ideas (pre-conceptions). The strangeness, the foreignness, the alienness of what comes through the clearing prised open by a new electric sensation is a result partly of its paradoxical temporal attributes. For this opening is created by attention, and through attentiveness we learn that the future creates the present.

It is the fact that an aesthetic object comes to be through a similar retroactive creativity that makes aesthetics relevant to ontology—and that is one (among several) reasons why indeed aesthetics should found ontology. For an aesthetic object is apprehended through the poetic principle that shapes it, insofar as every work teaches us how we should consider it. But the poetic principle that shapes each work (the principle we learn by attending to the work), is absolutely unique for each individual work—indeed it develops through the process of making/reading the work. To recognize that, however, is to acknowledge that it comes into being only through what it makes. The principle that guides the making of the work is constituted only retroactively, even though its existence is presumed by—and therefore prior to—what it brings into being. The poetic principle, insofar as it is unique in every poem, designates a particular configuration of experience that gives a poem its shape; but reciprocally, it comes into being through the poem itself. Thus, the principle of its be-ing is both presupposed by and derived from the poem.

Aesthetic experience, accordingly, makes generative temporality palpable, for generative temporality is a surface twisted into the form of a Möbius strip, in which the future generates the past even as the past brings forth the future. Generative time (unlike narrative time) is not composed of a series of "nows" strung out along a line—on the contrary, in generative time, the future creates the past from which the present is inherited. This generative time is the time of attention, of resoluteness: through resoluteness all my actions are inflected by an anticipation, for they are informed by my understanding that the future will inherit what I do. In claiming that resoluteness involves the understanding that the future will inherit my action, my deliberation is determined by my recognition of what it will mean for that action to belong to the past. Through resoluteness, then, the future brings the present into being through the mediation of a past which it (the future) creates for itself.

The reality of temporal convolution, in which the future creates the present through its influence on the past, is not the only ontological understanding that aesthetic objects furnish. Another results from aesthetic objects' capacity to make perception difficult. By making perception difficult, aesthetic objects also make us aware that human be-ing, which is an opening towards disclosure, is there to play both an interpretative and a constitutive role in bringing forth the meaning of beings—in *reading* beings. It restores to human be-ing that self-reflexive awareness that informs it of its primordially empty condition; recognition of our primordially empty be-ing, which human beings share with what lies beyond beings, grounds the possibility of human be-ing grasping the constitutive role it has in the be-ing of beings.

Formulating a thought is an act of violence—a violence that holds the eruptive, chaotic propensity of reality at bay. For a thought imposes a conceptual order on that which has no conceptual order—and the less genuine thinking is, the greater is this imposition. The character of the violence involved in formulating a thought can be understood through considering the analogy a common political situation offers. A law takes form as a means of stabilizing and perpetuating a relation between unequal parties—one nation wages war on another and loses; the victor then grants rights and privileges to the vanquished, guaranteed under treaty. The two parties are unequal, but, in the supreme act of the charity of human self-understanding, the accord is reached between them that fosters the illusion that both parties enter into the agreement with the measure of freedom requisite to assuming the obligations they contract to take on. The same occurs when law demands that the aggressor pay retribution to the victor.

The violence and charity of law is to place the weaker on an equal footing with the mightier—and of course, the prototype for this attribute that all positive laws evince is the moral law, which, by its universality, requires that the unlike all be treated alike. To the might of power, the law counterpoises the irrevocable demands of the humbled. The law brings both the victor and the vanquished, the mighty and humble, into an ungainly accord, the end of which is to quell any possible upheaval, to quiet any possible uprising.

So it is with thinking. All thinking, and all perception, is endangered by the object of thought, for the be-ing of any and all beings exceeds thought—that which elevates be-ing above beings is intimated in the resistance that a raw perception exhibits to being turned into a thought (a representation). Attention to these features of perception disclose that even though the subject participates in the transformation of the elemental into a percept, there is nonetheless a transcendental element associated with every object of perception which refuses to be reduced. That transcendental element is what, following Heidegger, I call "earth," and the creative transformation which perception effects results in the emergence of what, again following Heidegger, I call a "worldly" being. But perception, like all thinking, enters into a truce with beings; the truce is forged as one learns to cherish the gift of what is given in perception—learns that however troubling, upsetting, and violent perception is, human be-ing, through abiding with the gifts perception brings, may establish an ungainly, awkward peace with what brings these gifts, a peace wherein what is poorer and humbler, that is to say, consciousness, accedes to a status equal to that of the gifts that are given it. But against Heidegger, I insist that such an "abiding-with" is the result of a truce, a pact that a violence mightier than our own establishes with us, to grant us the time wherein we can complete the work of Be-ing.

Thinking does not passively render a pre-existent reality that lies before it. Rather perceiving transforms—violently transforms—what gives rise to it, by converting "what might be" into "what is." The violence of the conversion is that it reduces potentiality into actuality, possibility into determination, the infinite into the finite. Perception configures one particular arrangement out of the infinite possibilities that are implicit in the nothingness that hides itself in darkness. But this sacrifice of the infinite for the finite is also, like the Great Sacrifice, an act of charity, for it grants the beauty of all that comes to pass. It brings what is into be-ing.

Nonetheless, the primordial lies in darkness and is never disclosed as it is, for that element, in being perceived, changes its character—its nature changes when it enters into language.[1] The transformation by which a thematized being takes form and gains

1. To show this in my films I have often contrasted the dynamics of cinematic rhythms with the stasis of texts, by incorporating texts in my film.

membership in the world (that, is to say, since perception is a form of reading, when it becomes part of the "world-structured-in-language") results in the occultation of the earthly elements that go into its making. That process therefore has the nature of what I call an "apophantic process." The Pseudo-Dionysius wrote about this darkness, and its occultation by light in such an apophantic process:

> Darkness disappears in the light, the more so as there is more light. Knowledge makes unknowing disappear, the more so as there is more knowledge. However . . . the unknowing regarding God escapes anyone possessing physical light and knowledge of beings. His transcendent darkness remains hidden from all light and concealed from all knowledge. Someone beholding God and understanding what he saw has not actually seen God himself but rather something of his which has being and which is knowable. For he himself solidly transcends mind and being. He is completely unknown and non-existent. He exists beyond being and he is known beyond the mind. And this quite positively complete unknown is knowledge of him who is above everything that is known.[2]

Following Merleau-Ponty, I give to this earthly darkness, insofar as it is a faculty of disclosure, a faculty of the unveiling (*aletheia*) that grants us the perception of beings, the name "flesh."[3] The term "flesh" emphasizes the mutuality of the disclosure of self and other, the fact that the other is needed for the self to be. For flesh is at once a medium of experience and the ground that makes possible one's "being with" the world.

Flesh is the body antecedent to thematization—antecedent to being represented in thought. Flesh cannot be grasped through concepts. It is the evidence that cohesion in be-ing occurs without the mediation of any concept, that cohesion can defy the logic of form, and that, finally, cohesion is not the antithesis of dispersion. Flesh is what makes the body open to (or what, in a peculiar twist, is the same thing, prey to) influence

2. Pseudo-Dionysius the Areopagite, from the letters of the Pseudo-Dionysius, "Letter One: to the monk Gaius."

3. We call this process of unveiling truth, because through it the inscriptions of the λογοσ, which, as inscriptions belong to that category of entities of which can be qualified by truth or falsity, and yet through it beings come-to-be. "*Facta vera sunt*," Vico wrote—indeed that the objects Being makes are inscriptions is why we call Being the λογοσ.

through sensibility—for how could body grant sensation and consciousness except through the fact that body is not simply material, but also the possibility-of-knowing/sensing/feeling.

Flesh is what is brought into being through an *energeia* of a mutuality through which (as Merleau-Ponty was fond of pointing out) every grasping is also a "being-grasped," every touch a "being-touched." But flesh is also what disrupts the surface of being that the λογοσ creates. It can do this because flesh is non-coincident with itself; that is, it is not the same in pre-reflective consciousness as it is in self-reflective consciousness. It was Merleau-Ponty who was fond of pointing out this fact, to which he drew attention through his well-known example citing the presentiment that one has, by putting the fingers of one's right hand on one's left, of the possibility "of being able to touch [oneself] touching." However, he pointed out that this "reflection of the body upon itself always miscarries at the last moment: the moment I feel my left hand with my right hand, I correspondingly cease touching my right hand with my left hand" (9). What he describes as miscarriage is the transformation of a thought from pre-reflexive to a self-reflexive form—an apophantic process that eclipses that mutuality of thought and its object characteristic of pre-reflective thinking (the flesh's thinking) as thinking takes a thought as a thematized object. This transformation is a violent limitation for with it thought becomes self-enclosed.

Reality is a language activated in the dialogue between the earth and our flesh (which is anyway part of the earth) that I call "perception." The statements of this dialogue are enigmatic, because they interlace with each other over and over again, weaving a bewildering network of relations; in fact, they possess greater depth and variety of meaning than those which appear in a penetrating philosophic discourse on a profound topic, precisely because flesh, which is the basis of the communicative practice, is so mutable. It is its resistance to flesh's character, indeed to all that lies in darkness, that has made dominant cinema ("the movies"), like every other reactionary social form, hostile to ambiguity, lability, transformation, dispersal, contamination—those very attributes of flesh that the cinema was destined was embody.

For image and flesh are joined together in a unfathomable unity, each of which is just as strange as the other—the strange intimacy of the image is suited to unconceptualizable closeness of flesh. Accordingly, the true image is the very antithesis of narrative. Narrative valorizes the reduction of possibility into actuality, for that reduction provides narrative's founding form—the creation of a *diegesis*. Attention discloses the event of coming-to-be, the event whereby the Unlimited becomes limited, the Indeterminate becomes determinate. Attunement knows this reduction to be a sacrifice, an act wherein charity and violence mingle: attention requires that the sovereign self be deposed. Narrative, to the contrary, establishes the conditions under which the self legislates to perception by quashing all awareness of beings' coming-to-be. It demands—and in doing so places conditions on—the revelation of the future, in imposing expectations of what is to be.

Cinematography also reveals that the beautiful shines within the time-bound. To say that the beautiful shines within the time-bound is to say also that the beautiful can become dynamic—another lesson the cinema was created to convey. But if in the aesthetic of the cinema, the beautiful is dynamic, and if whatever is dynamic requires time, and time implies death, then in this aesthetic, beauty is allied with death—as closely allied to death as it is to life, as closely associated with violence as it is with charity. Thus, in this new aesthetic, beauty condemns what is beautiful to perish.

What is—that which is—shines with effulgence of the beautiful. But whatever else it is, the beautiful is still the result of a reduction in as much it is not as rich as What-might-be. The reduction involved in all thinking, all perceiving (and all artistic representations) speaks of the deficiency of what is in comparison with what might be. It is the pressure of what is greater than beings (that is to say, the Good), to manifest itself that accounts for this impulse to dismantle form and to liquefy all that is fixed (just as it is the pressure of what is beyond be-ing to manifest itself that impels beings to change). The violence of the process reveals the judgement of what might be on what is and the Good's striving for realization. The gap between what is and what might be is the real source of our intimations of deprival; it is that gap which draws our attention towards the Good. That is why genuine thinking cannot be simply a loving acceptance of the gift of the appearances (though true thinking must never dismiss the given, as scientific thinking does, and in fact must cherish the given). So perception must open itself even to the Violent Power that is beyond all that is, that would destroy whatever is. True thinking must be more than patient, loving attention toward all that is—more than a quiet listening that is chary of the tendency to impose upon things. Though we rightfully feel awe that anything whatsoever is, that there is that which is beyond beings is a cause for even greater wonder.

But of the arts, it is the cinema that is most disposed towards the elemental. If the cut is the formal sign of cinema's disposition towards fragmentation, the inner cause of that disposition is its affection for the world, an affection so profligate and so unjudging that it results in self-dispersal. The assimilation of reality that is the mission of film disposes it to contamination. Film is massively promiscuous, and as impure as all whose nature is promiscuity. Its readily-given affections carry it beyond itself, towards the other. Its proclivities, accordingly, result in dispersal. Its nature calls for forms that are fragmentary and incomplete; its promiscuity demands that works composed in the medium be dispersive opera, deploying multiple structures, plurisemic, incomplete, imperfect, unresolved, without closure. Their forms must be contaminated, impure, and full of strife. Each element in every moment must be foreign to every other. A film must allow text to contend with image, image to contend with sound, and sound to contend with text, and must do so without striving to reconcile the contention in something we conceive as good form. Films must incorporate the maximum of diversity for the cinematic medium is an outrageous violation of the ideal of purity. Furthermore, the cinema must favour repetition over narrative progress, for repetition shows contamination at work, by showing that the purity of self-identity is an impossible ideal (nothing is ever the same on two appearances). Repetition in art, because it demonstrates that any linguistic element is wrenched from self-identity with every reappearance, manifests violence at work.

The cinema itself is multiple—comprising image, movement, and sound (which, often, is itself multiple, comprising speech, music, and natural sounds). Accordingly, a film consists of constellations of elements that are alien to one another, and these constellations are arranged serially into higher-level constellations. Eisenstein taught, I think correctly, that each successive element in this serial constellation must be "estranged" from what preceded it, in order to incite strife. He also considered, correctly, that this strife was the mark of the cinema's essential constitution. For the cinema is multiple, and this multiplicity itself lays waste to any efforts at formal consolidation premised on purist ideals. The cinema's multiplicity opens it onto that which cannot be represented, which is similarly plural, similarly labile, similarly without identity. This multiplicity, accordingly, should be intensified, carried to the extreme. Its sensory elements, whether visual, aural, intensive, affective, rhythmic, tonal or even verbal (oral and written) must be made to contend, for that contention evokes the unrepresentable. The cinema has the ability to show process; it does so best by emphasizing speed which liquefies, by stressing dynamism's ability to dissolve boundaries and lay form to ruin, by animating light's searing destructive power (light's power to destroy what hides) through allowing changes in light to overwhelm spatial form, and by allowing cutting, which is the domain of mutability, instability, and ambiguity, to achieve the maximum of fragmentation. Only the cinema allows us thus to effect a *dérèglement de tous les sens*.

Perception that attunes itself to the process by which what the Infinite Beyond Be-ing becomes determinate is privy to the mystery of the incarnation—and to the mystery that, like The Incarnation, that incarnation, demands sacrifice. Sacrifice, it seems, is the condition of charity's being manifested. For there is still that which is left over, that excess of unrealized possibility, that which passes into nothing when a thought is configured, that which language consigns to silence. That excess subsequently rises against language, against thought, and against representation, to destroy them. Its violence is the violence that is characteristic of the revenge of the repressed. Perception that rises against preconceptions create a disposition towards a strange element foreign to perception, towards the uncanny that allows one to respond, however vaguely and indefinitely, to the return of the repressed. This vague sense of something beyond knowing vouchsafes an awareness that what is does not exactly coincide with what might be. Flow, speed, liquidity, dynamism, perpetual dynamism, transformation reveal the multiple possibility inherent in that which precedes beings, and so provoke a sense of the gap between what is and What-might-be.

As in many folk tales (for example, the Lorelei legend to which Heine gave poetic form), this call of the beautiful is also, though, a lure, that results in destruction. Its call is savage: "*Den Schiffer im kleine Schiffe / Ergreift es mit wildem Weh*" ("The boatman in his small boat / It seizes with unrestrained woe"). The violence of a perception is like the violence of the poetic principle: the unrepresentability of the poetic principle endangers thought only insofar as it exceeds any *a priori* precept. For through the poetic principle that which belongs to time becomes timeless, for the poetic belongs to the realm of ecstatic temporality; and in so doing, it comes to exemplify the nature of language. (That is also the very reason why the offspring of the Creator—who through some strange temporal twist is also identical with the Creator—is called the λογοσ.) So it is with cinematography: making the time-bound timeless, that act which cinematography accomplishes, is a violent act, for it puts that which is humble in a relationship of which it is not worthy; that exactly is what calls a regulatory principle into existence (for, as I have remarked, this inequality is the basis of law).

We apprehend the dynamics through which things come-to-be through the faculty for rhythm. An epistemology that accords thinking-through-rhythm primacy is far more sound than the currently voguish epistemologies based on narrative—in fact better than *any* other—because rhythm better reflects the discourse of Be-ing. We become aware of Be-ing in a certain throb, a certain stress, torsion, and flex we feel in our body, a sense of something whose very being is indefinite, but which we know with a certainty that quells all questions, something that participates in a pulse of something that is far larger than ourselves.

About the physicist David Bohm, David Peat wrote "That ability to touch preverbal processes at the muscular, sensory level remained with him all his life. It was not so much that Bohm visualized a physical system as that he was able to sense its dynamics within his body: 'I had the feeling that internally I could participate in some movement that was the analogy of the thing you are talking about'" (68). This form of corporeal thinking is close to what I mean by thinking-in-rhythm (as everything that has to do with the body is periodic). And at what does Bohm's theoretical physics arrive? That reality is process, and that mind and matter are inextricable—that same view we have been propounding. Our richest and deepest apprehension of flux, flow, dynamism comes through our capacity to respond to rhythm. For rhythm always discloses itself at once both as something beyond us, to which we give ourselves, and as something deep in ourselves. Thinking-through-rhythm thus reveals the mutuality of self and Other. Thinking-through-rhythm can engages us in prayer by which we tune ourselves to an alien, foreign pulse, to the pulse of an Other, the pulse of something wholly beyond us, and we woo It, while in response, It draws us ever more closely into its embrace. In responding to rhythm, something deep in us responds to some profound attribute of the dynamics of earth. Giving a place of privilege to thinking-though-rhythm changes thought's relation to its object. Thinking-through-rhythm allows multiple patterns to contend, without resolution. Thinking-through-rhythm belongs to the modality of the flesh's time. Rhythm makes time, and time is the fundament of our relation to alterity, to what lies beyond us. Time, and therefore rhythm, reveals to us that future is always without apprehensible content. It aims towards an *ideatum* that eludes being thought or perceived, for it is infinitely greater than the thought that thinks it. Thinking-through-rhythm reveals the future's transcendence, i.e., it discloses that beings and possibility cannot be thought together, and that beings require non-be-ing. The pulse of rhythm too has a violence at its core. For its throb can lay order and law to waste,

by accommodating the unexpected at the very heart of its being and, what is more important, by allowing the unexpected to arise continuously, from moment to moment. Rhythm, like all artistic form, invites regulation, only to undo the word of the law and the law of the word. The disordering of thinking that results from being-in-relation to the unapprehensible is an effective antidote to the self's desire to establish its sovereignty. The disproportion between the act of thinking itself and what the act aims at that summons the regulatory agencies of objective perception, and only the utmost of resoluteness, issuing in attunement, can forestall the violence of the imposition of law.

Thinking-through-rhythm uncovers what the be-ing of actual beings excludes; it discloses what is rejected by the order that thought imposes on experience. It acknowledges what is excluded from objective perception, cherishes the unwanted and the destitute, for it appreciates that the insignificant and absurd is that which cannot be reconciled with the conception of the world of objects as a standing reserve available to technique. Thinking-through-rhythm acknowledges the future is for the lowly, for time will raise them. Thinking-through-rhythm discloses that abjection and destitution lie closer to be-ing than do the vaunted and the celebrated. That proximity accounts for the redemptive power of the outcast and the rejected; and that proximity also explains why a humble cinema, a *cinema povera* (better names for the "experimental cinema") is needed.

Narrative thinking arises from the desire for totalization, from the desire to reduce reality to an ultimate unity through panoramic overviews and dialectical syntheses. Thinking-through-rhythm is dispersive: only it, therefore, can intimate the ungraspable and incomprehensive character of what is alien to rational thinking. Only thinking-through-rhythm can intimate the power of Other that breaks through the homogeneity of the familiar world and, with its unlimited power, shatters its totality. Only thinking-through-rhythm can intimate the violent potential of this intruder, this Other that encroaches on my familiar world, but can neither be experienced nor reduced to an object of knowledge.

Thinking-through-rhythm makes the time of the flesh palpable. Thinking-through-rhythm incorporates in the body what *dianoia*, rational thought of sort that practised in mathematical and technical subjects, can never apprehend, *viz.*, that which Plato, in the *Timaeus*, refers to as *khōra*, an element that defies the logic of *logos*, for it is neither intelligible nor sensible. *Khōra* (like earth) is an invisible element, that cannot be made present in a sensible form (i.e., cannot be made present-to-consciousness), yet it participates in the constitution of every worldly being—and does so even as it disrupts the process of its formation. "Earth," like *khōra*, is another word for what I ordinarily call "be-ing." Be-ing, I have said, is what is eclipsed by beings, for in order for a being to come forth, it is necessary for be-ing to withdraw into that darkness which is its element, in order to leave a lighted clearing in which beings can come to be—and of *khōra* Heidegger writes, "Might *khōra* not mean: that which abstracts itself from every particular, that which withdraws, and in such a way precisely as admits and "makes place" for something else?" (50–1). In light, the objective world is severed from observer, but beyond the range of illumination, *khōric* darkness reconciles what light has sundered. *Khōric* darkness is where the endless reproduction by acroamatic logic of narrative comes to rest. "In every word, there is a blaze of light"—against this we plead, again: "Let there be darkness."

Every work of art involves a contention between two impulses: toward form and against form. Every work of art exists simultaneously as, on the one hand, a disciplined structure, the order of which evolves out of a inner sense of the need for—or, better, a tropism toward—harmony and as, on the other hand, a process that exceeds all boundaries, refuses all containment, that dismembers syntax, destroys form, and lays representation to ruin. The necessary union between form (i.e., configuration, or what is the same, the spiritual dimension of the work) and matter in a work of art manifests the necessary unity between the timeless and the time-bound, a unity that can only be maintained by the violence of law. But this violence condemns the be-ing of an artwork to restlessness, to the instability of the uncanny, for as we have seen, the poetic principle which orders the work of art (both in the sense of giving rise to it and in the sense of shaping it), because it appears uniquely in every one of its appearances, is supremely unstable. The unity of form and content, Hegel opined, exemplifies the mystery of the incarnation, through which spirit is turned inside out, in order to enter the material realm and to take on a material dynamism. But incarnation, we know, requires a sacrifice.

We cannot assess a work of art by its *gestalt* form because it is restless and unstable, because it is inhabited by an element that does violence to representation and perception, that is to say, by the uncanny. The idea that artwork is an achievement of form was the old conception of art, and it has wasted itself in its constant effort to repress the dynamic element left over from perception, to hold at bay that excess of unrealized possibility left behind as be-ing emerges as a being (as an object), to obviate that which language consigns to silence, to ward off the return of that which passes into nothingness as a thought is configured, to expel from sensation that excess which rises against language, against thought, and against representation, to destroy them. Faced by the unremitting violence that is characteristic of the repressed, it has exhausted itself in the constant effort at pacifying that is required of it—it has become spent, it has had its day. Now we assume that the power of the work of art is measured by its capacity to mime the dynamics of the power of be-ing. Form serves to focus thought in order to create an opening towards the power of be-ing—it does this by engendering a stillness that fosters the grace one requires to respond to the violence the power of be-ing unleashes. By focussing attention, it enables the elemental to lay established patterns of thought in ruin. Thus, form creates an opening for the violence of the elemental—and it does so in order to enable that violence to liberate us from our customary ways of perceiving.

Every image, because it speaks of what is too luminous to be apprehended has an affinity with nakedness. But the relation of imagery's essential character with the nude body is more profound than this. Nudity makes us aware of the wisdom of modesty, which has its ground in the fact that our being is refractory to the light of analytic reason and available only to the super-rational understanding of the care human being solicits (a solicitation nudity renders more compelling). Nudity teaches us that our ordinary metaphorical system of historically-based rumination that privileges light over darkness is wrong: the strange intimacy of darkness that relates us to something we cannot apprehend makes darkness higher than light. Nudity flees the light, as be-ing slips away from the light of reason. Like nudity, be-ing seeks darkness as the condition for revealing itself. What is revealed by the modesty that nudity desires is that the Other is constituted in mystery; and just as every image of a nude person discloses the essential nature of imagery by its concern with fecundity, so every image of a nude discloses the nature of imagery. For the subject of every image withdraws into the modesty of non-disclosure even while it assigns to a double (that which shines forth in the image) the role of disclosure. The image of the nude, like every image, compresses the absence of what it depicts into a material force apprehensible by a sensibility.

An image of a nude body informs us, too, that our being is not external, and so is not apprehensible by the senses either. The image of a nude person offers paradigmatic proof of the non-reciprocal character of relation that obtains not just between a representation and the object represented but even between visibility and being: just as objects give us knowledge of representations, but representations do not afford knowledge of objects, so too, while be-ing produces visibility, visibility affords no understanding of be-ing. Just as the object withdraws from representation, so too be-ing withdraws from visibility. It is that lack of reciprocity that makes for that peculiarity that the frankness and explicitness of that special form of visibility we call nudity conceals be-ing, that the greatest of intimacy conceals a most profound alterity.

A nude implores us to caress; but a caress acknowledges that we cannot close the divide across which the Other resides. In caressing, or in imagining caressing, we acknowledge that erotic relations are not really reciprocal relations as our sense of justice would have us believe. Caresses tell us that *eros* is bound into an unintelligible, unfathomable condition (and so a condition that cannot be reduced to signification), for they tell us that our most profound, most creative ("self-making") relationships are to a being that not only is totally separate, but belongs to a different realm altogether. They tell us, then, that we are most deeply linked to what withdraws from us.

So profound is the gulf that separates us from the beings with which we form our most profound and most intimate relationships that our be-ing and that of the be-ing which, in soliciting us, creates us, belong to different orders of time. The status of the image makes this known to us as well, for, just as the image elicits expectation, so awareness of the Other (an awareness that, like all sensory experience belongs wholly to the immediate present) solicits a longing to give care to that which belongs wholly to the future. Thus, here we encounter again that twisted temporality, in which what comes later creates what comes before. But only a twisted temporality would be appropriate to the meaning of flesh, which is the revelation that the visible turns upon itself and that a carnal unity of the sentient with the sensed is antecedent to representation. The longing expressed in the futurity of the image is evoked not simply by the Other's voluptuousness (though it may be); rather the longing arises from all that separates me from the Other. The Other, speaking to me, in the present but from the future, constitutes the ground of time as process. What delights us in the erotic relation, and in the caress, is the tension (and so the anticipation) involved in sensing a relation that is sufficiently deep to constitute our identity, and yet that is not reducible to an identity (as the other in the relation remains ineluctably Other).

The cinema has an affinity for the faces and bodies—for the flesh of the other. We feel the other call out to us, to invite us to know her as an alike that is not alike. She calls out, invoking our desire, our sympathy, our hopes for an encounter. By the presence of an other, the film image calls out for a dialogue, and our inability to enter into a true dialogue with the other in the image—our inability either to integrate her into our world as real associate or to become a part of her world—makes us sense the gulf that separates what is closest to us.

The image of flesh, to which cinema is attuned, opens us onto the primordial realm which grants us being. The primordial grants us the recognition that the self and world unfold mutually. What accounts for this "togetherness" of self and world, of language and perception? It is, surely, that beings are always already articulate—that is they are dis-jointed. Darkness is one, but beings are many; and because they are many, they are configured similarly to the way language is—that is, non-sensible similarities exist among them. Flesh is the medium through which these non-sensible similarities are revealed; flesh is the medium that opens us towards the world, for it is the medium through which that which addresses itself to us emerges. Through the earthliness of flesh, beings emerge as worldly (that is, as belonging to the "world-structured-by-language"), for incarnation is a condition for having impressions through one's interaction with the world.[4] Flesh reveals the prediscursive configurations that pronounce themselves silently in each mute thing, and in which our bodies participate; these configurations are active—they are prediscursive activities that lay good form to ruins, that disperse all consolidated *Gestalten*, that dismember all patterns. But these revelations are vouchsafed to us by virtue of flesh only through adopting this silent language's manner of signifying. It is through conflict, discord, plurisemicity, irresolution, the refusal of closure that makes flesh felt (narrative, a form that achieved its present condition in the Enlightenment, invites none of these attributes). The cinema is disposed to flesh, and for this reason, the cinema should eschew narrative, and adopt rigorously plural—it should intensify the strife between the elements in the constellations that constitute it, by incorporating elements that are alien to one another. It should empha-size dynamism's ability to dissolve whatever forms might pacify the strife between these elements.

"Flesh" is the name for the condition of our "be-ing between." Awareness of flesh undoes the fiction that the reactionary forms of the dominant cinema are based on, the fiction of "outside spectator" (to use that term from Merleau-Ponty); repetition helps make the flesh evident, for repetition, like the flesh, is dynamized by passion—and it is passion that, ultimately, renders the sign mutable, unstable, labile, unsystematic (thereby rendering fatuous every hope for a project for a scientific semiology). Flesh

4. I say "have" because neither "create" nor "receive" is quite correct, for this "having impressions" involves both a creative and a receptive moment.

subjects the sign to passion; and passion makes every perception an interpretation. Flesh imprints itself on all that we perceive—and on our body (the worldly representation of the earthly element) and the body of the object alike, indeed on our body and the body of the object mutually. Flesh is an archive of passion-forms that, without actually being them (for they are earthly elements), informs our decoding of things. Flesh makes every perception a communicative act. "Flesh" names the physical pregnancy that issues in perception.

Darkness is required to divulge the interweaving of language and matter in perception. Why does it requires darkness to reveal this interpenetration? Because what blends language and matter together in perception is itself never perceived. The form of thinking which brings a work of art into being, however, lies much closer to the dark element than everyday thinking—scientific thinking or instrumental thinking—does. Accordingly, art has much to teach us about this essential togetherness of spirit and matter, form and content, language and perception, for which flesh is the primordial ground. Art is the consummation of language for it reveals there is, outside of language, no object of speech which language communicates. Similarly, there is no antecedent intention by which expression (or, better, configuration) can be limited, no external gauge by which it can be measured—we communicate *in* language, not *through* language. Language does not describe a pre-existing reality; rather, language transforms what stands before it, and through this transformation, summons beings to be-ing, and gives them membership in the world (i.e., the "world-structured-by-language"). Beings come into being through λογοσ, the home that harbours them. But this charity, as we have pointed out, is also a sacrifice, for it reduces be-ing to beings, potentiality to actuality, indefiniteness to definiteness.

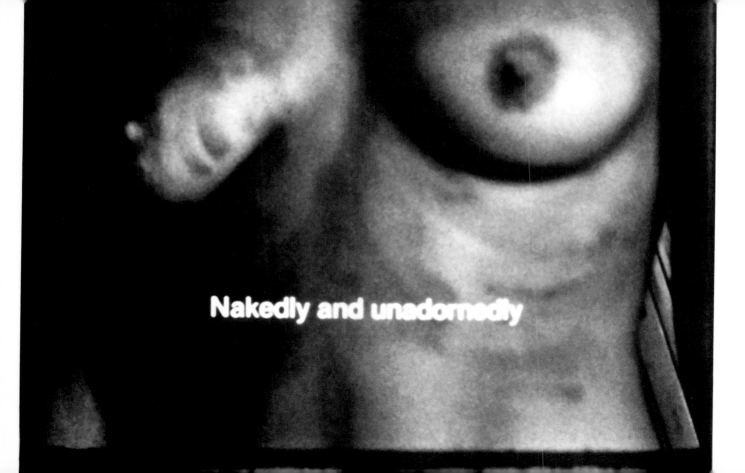

Flesh is an infinite surface, on which an infinitude of terms can be inscribed—but though it is infinite, it is bounded, for we can discover that there is that which language cannot say, or what is the same, that we cannot experience. In fact, there are an infinite number of these infinite surfaces. We call them collectively by the name "flesh," which, then, must be both one and infinite in number. Flesh entwines itself with be-ing; for it is through flesh, which is the ground of the unity of the physical and the psychical, that consciousness arises out of matter, out of "earth," really, and that thereby the world is erected. We cannot posit a single sensible thing without recognizing the role that flesh has in its disclosure, for flesh is the surface on which every inscription is inscribed. Flesh is prior to beings; yet, without beings, flesh cannot disclose its essence—Can you imagine a consciousness that has utterly withdrawn itself, a consciousness out of relation to anything and everything? The impossibility of imagining that is another reason why I describe flesh as an *entre deux*, and why I have concluded that it actualizes itself only in conjunction with the world.

The thinking that makes art belongs to the flesh. That is what spares art from being self-expression—self-expression that would eclipse the Infinite. The poetic principle is prior to all reflection, including self-reflection. The operation of the poetic is prior to thought, prior to reflection, prior even to the self. When the evangelist says, "Not I, but Thee in me, knows...," he is acknowledging being possessed by this prior-to-self anonymity, by a grandeur that shatters the vessels of self. The flesh is one; all flesh is the same flesh—it is made one through the reciprocity of sense, that is, through an utterly anonymous and therefore common sensibility inhabiting all humanity. So far as artworks reach towards the flesh, they reach towards something that is common to all, something that is prior to the self. Self-expression concerns what separates one individual from another; cleaving to flesh reaches towards a numinousness that binds all together in an anonymous universality.

The elements of the primordial are connected to each other in a genuine time that I have called time of the flesh. So I have emphasized rhythm and rhyme and flow over good spatial *Gestalten*. Indeed, I believe that the cinema is first and foremost an art of time, and not an art of space; and that the emphasis on the spatial design of the image, more than on its dynamic flow, is the most deleterious feature of most current cinema pedagogy. The awareness of that time is elemental, is productive; that beings come forth in time only, and would not be without time, is a secret that cinema was invented to disclose. This elemental factor with which every work of art engages is also what Dennis Lee refers to as "cadence." He writes

> Most of my time as a poet is spent listening into a luminous tumble, a sort of taut cascade. I call it "cadence." If I withdraw from immediate contact with things around me, I can sense it churning, flickering, thrumming, locating things in more shapely relation to one another. It feels continuous, though I may spend days on end without noticing it.
>
> What I hear is initially without words. But when a poem starts to come, the words have to accord with that energy or I can't make a poem at all. (I speak of "hearing" cadence, but the sensation isn't auditory. It's more like sensing a constantly changing tremor with your body: a play of movement and stress, torsion and flex—as with the kinaesthetic perception of the muscles.) More and more I sense this energy as presence both outside and inside myself, teeming towards words. (3–4)

The image of nude is a cause for exultation, because, in revealing a human being, it also reveals that human be-ing, as an opening towards disclosure, completes the work of creation by enabling what is mute, or what became mute through the Fall (in which

God's word curses the ground), to speak. For, as Walter Benjamin stated, muteness is "the deep sadness of nature." "It is a metaphysical truth," Benjamin wrote, "that all nature would begin to lament if it were not endowed with language.... Speechlessness: that is the great sorrow of nature (and for the sake of her redemption the life and language of *man*—not only, as is supposed, of the poet—are in nature).... Lament, however, is the most undifferentiated, impotent expression of language; it contains scarcely more than the sensuous breath; and even where there is only a rustling of plants, in it there is always a lament. Because she is mute, she mourns" (1979, 329).

Naming beings summons them into being by making them definite and distinct—that, I believe is why Benjamin proposed that "*in naming, the mental being of man communicates itself to God.*" For in doing this, human be-ing extends what the λογοσ inscribed at the time of the creation (Benjamin 1979, 318). So Benjamin concludes from considering the difference between human language and the language of things:

> The quintessence of this intensive totality of language as the mental being of man is naming. Man is the namer, by this we recognize that through him pure language speaks. All nature, insofar as it communicates itself, communicates itself in language, and so finally in man. Hence he is the lord of nature and can give names to things. Only through the linguistic being of things can he gain knowledge of them from within himself—in name. God's creation is completed when things receive their names from man, from whom in name language alone speaks. (1979, 318–9)

Aesthetic objects help us to understand a peculiarity in this discourse of things. Through aesthetic experience we have come to understand that art objects often concern the medium in which they are realized and the process of their coming-to-be. But the discourse of things has similar intentions: the λογοσ creates the world, and its icons, the objects of the world, speak of the λογοσ. Thus, language of things speaks of the λογοσ; or, to put it otherwise, the language of objects speaks of the word, of language itself; that language speaks of language itself is another ontological revelation the aesthetic experience allows us to understand.

The cinema's mission, I contend, is to reveal the discourse of things. Cinematography, the duplication of the order of creation, helps human be-ing complete this work for the sake of which human be-ing is in nature. Nature finds consolation for lamentation in cinematography, and by reason of this consolation, it exults. Benjamin might have understood that order. He realized that inversion of the proposition, "because she is mute, nature mourns," is even truer: "the sadness of nature makes her mute." Cinematography discloses the beauty of the λογοσ' inscription, and makes her glorify Him. To glorify the Creator is the reason of all exultation.

Nature, the order of things, speaks only mutely. Cinematography, the duplication of the order of things, translates this mute speech into an audible language. The secret language of things is vouchsafed only to those who can abide in that form of contemplation that allows the be-ing (the first actuality) of beings to enter into human be-ing, who can endure the violence of that form of charity which Keats called "negative capability." Hearing the mute language of things demands an openness, to allow the gifts of be-ing to come to presence—the receiving of which is the mission of photography. That practice perhaps is not creative, but is something higher, for it is a practice which enables the fugitive discourse of things to be preserved. This miracle should not be shunned; rather but to be taken up as the wonder it is.

But even as the image, the "seen" form, enters into human be-ing in this wondering abiding with things, and even as the "unseen" but visible *gestalt* form enters into human be-ing at the same time, so too does an unseen and invisible principle. That unseen, invisible principle is an activity, an *energeia*, indeed a violence that actualizes all that becomes present. It operates according to an apophantic logic, as it discloses itself only by withdrawing. It operates behind the constraints of repression, and is known only through the phantasmic constructions which it produces, and which, more often than they straightforwardly reveal, reveal it only by concealing it.

Against the present climate of despair, I continue to believe that language is grounded in truth. I cannot accept that nothing fastens words and things, that language is free play. To quote Benjamin again:

> Hölderlin's translations from Sophocles were his last work; in them meaning plunges from abyss to abyss until it threatens to become lost in the bottomless depths of language. There is, however, a stop. It is vouchsafed to Holy Writ alone, in which meaning has ceased to be the watershed for the flow of language and the flow of revelation [that is language and revelation flow in the same direction in the Holy Writ]. Where a text is identical with truth or dogma, where it is supposed to be "the true language" in all its literalness and without the mediation of meaning, this text is unconditionally translatable.... Just as, in the original, language and revelation are one without any tension, so the translation must be one with the original in the form of the interlinear version, in which literalness and freedom are unity. For to some degree all great texts contain their potential translation between the lines; this is true to the highest degree of sacred writings. (1969, 81–2)

But the λογοσ also wrote all things, into the book of Creation. The discourse of things also constitute a Holy Writ. The cinema was born to make evident that visible objects constitute the signs of a language, and to do so simply by repeating them. Or, as

Benjamin might have had it, translating them. Because it is without the mediation of meaning, this text is unconditionally translatable. "Cinematography" is the name for the immediate process of translating the discourse of things, of filling in the translation between the lines in the sacred text which the λογοσ composed—an activity that results in a sort of interleaving of the translated images of things with things themselves. In the course of making that translation, I too am translated, as Bottom realized.

> Let us think of love, whether we are speaking of divine or angelic or intellectual or psychic or natural love, as a certain unitive and continuative power which moves the higher things to provide for the lower, and again those of equal form to exercise a close influence upon one another, and those things which are placed lower to turn to those that are better and are placed above them. —The Pseudo-Dionysus, "Amatory Hymns"

Walter Benjamin (1969)
The Task of the Translator
Illuminations
New York: Schocken Books

——(1979)
On Language as Such and the Language of Man
Reflections: Essays, Aphorisms, Autobiographical Writings
Peter Demetz, ed.
Edmund Jephcott, trans.
New York: Harcourt Brace Jovanovich

Martin Heidegger (2000)
Introduction to Metaphysics
Gregory Fried and Richard Polt, trans.
New Haven: Yale University Press

Dennis Lee (1988)
Cadence, Country, Silence
Body Music
Toronto: Anansi

Maurice Merleau-Ponty (1969)
The Visible and the Invisible
Alphonso Lingis, trans.
Chicago: Northwestern University Press

F. David Peat (1996)
Infinite Potential: The Life and Times of David Bohm
New York: Helix Books

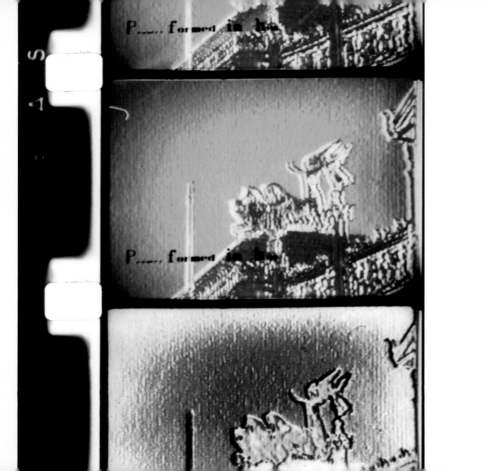

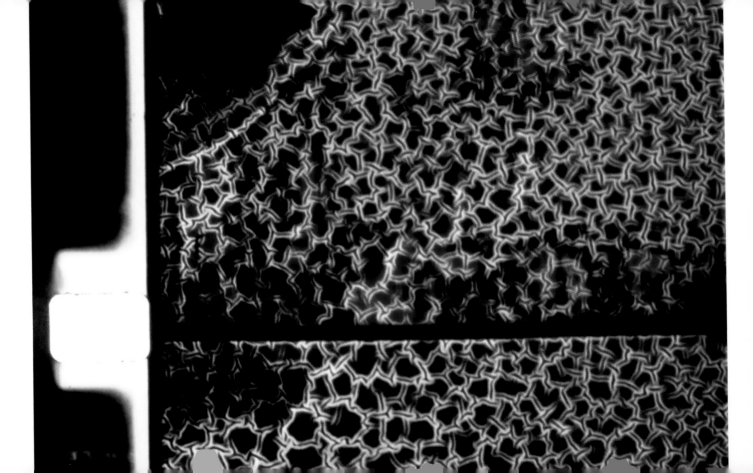

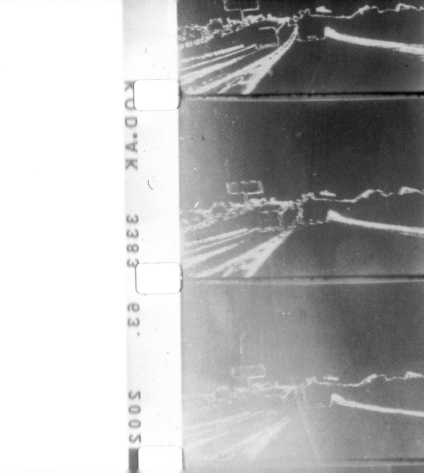

A NAME ON A PAGE
Jack Lewis and John Greyson

Zoology. feeding on

-VOROUS]

have sexual intercourse

al intercourse. **3.** *Slang.* a

specified competence or exp

care or give a fuck. not to car

xpression of strong disgust or

s such as **fuck you! fuck** it! etc.).

Middle Dutch *fokken* to strike]

adv.) *Offensive taboo slang.* 1. (*in*

anner. **2.** (*tr.*) to treat (someone)

lang a despicable or obnoxious

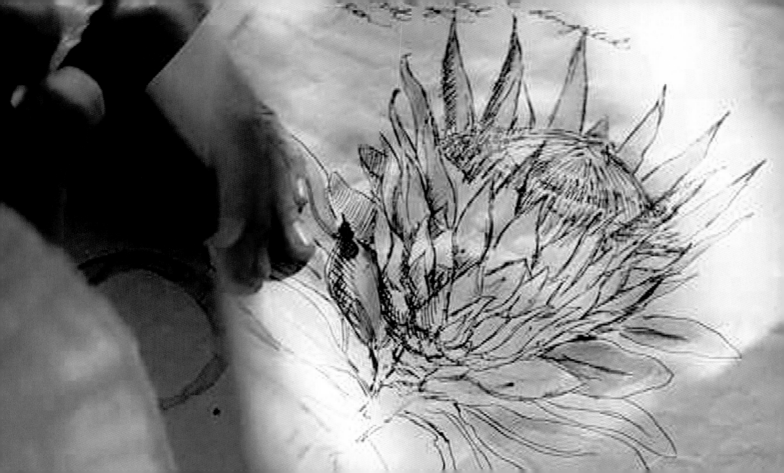

Ten years ago, the handwritten middle Dutch transcript of a 1735 trial was discovered in the Capetown city archives. It detailled the proceedings against two Robben Island convicts, accused of committing the *crimen nefandum* (mute sin) of sodomy. They were Rijkhaart Jacobsz, a Dutch sailor, and Claas Blank, a Khoisan (Hottentot) youth. The following scenes are from the film *Proteus* (Jack Lewis/John Greyson 2003), inspired by the transcript.

———————

Northern Cape, 1725: Scottish plant collector Virgil Niven is sketching a King Sugarbush from nature. Engrossed in his work, he doesn't notice a Khoisan youth, Claas Blank, running madly across the distant hillside.
Weeks later. Blank is caught and incarcerated on Robben Island, the Cape penal colony. Niven secures the use of the prison garden to acclimatize and propagate sugarbush cuttings for the European market, under the direction of his mentor, Swedish botanist Carolus Linneaus. Eager to learn the native names for and uses of the flower, Niven shows Blank his sketchbook.

NIVEN: What is the Bushman name for this King Sugarbush?

[Blank pauses carefully before answering.]

BLANK: #Nuis. [cunt]

NIVEN: *#Nuis?*

BLANK: Yes sir, #Nuis.

NIVEN: *#Nuis*. [to his assistant Lourens] Can you write that down? *#Nuis*. #Nuis.

In 1870, three */Xam* (bushmen) convicts named //Kabbo, /Han=kasso, and Dia!kwain, were serving sentences of hard labour in Capetown. A German linguist, Dr. W. H. Bleek, intent on recording the near-extinct language and oral traditions of the */Xam*, had them transferrred to his service. For the next five years, he and his sister-in-law recorded their stories, songs, and folklore, devising a painstaking phonetic system for transcribing and then translating this ancient African language. The results totalled 12,000 hand-written pages.

In 1991, Capetown poet Stephen Watson adapted some of these transcriptions into a series of poetic *versions*, his own translations of Bleek's translations. With great subtlety, he rendered his sense of the originals in the hope that "at least some echo of the */Xam*'s all-important presence on this earth may still be heard."

ORIGIN OF THE MOON
[//Kabbo via Bleek via Watson]

The moon was a shoe, *veldskoen* of the Mantis,
long ago in a time when the Mantis still wept.
The creature he'd made, the Eland he'd loved,
had been killed by the Meercat, cut into pieces...

So he took off his shoe, threw it into the sky.
He said: "I am the Mantis, I am called Mantis,
but my shoe up there, shining red in the dark,
will now be the moon, will shine as the moon,
lighting a path through the dark of the bushes,
lighting the earth, that I may return home."

——————

NIVEN: Tell me the legends of the King Sugarbush.

[Claas remembers stories told him by his mother, /Kaness, at night by the fire. She is Nama, but her father was */Xam*.]

/KANESS: Sa outab ge ge mi.... [Your grandfather said]

CLAAS: My mother said, that my grandfather said...

/KANESS: !am-//gôuab ats ga ke o [if you look at Mantis]

CLAAS: ...if you look at Mantis

/KANESS: ...ob ge //khâba ni //aixa tsî ni [then the moon would get angry]

CLAAS: ...the moon would get angry

/KANESS: …!khaeb !nâ ni xû da, /anni !nâ. [and hurl us into the smoke]

CLAAS: …get angry and…make the sugarbush blossoms bitter.

NIVEN: Wait…good! The moon would get angry, and make the sugarbush blossoms bitter. Bitter like lemon?

CLAAS: Yes, like lemon.

NIVEN: Just the flowers or also the roots?

CLAAS: Just the flowers.

NIVEN: Very good, proceed.

/KANESS: //Khâb ge /apa !am-…[the moon is red]

CLAAS: The moon is red…

/KANESS: …-//gôuab ti //haros !aroma, [because it is the shoe of Mantis]

CLAAS: …because it is the…King Sugarbush blossom of Mantis…

/KANESS: …//ib ge /Kaggen…[who is /Kaggen]

CLAAS: ...who is /Kaggen

/KANESS: ...tsira !hau !khaeb !na tsi //ib ti //harosa ra #noa !apa /hommi //ga, tsis ge //harosa /apase ra #hai !aromas /Kaggenni go !garob !na !gû kai /urib tsharab !aroma. [Who got mad at the darkness and threw his shoe up into the sky, and it shines red because the shoe is covered with the red dirt from where /Kaggen walked on the veld.]

CLAAS: who threw his...his sugarbush blossom, his red sugarbush blossom, up into the sky.

NIVEN: You go too fast. He threw his red blossom...

Path of the scene:
//Kabbo (/Xam speaker)
via Bleek (transcriber)
via Watson (poet)
via Greyson/Lewis (script)
via Johan Jacobs (Nama translator)
via Katerina Kaffer (actor in Nama)
via Rouxnet Brown (actor in English)
via Roslyn Kalloo (editor)
via Kelly Morris (online subtitles)

———

[Court of the Cape Colony, Jurisdiction of the Dutch East India Company, Cape Governor presiding (assisted by three stenographers).]

GOVERNOR: Rijkhaart Jacobsz, a sailor of Amsterdam, did testify that in the prescence of Sergeant Willer, he did cry out the filthy and abominable words: *Send mij maar op, ik het hom in't gat geneukt.*

RIJKHAART: *Send mij maar op, ik het hom in't gat geneukt.*

ELISE: *het hom in't gat geneukt.* That's like the Afrikaans, ne, to hit to strike?

BETSY [consulting her phrase book]: Here...*fucked.* In Dutch, *geneukt* only meant fucked.

ELISE: Oh Betsy! That makes it sound so modern!

TINNIE: Very contemporary!

BETSY: *het hom in't gat geneukt.* I fucked him up the arse.

TINNIE: What about *buggered*?

BETSY: Right here, see? *Fokken*, to hit, to strike. Perfectly good sixteenth-century middle Dutch.

TINNIE: But it sounds so modern, Betsy.

ELISE: We could use that slang from geneukt: *ny...holnaaier...to sew a hole*. It's a euphemism.

BETSY: Fucked.

TINNIE [consulting her phrasebook]: Oh! Howsabout: *Send me up, I used the native against nature?*

ELISE: Or maybe, *I performed crimen laesae naiestatis tam naturae quam divinae*, an offense against God and man alike?

BETSY: Fucked, darlings.

ELISE: Here: *I carried out the mute sin of crimen nefandum, from behind.*

TINNIE: Perhaps: *I executed sodomy on his person.*

GOVERNOR: Stilte asseblief! [Silence!]

[Niven is sketching Claas in an approximation of traditional Khoisan garb, a prison blanket standing in for a *kaross*, a hankerchief improvising a cache-sex.]

NIVEN: Mr. Blank, I have decided on a family name for my flowers, and the idea came from you. Proteaceae.

CLAAS: That's not from me, sir.

NIVEN: From your Mantis, your /Kaggen. After Proteus, the Greek shepherd of Poseiden's seals. What do you think?

CLAAS: /Kaggen's not a shepherd, sir.

NIVEN: Ah, but like your /Kaggen, he was a shapeshifter who could change at will into any manner of creature: an eagle, or a hideous gorgon, or a panther. Equally, Proteus had the gift of foretelling the future, though he was loathe to do so.

CLAAS: My leg's getting tired, sir.

NIVEN: Ah, yes, of course.

[Niven shows his portfolio of drawings to Claas, each species named after a family member or friend.]

NIVEN: Protea Virgil. Protea Lourens. Protea Katherina. Protea Adriaana. Protea Hendrikia.

[Claas recognizes his name, and points to the final illustration.]
CLAAS: Blankia.

NIVEN: Protea Blankia. It's one of the rarest in the family, one of the most beautiful. It's certainly the hardest to find, as it only blooms at night.

CLAAS: Only at night.

NIVEN: I'm going to miss you, Mr. Blank, more than you might imagine. You've been a marvelous assistant, of course, but more than that, I can't think of the name.

CLAAS: I'm proud to be a name, sir.

———————

In 2000, the ANC government unveiled the new South African Coat of Arms, featuring the *!Xam* motto: *!ke e: /xarra //ke* (unity in diversity). A disgruntled Khoisan chief claimed that the translation was garbled and it actually meant: "piss on your grave." Though the chief himself spoke no *!Xam*, his unfounded accusation became an oft-repeated urban myth. The ANC translation was backed up by voluminous scholarship, but it was still hard to refute the chief's claim since no one actually speaks *!Xam* today: the language has been extinct for a century.

———————

Ten years later, Niven brings Claas a copy of his monograph of the Proteus family. As a condition of publication, he had to deem his mentor Linneaus the author. In turn, Linneaus renamed all of the flowers. Thus *Protea Blankia* has become *Protea Humiflora*.

NIVEN: It's just a name on a page. It's just a page. I mean, a name.

———————

Path of the scene:
Dia!kwain (*/Xam* speaker)
via Bleek (transcriber)
via Watson (poet)
via Greyson/Lewis (script)
via Johan Jacobs (Nama translator)
via Katerina Kaffer (actor)
via Roslyn Kalloo (editor)

OUR BLOOD MAKES SMOKE [excerpt]
We would know it by our bodies, by a blood within, which trembling, shaking, would start to make the smoke, a smoke which then would sit before us, burning in our eyes—it was by blood, by smoking blood, we knew the danger near.

/KANESS: #âi xo tai eb go misa? !ui /anni ge /ao /anna, sa /aub ga /khûo o i ge ra /an, tsi sa mûde ra #hubi, Tsira mîba tsi //khô-//khôsasib /guse hâ !khaisa. Sa autab ge ge mî sada ti sorodi ga tsausa o, tsi !hub-aib ga /â tsi /apa o i ge /ana sada /aoba xu nî sôu da. [Remember what he'd say? White smoke is blood smoke, when you feel your blood tremble, that's when it makes smoke, burning your eyes, telling you that danger is near. Your grandfather said, when our bodies are exhausted, when the earth is wet and red, then the smoke from our blood will come and hide us.]

NIVEN: . . . *his red blossom into the sky*. There. Very good, proceed.

CLAAS: No. That's it. There's no more.

––––––––––

CAROLUS LINNAE

PROTEACEAE
AFRICANUS

VIRGILIO NIVENO

BLUE: ARCHIVE OF DEVASTATION
Deborah Esch

Every view ends in illness, the whole world staggering into the grave just a little too soon. It should have begun in ten years' time, but started ten years ago and now it's all but over. I wonder if any of this will be remembered; probably not....

—Derek Jarman, *Smiling in Slow Motion*

In January 1993, Derek Jarman recorded in his journal his thoughts on the difficulty of translating HIV/AIDS, whether in autobiographical or more broadly historiographical terms, onto film:

> No ninety minutes of cinema could deal with the eight years HIV takes to get its host. Hollywood can only sentimentalize it, it would all take place in some well-heeled West-coast beach hut—the reality would drive the audience out of the cinema. We don't lack images—just good ones.... Even documentaries cannot tell you of the constant, all-consuming nagging, of the aches and pains. How many times I've stopped to touch my inflamed face even while writing this page. There's nothing grand about it, no opera here, just the daily grind in a minor key. (Jarman 2000, 290)[1]

For Jarman, the problem of rendering the "awful devastation of AIDS" (2000, 139), which he had been endeavouring to do in his writing and painting since his diagnosis as seropositive in December 1986, was not simply a function of the resistance of a practically invisible virus to visualization, nor of the pitfalls of pathos and sentimentality that would likely attend any quasi-realistic representation of its effects: both predictable dilemmas for an artist working in any medium. Rather, it was a matter of a fundamental incommensurability between the temporality of the virus (here, "the eight years HIV takes to get its host") and that of the medium in question, in this case feature film ("ninety minutes of cinema"). A version of that incommensurability, the mutual untimeliness invoked in the journal as the obstacle to be overcome, is arguably the predominant

1. Jarman's biographer, Tony Peake, cites an unedited version of the same journal entry in which the filmmaker observes (following "the reality would drive the audience out of the cinema") that "no one viewpoint could mirror the 10,000 lives lost in San Francisco to date," and further (following "just the daily grind in a minor key") that "we would wish our lives to be recorded in an oratorio by a Beethoven or Mozart not in the auction sale of Keith Haring tea towels" (Peake, 514–5). The biography is especially valuable for the access it affords to a range of Jarman's unpublished writings.
2. Cf. Jarman's earlier journal notation on a projected final film: "Wild dreamings through the night: some last film full of vanishing incoherent sequences, the images crystal clear but so strange I cannot decipher them. They fall off the screen into the audience, who are frozen in their seats" (1991). Peake quotes from a subsequent, unpublished journal entry: "Behind the façade I've been in turmoil...the waiting

theme as well as the signature of Jarman's late work, most emphatically in the instance of his final film, *Blue*, released less than a year after the journal entry was written, and only months before his death.[2]

The gestation of the film that would eventually be realized as *Blue* is a lengthy one, traceable through notes and proposals dating from as early as 1987, as well as through the range of possible titles Jarman considered at various stages, including *Bliss*, *Blueprint*, *A Blueprint for Bliss*, *International Blue*, *Forget-Me-Not*, *Speedwell Eyes*, *Bruises*, *Blue protects white from innocence*, *0*, *Into the Blue*, *My Blue Heaven*, and *Blue is Poison* (Peake 398, 435, 510).[3] In a proposal written in August 1987, preserved in the archive of his production company, Basilisk, he adumbrates

> [a] fictional film exploring the world of the painter Yves Klein, inventor of the void, *International Blue*, the symphony monotone. A film without compunction or narrative existing only for an idea. In the cacophony of images Yves found the silence of the immaterial, expressed in a series of symbolic gestures performed in six short working years before his early death [in 1962] at 32. Yves is mercurial, enigmatic...a devotee of St. Rita, the patron saint of lost causes.... The proposal is to develop a feature length film in 35 mm exploring further the juxtaposition of sound and image that exists in *The Last of England*, but unlike this film to produce an atmosphere of calm and joy. A world to which the refugees from that dark space might journey. (Peake 398)

In the aftermath of his HIV diagnosis, Jarman found fresh inspiration in the abbreviated career of Yves Klein, particularly in the latter's pursuit of the immaterial in and through his monochromatic paintings rendered in the vibrant ultramarine he would come to copyright as "International Klein Blue," or IKB. In *Chroma*, written in 1993, Jarman invokes

is characterized by indecision. My mind darts this way and that, is full of non-sequiturs.... I toyed with the idea of a last film. Need it be a last film?... What's happening? What's happening? I skate across the surface. The depths are too deep to plumb. A pandemonium of images floated past through the summer and every idea brought its own doom.... I feel my work is in ruins—or rather should I say which way to go?... Am I getting beneath the surface or is this just maudlin self-obsession?... What to do?... or Yves Klein the great blue film of the image a cop out?... What would you do?" (405–7).

3. Indeed, *Blue is Poison* was one working title for *Caravaggio* (1986), Jarman's cinematic portrait of the painter who chose red rather than the conventional (and expensive) blue to paint the Virgin's dress, in the conviction that "blue is poison."

"The great master of blue—the French painter Yves Klein. No other painter is commanded by blue, though Cezanne painted more blues than most" (Jarman 1994B, 104). Though *Blue* was initially conceived as an imageless homage to his predecessor, accompanied by a "sophisticated Dolby stereo soundtrack which would tell the Yves Klein story in sound and jazzy be-bop," the obvious difficulty of funding such a project led Jarman to consider other, very different scenarios, including an elaborate masque dedicated to Klein that would involve a host of *dramatis personae*, historical pageantry, and image montages (Peake 399).[4] Always, the soundtrack was integral to his plans for the film; at one stage, "Jarman dreamed of recording the actor Matt Dillon's heartbeat for the soundtrack: 'it would make a great first credit'"; at another point, he "thought the film might follow the sound of footsteps, a journey with the continuous murmur of lazy waves, sea breezes, thunder, and stormy growlers" (Peake 435).[5]

In the name of "the admirable austerity of the void," however, the filmmaker would ultimately revert to his original conception of a blue screen devoid of images. Where for Caravaggio, the protagonist of his film of 1986, the colour had been "poison," Jarman himself came to exploit the potential of blue as pharmakon: simultaneously pathogen and remedy, and strictly neither, but a potent distillation of autobiography and historiography, "subjective memory and documentary reality," in "a fragment of an immense work without limit. The blue of the landscape of liberty."[6]

A journal entry dated 2 March 1993 registers Jarman's satisfaction on completing the film whose possibilities he had been contemplating for years:

> We sit in the *Blue*. . . . Intricate landscape of pain, all at sea, leaving one's senses. We finished *Blue* just before midnight. . . . I think the film is magnificent—it's the first time I've been able

4. The various scenarios that Jarman contemplated over the years are detailed in Peake (especially 399–400, 475–6).

5. In the final version, the voiced sound track preserves elements of the earlier scenario:"I'm walking along the beach in a howling gale—/ Another year is passing / In the roaring waters / I hear the voices of dead friends / Love is life that lasts forever" (Jarman 1994A, 5).

6. Unpublished proposals in the Basilisk archive (Peake 475, 515).

7. "Marco Polo stops and sits on a lapis throne by the River Oxus while he is ministered to by the descendants of Alexander the Great. The caravan approaches, blue canvasses fluttering in the wind. Blue people from over the sea—ultramarine—have come to collect the lapis with its flecks of gold" (Jarman 1994A, 13).

8. *Blue* recalls Jarman's earlier, mediated encounter with blindness: "As a teenager I used to work for the Royal National Institute for the Blind on their Christmas appeal for radios, with dear Miss Punch, seventy years old, who used to arrive each morning on her Harley Davidson...Miss Punch Leather Woman was the first out dyke I ever met. Closeted and frightened by my sexuality she was my hope. 'Climb on, let's go for a ride'" (Jarman 1994A, 13–4). In a journal entry from December 1992, Jarman records his reply to a German producer who has been unable to shepherd *Blue* past her editorial board to production: "I told her it would be great for her blind viewers, as indeed it would" (Jarman 2000, 259). Subsequently, Jarman himself becomes one of the blind viewers of the film: "I can no longer see straight, dizzy, with one eye missing.... [HB] learned how to connect the drip of Gancyclovir, about thirty procedures including mixing the drug. In the afternoon we watched *Blue*, this cheered me up" (Jarman 2000, 315).

to look one of my films in the eye. Cinema catches up with the twentieth century, this is the first feature to embrace the intellectual imperative of abstraction, it's moody, funny and distressing;...it takes film to the boundary of the known world, the River Oxus. The film is dedicated to HB and all true lovers. (Jarman 2000, 320)[7]

For the reader of the journals written from 1991 to 1994, and published posthumously as *Smiling in Slow Motion*, there is no small irony in the figuration that has Jarman, for "the first time," looking his last film "in the eye" (and that has cinema, in and through *Blue*, "catch[ing] up with the twentieth century," as the virus whose appearance is dated from the 1980s catches up with its director). For, by this point, HIV has more than once cost him (among much else, certainly) his sight.[8] The journals of this period chronicle a series of opportunistic infections that deprive him of visual perception, as well as the treatments administered to ward off the encroaching blindness. In August 1992, in language that will resurface in *Blue*, Jarman notes:

> Dr. Mark thought that he could detect lesions in the back of my retina, and put the stinging drops in....
>
> Eyes again, a terrible blinding light. I was put on a succession of machines. "Look left, look up, look down, look right." The torch was blinding, but worse was to come, as the CMV, now diagnosed, was photographed. A blinding flash into the eye while you concentrated on a small flashing red and green light, a green moon after-image and then the world turned magenta. The photos of my eyes looked like one of those colour photos of a distant planet. "Like a pizza," said the doctor. "We often use culinary terms in the hospital...."
>
> A young South African doctor came to inspect the damage. I won't get the vision back this time, though when the bleeding in the eye is stopped it might improve slightly. Blindness

in on the cards. I'm relieved that I know what is happening, the worst is the uncertainty. I think I have played this scenario back and forth nearly every day for the last six years. (Jarman 2000, 189)[9]

Shortly thereafter, he resolves to play the hand he has been dealt, and to stay true to his vision even in the absence of his sight: "I think I have to come to terms with my blind fate, there is so much to do, if Beethoven could write the ninth without hearing, I'm certain I could make a film without seeing.... I wonder how long it takes to learn Braille" (Jarman 2000, 192).[10]

It was a year later, in August 1993, that Jarman gave an interview to John Cartwright of the British Arts Council, filmed in his art dealer's studio against the backdrop of one of his last paintings and released under the title *There we are, John*.... In response to a question about his most recent feature, Jarman observes: "It is a film.... Technically speaking, it shouldn't be." His spare formulation underscores the fact that *Blue*, with its "roots in painting" (it began as a film loop of a Klein monochrome in the collection of the Tate Gallery), has a singular status in the annals of cinema.[11] For not only is it a film without images, whose sole visual content is a blue colour field that approximates IKB. It did not, moreover, ultimately result from any activity of filmmaking as conventionally conceived and practiced: in the event, the film loop was set aside, and the colour produced in a lab. *Blue* thus stands in stark contrast to the director's earlier endeavours, notably *The Last of England* and *The Garden*, with their highly-wrought image montages and internal references to their own filming.

Jarman spent much of September 1993 in the hospital, where he underwent two eye operations that temporarily postponed the loss of his sight. In the same month, according to his biographer,

9. Cf. Jarman 1994A, 4, 6.
10. Cf. Jarman 1994A, 9.
11. Jarman's earliest medium of choice was painting, which he studied at the Slade and to which he returned time and again, particularly in the last years of his life.

as if to celebrate this respite, *Blue* was given a last-minute release in central London before its simulcast on Channel 4 and Radio 3 [19.9.93]. Radio listeners were invited to write in for a blue postcard at which to stare for the length of the broadcast, while on television the film was shown without pause for commercials, a breakthrough as far as Jarman was concerned. Of the 252 calls taken by the Channel 4 duty officer after the screening, the majority expressed horror and disappointment. Ten queried problems with transmission and four declared a preference for red. Jarman's old sparring partner the Sun was predictably, punningly dismissive: "It may be Blue, but it's no movie" [18.9.93]. Elsewhere, the film met with a generally positive reaction, especially from those who felt that by dispensing with the image, Jarman had made a different film for each and every member of his audience. (Peake 527)[12]

That ten members of the simulcast's audience should query "problems with transmission" of a film that "treats" the effects of HIV is ironic enough (it is also worth observing that because of *Blue*'s lack of images and hence of a visual sequence, it would be impossible to verify the simultaneity of the simulcast on Channel 4 and Radio 3). Anticipating in effect the "preference for red" expressed by four others, Jarman himself mapped out a sequel to *Blue*, "a scarlet film in choking hellfire: smashing glass, madness, a horror film with HIV as a conscious beast rustling round, hysteric laughter, Beelzebub, legions, PCP is summoned, HELL ON EARTH, red generated from sulphur, demonology" (Jarman 2000, 312). Moreover, the tabloid reviewer's characteristically uninformed opinion ("It may be Blue, but it's no movie") proves a weak, unwitting echo of the filmmaker's own judgement, in *There we are, John...*, that "It is a film.... Technically speaking, it shouldn't be." And *Smiling in Slow Motion* lends some specificity to the "generally positive reaction" alluded to by Jarman's biographer: "*Blue* has been a great success; some of the

12. Peake notes further that a week after the transmission of *Blue* Jarman heard from Potsdam that he had been awarded the first Rainer-Werner Fassbinder prize for his "extraordinary artistic oeuvre" (527).

reviews have been a bit over the edge for such a modestly conceived film; of course I'm thrilled.... Everyone happy, not least a young man who told me it had stopped him committing suicide at a moment of great depression, something that had happened since he was the victim of a hit-and-run driver" (Jarman 2000, 377). The young viewer's testimonial does more than recall the near-miss recounted early in *Blue*, accompanied on the soundtrack by a cacophony of traffic noise: "I step off the kerb and a cyclist nearly knocks me down. Flying in from the dark he nearly parted my hair. I step into a blue funk" (Jarman 1994A, 3). It bespeaks the life-and-death stakes of a work whose aim and achievement is to bear witness to the awful devastation of the pandemic.[13]

Near the end of *Blue* the spoken soundtrack narrates a brief passage that also appears in a number of Jarman's earlier writings, including the journals of 1989–90, published under the title *Modern Nature*.[14] The unmarked quotation is one more instance of the author's citing himself, resurrecting his recorded past, as he does so frequently in his written work as well as his films. Indeed, the text of *Blue* (reproduced in a volume published in 1994) cites copiously from "Into the Blue," the chapter Jarman devoted to the colour in *Chroma*, and from the journals he kept prior to completing the film in 1993.[15] In the quotidian terms that characterize his diary entries, the passage in question figures the time remaining to Jarman, the proscribed life expectancy of one whose every day could be his last[16]: "I caught myself looking at shoes in a shop window. I thought of going in and buying a pair, but stopped myself. The shoes I am wearing at the moment should be sufficient to walk me out of life" (Jarman 1994A, 28). The poignancy here is in part an effect of Jarman's configuration of the life span of the shoes he is presently wearing with his own future, foreclosed as it is by the virus.

13. Immediately preceding the narration of the near-miss, the spoken soundtrack asks: "What need of so much news from abroad while all that concerns either life or death is transacting and at work within me?" (Jarman 1994A, 3).

14. I attempt a more extended reading of *Modern Nature* in the final chapter of *In the Event: Reading Journalism, Reading Theory*.

15. In the text of *Chroma*, Jarman quotes the familiar couplets "Something old, / Something new, / Something borrowed, / Something blue..." which link the colour with citation's borrowing in the present from the past (1994B, 106).

16. "I can never quite forget my illness, it gives a finality to every gesture—is this the last flower I will plant? Will this be my last flying trip into my past—the Heath? I go to spite the present" (Jarman 2000, 33).

There are multiple allusions in *Blue* to the limit set on life expectancy: some, like the passage just cited, are specifically autobiographical; others are more inclusive, even abstract, in keeping with the visual content of a film that "embrace[s] the intellectual imperative of abstraction." In the first category would number the calculation: "If I had to live forty years blind, I might think twice" (about participating in a risky experimental drug trial for oral DHPG) (Jarman 1994A, 24). The second category would include the epigrammatic formulations "Love is life that lasts forever" and "Blue transcends the solemn geography of human limits" (Jarman 1994A, 5, 7), as well as a passage that once again borrows from in *Modern Nature*:

> Ages and Aeons quit the room
> Exploding into timelessness
> No entrances or exits now
> No need for obituaries or final judgements
> We knew that time would end
> After tomorrow at sunrise
> We scrubbed the floors
> And did the washing up
> It would not catch us unawares. (Jarman 1994A, 26)

But the language in which Jarman projects a delimited future for his shoes and himself—"The shoes I am wearing at the moment should be sufficient to walk me out of life"—provides a pivotal link to other telling passages in *Blue* and elsewhere in the corpus. Its figuration of life as a perambulation whose final step traverses the threshold of death is of course rooted in an ancient rhetorical tradition. But in Jarman's unsettling reinscription of the topos, the journey is without prescribed direction or destination. In *Kicking the Pricks*, a volume contemporaneous with *The Last of England* (1987), he observes that the film's allegorical structure "suggests a journey: pages turn in a book bringing with them new turnings in direction, building up an atmosphere without entering into traditional narrative" (Jarman 1987, 188). In another instance, a draft proposal for *Blue* that found its way into the opening voiceover from his film *The Garden* (1990) reads:

> I want to share this emptiness with you
> Not fill the silence with false notes
> Or put tracks through the void
> I want to share the wilderness
> Without fences
> The others have built you a highway
> Fast lanes in both directions
> I offer you a journey without direction
> Where our paths cross for a moment
> Like the swallow that flies through
> Our ancestors' mead hall
> Arm yourself like a Beowulf
> For a journey into the unknown
> I offer you uncertainty
> No sweet conclusions
> When the lights give out
> There are many paths and many directions
> I went in search of myself. (Peake 400)[17]

17. Jarman's biographer observes that this poem "refers to Klein's Theatre of the Void, to which he dedicated a specially prepared edition of a Sunday newspaper." He cites further from Jarman's draft proposal: "Silence is golden / Silence falls on the pandemonium of images / An infinity of silence / Without compunction / At the world's end / I pick up a paintbrush / And demonstrate the evolution / Of the immaterial / For the astronauts of the void / Lost in time and space / I dream of a blue heaven / Where dead souls whisper / Silence is golden" (Peake 400).

The narration in *Blue* has further recourse to the same figuration: "The Gautama Buddha instructs me to walk away from illness. But he wasn't attached to a drip" (Jarman 1994A, 9). (The soundtrack here also features a chorus of women's voices intoning "walk away from this.") Subsequently, the prior male voice poses the plaintive and pressing question: "How can I walk away with a drip attached to me? How am I going to walk away from this?" (Jarman 1994A, 10).[18]

The intravenous drip, long since a fact of life for Jarman, is here the mechanism that delivers one of his medications, DHPG or Gancyclovir, which targets the encroaching blindness, and whose side-effects the soundtrack enumerates in a harrowing passage punctuated by the rhythm of an oxygen machine:

> The side-effects of DHPG, the drug for which I have to come into hospital to be dripped twice a day, are: low white blood cell count, increased risk of infection, low platelet count which may increase the risk of bleeding, low red blood cell count (anaemia), fever, rash, abnormal liver function, chills, swelling of the body (oedema), infections, malaise, irregular heart beat, high blood pressure (hypertension), low blood pressure (hypotension), abnormal thoughts or dreams, loss of balance (ataxia), coma, confusion, dizziness, headache, nervousness, damage to nerves (paraesthesia), psychosis, sleepiness (somnolence), shaking, nausea, vomiting, loss of appetite (anorexia), diarrhoea, bleeding from the stomach or intestine (intestinal haemorrhage), abdominal pain, increased number of one type of white blood cell, low blood sugar, shortness of breath, hair loss (alopecia), itching (pruritus), hives, blood in the urine, abnormal kidney function, increased blood urea, redness (inflammation), pain or irritation (phlebitis).
>
> Retinal detachments have been observed in patients both before and after initiation of therapy. The drug has caused decreased sperm production in animals and may cause

18. Elsewhere in *Blue*, the journey is inflected as quest: "I have walked behind the sky./ For what are you seeking?/ The fathomless blue of Bliss" (Jarman 1994A, 15).

infertility in humans, and birth defects in animals. Although there is no information in human studies, it should be considered a potential carcinogen since it causes tumours in animals.

If you are concerned about any of the above side-effects or if you would like any further information, please ask your doctor. (Jarman 1994A, 18–9)

As *New York Times* critic Stephen Holden observed after a screening of *Blue* at the New York Film Festival in October 1993, "The recitation of the possible side effects of an experimental drug is horrifying: many sound far worse than the blindness the drug is intended to thwart" (16). It also leaves the patient facing blindness in a cognitive predicament figured in the narration in terms of visual perception: "In order to be put on the drug you have to sign a piece of paper stating you understand that all these illnesses are a possibility. / I really can't see what I am to do. I am going to sign it" (Jarman 1994A, 19).

But in *Blue*, crucially, the IV drip is also more or other than a medical technology, for "The drip ticks out the seconds, the source of a stream along which the minutes flow, to join the river of hours, the sea of years and the timeless ocean" (Jarman 1994A, 18). The drip now attached to Jarman functions here and elsewhere as a kind of prosthetic timepiece that measures or marks time remaining, on the order of a watch, a clock (at this stage, the soundtrack reproduces the differential ticking of multiple clocks), and eventually a calendar.[19]

Indeed, these passages in *Blue* recall a series of journal entries dating from July 1990, when, as he writes, "I was taken into hospital...for an emergency brain scan, which picked up the toxoplasmosis that had destroyed my sight in the previous days" (Jarman 1991, 304). *Modern Nature* records an early stage in Jarman's gradual loss of vision

19. Note on watch in SISM and on perpetual calendar *Today and Tomorrow*. Cf. *Blue*: "The darkness comes in with the tide / The year slips on the calendar" (Jarman 1994A, 20).

under the assault of successive opportunistic infections, chronicled further in *Smiling in Slow Motion* and both thematized and figured in *Blue*. Because the language here informs so much of the artist's subsequent writing, painting and film, it warrants citation at some length:

No books to read, no newspapers. So, what did I think about during the long hours?

I watched the clock.

On the first day its face was a fuzzy halo, the digits telescoped and disappeared.

On the second day I could see the red second hand move in a jumble of black.

On the third day I paused, looked and looked again and read the time.

On the fourth day I could read the numbers round the dial. . . .

Beware of very hot water reads the sign above the basin. The number 13 in the corridor slowly came into focus. It's 11:25, I have written three pages. My writing is illegible. It is remarkably easy to lose your sight: a bad headache on a Friday evening and words slide off the pages. Within a few days they disappear altogether.

In the waiting room of the West London Eye Hospital I was barely aware of the drip sticking in my arm watched by curious children. I read the flashing dot in the machines and longed to get back into my bed. . . .

I feel I should be able to record more than I have or more deeply and find I cannot. . . .

My symptoms are a first. I will be written up in the BMJ. . . .

I see the blue sky veiled with shadows. . . .

The nurse said today that this must be a frightening experience. It isn't, just aggravating—so silly to lose your eyes. I can write clearly and in straight lines across the gloomy page. How many aftershocks must I endure till my body, broken, desiccated, and drained of colour, fails to respond. I live in a permanent hangover, after years of good health. A little green light flashes in the drip, the cool poison runs into my arm. . . .

Blind as a bat he took to finding his way with sonar, flitting this way and that across the empty page, the starchy whiteness of a page of St. Mary's foolscap. Silent as the salt lakes, dazzling, blinding white to the horizon.

Waves of icy sulphadiazine breaking on the farther shores after we have crossed over in a blizzard of pills, a rainbow-coloured confetti of serpent poisons, sharp-toothed as the adder. Words, no longer strung out on the lines of narrative, escape and hang round corners waiting to jump out of the dictionary, restore primal disorder. The emerald apple sits on my bedside table, its perfection disordered in my mind's eye. . . . Apple of my eye.

Someone else says losing your sight must be frightening. Not so, as long as you have a safe harbour in the sea of shadows. Just inconvenient. If you woke on a dark day, had only the mind's eye with which to see your way, would you turn back?

My drip ticks away a long afternoon. The sulphadiazine battles with the cysts to bring me second sight. By tea time the migraine takes over. They play the "theme tune" from Death in Venice as I enter the brain scan. . . .

My eyes are back, I can read. Though the grey shadows circle at the periphery, and the drugs make me dizzy and disorientated. . .I could be out by Saturday. I'm stronger, have put my weight back on; but feel like an invalid. I can't believe I'll ever be well again. The drugs have brought on a rash. I'll be on them for life, and how long will that be?

The lilies Lynn sent me have lasted eight days.

A woman leads a blind child slowly down the stairs.

In the vision field you gaze for an eternity at small bright lights andpress a buzzer each time lights flash on and off. It is confusing and my eyes, heavy with antihistamine, fall asleep. An eye for an eye. I return to the waiting room. . . .

20. Cf. Jarman's account of an adventure in Manchester during an exhibition of his paintings in the city: "HB mounted an expedition through a window and across a precarious ledge. He climbed the clock tower, found the handle which wound up the clock and immediately put the whole of Manchester at sixes and sevens, leaving each of the faces reading a different time" (Jarman 2000, 125).

21. Much of Jarman's film-making, painting, and writing assumes the responsibilities of the historian of crisis in what *Blue* terms "these uncaring times" (Jarman 1994A, 21). At the end of *At Your Own Risk: A Saint's Testament*, for example, he addresses his readership: "Please read the cares of the world that I have locked in these pages; and after, put this book aside and love. May you of a better future love without a care and remember that we loved too. As the shadows closed in [complete citation ref]. More often than not, his mode of historiography comprises an autobiographical dimension, as in a

I wish I had brought a video and recorded these last weeks here....

What the eye doesn't see the mind doesn't grieve for....

The day of our death is sealed up. I do not wish to die...yet. I would love to see my garden through several summers....

I view the world through drunken eyes....

The horizon has closed in....

X-rays take an age. I hate this waiting room.... A sign says *Come Early, Save Time.* (Jarman 1991, 304–12)

The language of these entries and others like them affords an opportunity—and imposes an obligation—to *read Jarman reading*, as it links the threat of blindness posed by HIV not merely with a *de rigueur* clock-watching[20] "during the long hours" in hospital waiting rooms and wards, but with an imperative to *read the time* even as he continues to record "across the empty page" a time that is "all awry" ("My weakness is my inability to grasp that literate and intelligent people could do anything but agree that this time is all awry" [Jarman 2000, 111]).[21] And the responsibility to read the time is not Jarman's alone. Indeed, its urgency is not confined to those already suffering the incalculable effects of the virus, foremost among them the foreclosing of the horizon. The journal's intermittently apostrophic mode—here, "If you woke on a dark day, had only the mind's eye with which to see your way, would you turn back?"—directs the imperative not only to its eventual readers, but more generally to all persons of voice: first, second, and third. By way of a question that, once again, is neither simply rhetorical nor strictly hypothetical, the imperative is further linked, through the prospect of blindness, to the perhaps compensatory and certainly allegorical figuration of a supplementary "vision"[22] (the "mind's eye," "second sight," an "eye for an eye"), allowing for the possibility that

characteristic entry in *Smiling in Slow Motion*: "As the Establishment always writes the history, I wonder how I'll come out. A bitter man who resented life? Took it out on those nearest? Put the clock back for homosexual reform? If you read *Peers, Queers, and Commons* there is a vital element missing: its thesis is that the steps forward will occur through parliamentary legislation. This is a mistake, steps forward came by the example of our lives, one David Hockney in 1960 was worth more than the 1967 act and did more to change our lives. The aim is to open up discourse and with it broaden our horizons; that can't be legislated for" (Jarman 2000, 43). 22. Cf. *Blue*: "The retina is destroyed, though when the bleeding stops what is left of my sight might improve. I have to come to terms with sight-lessness./If I lose half my sight will my vision be halved?" (Jarman 1994A, 7).

"blindness may be a blessing, even the gift of poetic and political clairvoyance, the chance for prophecy" (Derrida 128).[23] All as the drip delivers the drugs that Jarman will be on "for life, and how long will that be?", even as it "ticks away a long afternoon." Appearing three years later, his last film will allude (again, apostrophically) to the long duration of the brief time remaining: This illness knocks you for six / Just as you start to forget it / A bullet in the back of the head / Might be easier / You know, you can take longer than / The second world war to get to the grave" (Jarman 1994A, 26).

In a proposal dated May 1991, Jarman contemplates a scenario for *Blue* in which the only trace of "the original Klein idea" would be a "sea of time, presented as a blue void" (quoted Peake 475). The relationship between the "blue void" and the "sea of time" it is meant to present is not so much metaphorical as allegorical, unfolding over time: in the event, not ninety but seventy-seven minutes of a feature film that translates the devastation to which Jarman has been witness. To the extent that *Blue* succeeds not so much in surmounting the obstacle of incommensurability ("No ninety minutes of cinema could deal with the eight years HIV takes to get its host") as in rendering the predicament itself on film, the difficulty and the responsibility to address it become the viewer's own. If the "blue void" that is the sole visual content of this film without images figures (among other things[24]) a "sea of time," how do we, erstwhile survivors of the pandemic, *read* this time, which subsumes the multiple temporalities inscribed in the passage in which "The drip ticks out the seconds, the source of a stream along which the minutes flow, to join the river of hours, the sea of years and the timeless ocean" (Jarman 1994A, 18)? How do we read what in *Blue* is more and other than a theme: the possibly illegible signature of Jarman's last film?

23. In his journals, Jarman was consistently clairvoyant—at times poetically, at times more brutally—about his own fate: "When the author of these scowling canvasses has gone the heat will be turned off and all that will be left is the ash. My mind, unable to concentrate, grey as cinders" (Jarman 2000, 111). A journal entry dated July 1991 presages in political terms the disastrous dimensions the pandemic would assume in sub-Saharan Africa: "Spent the morning at St. Mary's. My doctor had returned from an AIDS conference in Florence. Africa is facing huge problems—a health budget of twenty-seven pence per person per annum. Here things are very different, St. Mary's one of the finest hospitals, patients live longer. We dwell on a little futurology, three to six years are the best forecast, the worst next week. On the way home I decide to try to make the millennium." (Jarman 2000, 29)

24. At various points, the film's spoken sound track hints at what else blue may figure for Jarman: "Blue bottle buzzing /

Lazy days / The sky blue but-
terfly / Sways on a cornflower /
Lost in the warmth / Of the
blue heat haze / Singing the
blues / Quiet and slowly / Blue
of my heart / Blue of my
dreams / Slow blue love / Of
delphinium days / Blue is the
universal love in which man
bathes—it is the terrestrial
paradise" (Jarman 1994A,
4–5). See also "Into the Blue"
(Jarman 1994B, 103–24).
25. The entry continues: "All
steps forward have been made
by those of us trying to grapple
with the problems in our daily
lives. Life was not *The Sound
of Music*; if you climbed a
mountain it was a sweaty affair
and you might not reach the
summit. The great queer artists
dealt with the negatives, that
is why Pasolini and Genet will
last long after *Gay Times* is
forgotten in a world of false
hope and illusion fed by
adverts. A film like *Salo* is a
necessary antidote, you could
hardly call Pasolini 'gay.'
The word is an illusion, it was
a necessary rallying point in
1970; with it came 'gay community' to give us focus but
it soon became a method of

One hypothesis might be ventured based on the film's association of blue with the telling phenomenon of the after-image: "The shattering bright light of the eye specialist's camera leaves that empty sky blue after-image. Did I really see green the first time? The after-image dissolves in a second" (Jarman 1994A, 27). Jarman's final film is of a time after the time of images, in several possible senses. One of these, perhaps the most readily legible, is a function of its position in his trajectory of filmmaking: it completes the notional trilogy whose earlier components, *The Last of England* and *The Garden*, partake of his characteristic image montages that configure past (e.g., in their incorporation of Jarman's earlier Super-8 films and his father's home movies), present (e.g., in their depiction of the Thatcher era in Britain), and future (in their respective prophetic elements), conjugating these three tenses as they unfold over their feature length. *Blue* concludes the Dantesque sequence in which "The first film represented the underworld, the second the real world, *Bliss* paradise" (Peake 475). In this sense, its serene colour field comes after the time of images in Jarman's filmography.

It does so, too, insofar as the "age of AIDS" conceived as a historicist periodization follows an era characterized by the project of gay liberation and its vaunting of "positive images," a nomenclature that certainly failed to stand the test of time from one decade to the next. As Jarman attests in *Smiling in Slow Motion*, "The concept of positive images was born out of gay liberation in the 1970s. . . . There was a disgraceful review of my films by the [*Gay Times*] positive image 'film critic' Steven Bourne. Positive images are an illusion, like commercials—they are not the stuff of art" (Jarman 2000, 168).[25] What he deplores in a reliance on such images is the failure to engage with the graphic realities of homophobia in a tactic that seeks to counter bigotry through a mimicry of the acceptable: youth and health being constitutive components of the putatively positive.

For Jarman, the political and historical matter of "positive images" was inseparable from the filmmaker's ever-present pragmatic dilemma, as he noted in preparing to shoot *Wittgenstein*: "how do you make images resonate? They can't be illustrative, there's not much point in making a film 'about' something" (Jarman 2000, 133).[26] (It was also at times difficult to disentangle from the problematic "visual illiteracy" he deplored in the London passersby [Jarman 2000, 177]).

Because, as he attests in the journal entry with which this essay begins, "We don't lack images—just good ones," because "The image is a prison of the soul, your heredity, your education, your vices and aspirations, your qualities, your psychological world" (Jarman 1994A, 15), *Blue* foregoes visual imagery, presenting its viewers instead with a blue after-image sustained beyond its ephemeral lifespan for seventy-seven minutes:

> In the pandemonium of image
> I present you with the universal Blue
> Blue an open door to soul
> An infinite possibility
> Becoming tangible. (Jarman 1994A, 11)

The supplanting of image by the "infinite possibility" of *Blue* is further linked to Jarman's own history, and specifically to his ambivalent sense that (like Yves Klein's) it is drawing to a premature close: "Some part of me dares this blindness to progress, it says I've seen enough" (Jarman 2000, 230). For himself, for his contemporaries, he seeks relief from the "cacophony," the "pandemonium of image":

> Over the mountains is the shrine to Rita, where all at the end of the line call. Rita is the Saint of the Lost Cause. The saint of all who are at their wit's end, who are hedged in and trapped by the facts of the world. The facts, detached from cause, trapped the Blue Eyed

marketing nightclubs and clothing. . . . / I didn't discover my sexuality to sell in—I want change. 'Gay' itself was a problem for artists I knew, it did not describe us. If we had come up with 'difficult' that would have been better. . . one day maybe we will dispense with boundaries and categories. I was never gay, queer maybe, difficult certainly, with good reason. . . . / I wish it were raining, rain concentrates the mind, the blue sky is an illusion, behind lies an infinite black" (Jarman 2000, 168–9). On the vexed question of "boundaries and categories," cf. *Blue*: "I am a cock sucking / Straight acting / Lesbian man / With ball crushing bad manner / Laddish nymphomaniac politics / Spunky sexist desires / Of incestuous inversion and / Incorrect terminology / I am a Not Gay" (Jarman 1994A, 21–2).

26. During filming of *The Garden* in December 1989, Jarman noted in his journal: "David Lewis asked me on the way home if I had an image which I worked to. The answer is No. I have no idea how the

scenes will work, and no wish to" (Jarman 1991, 200). And further: "Watched another hour of the film rushes last night. They depress me. So many fleeting moments lost to the camera, which seems destined to point in the wrong direction" (Jarman 1991, 210).

27. In his journals in particular, Jarman took to heart the diffi-cult task of filling the empty page, as for example in the first entry reproduced in *Smiling in Slow Motion*: "For days now I have tried to restart this diary, but the clatter of my existence has interrupted; the first mark on the page eludes me, it is easy to put off" (Jarman 2000, 3).

28. Cf. *Blue*: "The archaeology of sound has only just been perfected and the systematic cataloguing of words has until recently been undertaken in a haphazard way. *Blue* watched as a word or phrase material-ized in scintillating sparks, a poetry of fire which cast everything into darkness with the brightness of its reflections" (Jarman 1994A, 13).

Boy in a system of unreality. Would all these blurred facts that deceive dissolve in his last breath? For accustomed to believing in image, an absolute idea of value, his world had forgotten the command of essence: Thou Shall Not Create Unto Thyself Any Graven Image, although you know the task is to fill the empty page. From the bottom of your heart, pray to be released from image. (Jarman 1994A, 15)[27]

Saturating the screen with the "Bliss in [his] ghostly eye" (Jarman 1994A, 29), Jarman releases his viewers from image as an affront to sore eyes. But his caveat to the com-mandment invokes the ongoing "task" of writing, and with it the inevitable, invisible images in the language enlisted "to fill the empty page": the images we hear rather than see in *Blue*. As Derrida reminds us in his *Memoirs of the Blind*:

One must always remember that the word, the vocable, is heard and understood, the sonorous phenomenon remaining invisible as such. Taking up time rather than space in us, it is addressed not only from the blind to the blind, like a code for nonseeing, but speaks to us, in truth, all the time of the blindness that constitutes it. Language is spoken, it speaks to itself, which is to say from/of blindness. It always speaks to us from/of the blindness that constitutes it. (3)[28]

Neither does the film spare us the related task of accounting for the other crucial incommensurability it renders: that between the time of its recorded testimony and the time of the experience to which it testifies and with which it cannot coincide. *Blue*'s blind address to the blind calls us to hear the difference as the spoken sound track reverts to the past tense:

The virus rages fierce. I have no friends now who are not dead or dying. Like a blue frost it caught them. At work, at the cinema, on marches and beaches. In churches on their knees, running, flying, silent or shouting protest. It started with sweats in the night and swollen glands. Then the black cancers spread across their faces—as they fought for breath TB and pneumonia hammered at the lungs, and Toxo at the brain. Reflexes scrambled—sweat poured through hair matted like lianas in the tropical forest. Voices slurred—and then were lost forever. My pen chased this story across the page tossed this way and that in the storm. (Jarman 1994A, 7–8)

It calls us as well to register the prophetic cadences of the outraged witness:

How did my friends cross the cobalt river, with what did they pay the ferryman? As they set out for the indigo shore under this jet-black sky—some died on their feet with a backward glance. Did they see Death with the hell hounds pulling a dark chariot, bruised blue-black, growing dark in the absence of light, did they hear the blast of trumpets? David ran home panicked on the train from Waterloo, brought back exhausted and unconscious to die that night. Terry who mumbled incoherently into his incontinent tears. Others faded like flowers cut by the scythe of the Blue Bearded Reaper, parched as the waters of life receded. Howard turned slowly to stone, petrified day by day, his mind imprisoned in a concrete fortress until all we could hear were his groans on the telephone circling the globe. (Jarman 1994A, 16)[29]

In a journal entry dated August 1993, written contemporaneously with preparations for the "release" of *Blue*, Jarman alludes to the temporal asymmetry between perception and attestation in experiential rather than conceptual terms: "The stinging eye drops are in, the reading chart which has a flaw—as if you read with your good eye first you can remember the letters, to whose benefit? My illusions.... Eleven o'clock and still waiting for the dragging minutes to pass.... I feel less and less like fighting, giving up, giving in. Writing blind now.... Yawning void" (Jarman 2000, 224). For the blinded Jarman, of course, visual perception belongs to recollection, as the editor's preface to

29. Or again: "We all contemplated suicide / We hoped for euthanasia / We were lulled into believing / Morphine dispelled pain / Rather than making it tangible / Like a mad Disney cartoon / Transforming itself into / Every conceivable nightmare" (Jarman 1994A, 17).
30. In *Memoirs of the Blind*, Derrida poses "a thoughtful question: what would a journal of the blind be like? A newspaper or daily of the blind? Or else the more personal kind of journal, a diary or day-book? And what about the day, then, the rhythms of the days and nights without day or light, the dates and calendars that scan memories and memoirs? How would the memoirs of the blind be written?" (33). *Smiling in Slow Motion* answers Derrida's questions by and for example, in chronicling the rhythms of Jarman's final days and nights without day or light.

the posthumously published *Smiling in Slow Motion* confirms: "In the final diary he wrote without vision, his semi-legible scrawl only possible from his memory of the scratch of nib on paper" (Jarman 2000, np).[30]

In his journal of the blind, as in his film without images, Jarman gives us to understand that he has finally seen enough:

> [t]he blind man thus becomes the best witness, a chosen witness. In fact, a witness, as such, is always blind. Witnessing substitutes narrative for perception. The witness cannot see, show, and speak at the same time, and the interest of the attestation, like that of the testament, stems from this dissociation. No authentification can show in the present what the most reliable witness sees, or rather, has seen and now keeps in memory. (Jarman 1991, 104)[31]

Nearing the end of his journey without destination, with no prospect of an afterlife beyond the horizon, Jarman finds that no image can show in the present what he has seen and now keeps in memory. In place of the "pandemonium of image," he bequeaths his viewers an imageless archive: one that preserves a time that was (and remains) "all awry," along with its own fundamental incommensurability, as testimony, with the awful devastation of AIDS.

31. Jarman's paintings, the last of which he executed while blind, also serve to bear witness: see for example his artist's statement for a 1992 exhibition in Manchester: "My spirit guide is Goya, I saw this, this is the present in which my friends were lost, they died in these headlines behind the cups of sugary tea. Which blood? Which books? What revenge? What vice? What virtue? / I painted these pictures with no hope and wild laughter, you are the jokers, the laughter is on you. Tears fall behind the headlines. "Discover yourself" they said at school. I found a terrible subject. Was my sex ever safe? / Shed no tears over this work" (Jarman 2000, 88).

Jacques Derrida (1993)
Memoirs of the Blind: The Self-Portrait and Other Ruins
Chicago: University of Chicago Press

Deborah Esch (1999)
In the Event: Reading Journalism, Reading Theory
Stanford: Stanford University Press

Stephen Holden (1993)
The New York Times (October 2)

Derek Jarman (1986)
Caravaggio
United Kingdom: British Film Institute

——(1987)
Kicking the Pricks
London: Vintage

——(1991)
Modern Nature
London: Vintage

——(1993)
At Your Own Risk: A Saint's Testament
Woodstock: Overlook Press

——(1994A)
Blue: Text of a Film by Derek Jarman
Woodstock: Overlook Press

——(1994B)
Chroma
London: Vintage

——(2000)
Smiling in Slow Motion
London: Century

Ken McMullen (1993)
There we are, John...
United Kingdom: The British Council

Tony Peake (1999)
Derek Jarman
London: Little, Brown

It's the end of cinema.

AFTERWORD

FILMING TRANSLATION (THE MOST EXEMPLARY FILM)

Ian Balfour

It is not possible to see a version of Jean-Luc Godard's *Le Mépris* (*Contempt*) without subtitles.

The point of departure: a French screenwriter is being courted, in Italy, by an American producer to work on the script of a film version of the classic Greek epic *The Odyssey*, to be directed by a German director (no less than the real Fritz Lang). Crucial to the dynamics is the work of the Italian translator (not by accident, a woman) who almost never speaks Italian. Her job is to see that the French, German, and American parties understand each other. One of the few words she ever says in Italian is *strano*, when Fritz Lang asks what the word is for *étrange*.

Translation usually reproduces the words of one language in another and the translator is most often thought to be in the service of the original. Yet Godard's translator sometimes evinces a certain priority, a violent priority. More than once she translates phrases in advance of their being spoken by the person whose words she is supposed to be translating. The "original" echoes the "translation" that pre-empted it. Foreignness comes to inhabit what seemed not foreign in the first place.

Or sometimes the translation is simply boldly interpretive, in a way that exceeds the original. When the producer Prokosh (Jack Palance) laments that he had to sell the land the film studio is on and notes that "they are going to build a 5 & 10 cent store on this, [his] lost kingdom," the translator "translates": "C'est la fin du cinéma": "It's the end of cinema." Not a literal translation in any sense, it does nonetheless convey a version of the original while going well beyond it, to a resonant allegorical pronouncement on the precarious state of cinema itself. The film's internal "subtitles" precede the actual subtitles to come, raising all the problems of translation in advance of their inevitable re-staging in the circulation of the film as foreign.

The near-ubiquity of translation from one given tongue to another alerts us to the presence of an almost vertiginous series of translations from one genre, from one thing to another:

from Homer's epic to Fritz Lang's film of it

from ancient Greece to modern Italy

from Greek art to Roman, real or fake

from living gods to immobile, eyeless statues

from the theatre to the screen (the screenwriter, a novelist, really wants to write plays)

from novel to screen (Godard's whole film is a translation of Moravia's novel).

Translation is everywhere, in and out of and into language.

We are used to thinking of subtitles as a kind of afterthought, a supplement to the original language of the film, a supplement which could be added to the original, depending not least on market forces. But Godard changes all that. In its extremity, *Contempt* tells the truth about film and films, even those seemingly oblivious to the question of translation. Subtitles are the marks of difference, the written words that visibly render the voice of another language, and in such a way as to render the original foreign from the very start.

The final word of *Contempt*: SILENZIO.

STEPHEN ANDREWS was born in 1956 in Sarnia, Ontario. He has exhibited his work in Canada, the US, Brazil, Scotland, France, and Japan. He is represented in the collections of the National Gallery of Canada and the AGO. His work deals with memory, identity, surveillance, and their representations in various media.

IAN BALFOUR teaches in English and the Graduate Programme in Social & Political Thought at York University. He is author of *The Rhetoric of Romantic Prophecy* and with Eduardo Cadava co-editor of *And Justice for All? The Claims of Human Rights.* He is currently completing a book on the sublime.

RUSSELL BANKS is the author of many novels, including *Continental Drift, Rule of the Bone,* and *Cloudsplitter,* and five collections of short stories, most recently *The Angel on the Roof.* Two of his novels, *The Sweet Hereafter* and *Affliction,* have been made into award-winning films. His work has been widely translated and anthologized.

KASS BANNING teaches Cinema Studies at the University of Toronto. She has written extensively on diasporic cinemas and is completing a study on minoritarian film and new media practices. Banning co-founded and co-edited *CineAction* and *Borderlines* for a decade and is co-editor and contributor to *Gendering the Nation: Canadian Women's Cinema.*

MARIE-AUDE BARONIAN is an assistant researcher at the University of Amsterdam and a member of the Amsterdam School for Cultural Analysis. She has written and lectured on Atom Egoyan's cinema, and on representation, testimony, and memory. Her current project is titled *Image, Mémoire et Transmission: Sur la (non-) représentation du génocide Arménien.*

A radio and television producer, director and talk-show host, HENRI BÉHAR is also a writer (*Hollywood on the Riviera: The Inside Story of the Cannes Film Festival,* 1992) who has extensively covered the North American cultural scene for such French publications as *Le Monde* and *Paris-Vogue.*

RAYMOND BELLOUR is a Director of Research of CNRS, Paris and was a founder of du Centre Parisien d'Etudes Critiques where he still teaches. Recent publications include *L'Entre-images, Jean-Luc Godard: Son + Image, L'Entre-images 2* and *The Analysis of Film.* In 1991, with Serge Daney, he created the cinema review *Trafic.*

JORGE LUIS BORGES, 1899–1986, was an Argentine poet, critic, and short-story writer. Borges has been widely hailed as the foremost contemporary Spanish-American writer. He helped to found three avant-garde journals and was director of the National Library and professor of English at the University of Buenos Aires.

ANNE CARSON is a much-heralded poet and McGill University classics professor who has been acclaimed by her peers as the most imaginative poet writing today. Carson won the 2001 Griffin Poetry Prize. She is the author of *Men in the Off Hours, The Beauty of the Husband,* and *Autobiography of Red.*

ERIC CAZDYN is Associate Professor of Comparative Literature, East Asian Studies and Cinema Studies at the University of Toronto. His book *The Flash of Capital: Film and Geopolitics in Japan* was published by Duke University Press in 2002 and he is presently thinking about "crisis" and "preemptivity" across various fields

CLAIRE DENIS is at the forefront of a new wave of French women filmmakers. She has directed, among other films, *Beau Travail* (1996), *U.S. Go Home* (1994), *No Fear No Die* (1990), and *Chocolat* (1987).

MARY ANN DOANE is George Hazard Crooker Professor of Modern Culture and Media at Brown University. She is the author of *The Emergence of Cinematic Time: Modernity, Contingency, the Archive, Femmes Fatales: Feminism, Film Theory, Psychoanalysis,* and *The Desire to Desire: The Woman's Film of the 1940s.*

ATOM EGOYAN has written and directed film, television, theatre, and opera. Egoyan's most recent work includes the feature films *The Sweet Hereafter, Felicia's Journey,* and *Ararat,* as well as the screen adaptation of *Krapp's Last Tape.* He is presently involved in the Canadian Opera Company's production of Wagner's *Ring.*

BRUCE R. ELDER teaches in the Ryerson/York Graduate Programme in Communication and Culture. His films have been shown at the Museum of Modern Art (New York), Centre Pompidou (Paris), Kino Arsenal (Berlin), and in numerous retrospectives, including two at Anthology Film Archives. His most recent book is *The Films of Stan Brakhage.*

KENT U. ENNS is a lecturer on the history of philosophy and political thought with the University of Toronto School of Continuing Studies. He is also author of the novel, *Song of the Liquid West* (forthcoming).

DEBORAH ESCH teaches reading and theory at the University of Toronto. She is the author of *In the Event: Reading Journalism, Reading Theory* (1999) and the forthcoming *The Brevity of Life: What AIDS Makes Legible.*

SARAH NIXON GASYNA is a doctoral student at the Centre for the Study of Drama at the University of Toronto. Her dissertation examines the ways in which death was mediated through dance in late eighteenth- and early nineteenth-century France (from the Revolution to the establishment of the Romantic Ballet).

JOHN GREYSON is a Toronto film/video artist whose works include the video opera *Fig Trees* (2003), the sodomy epic *Proteus* (2003), the circumcision fable *Uncut* (1997), and the AIDS musical *Zero Patience* (1993).

JENNIFER HARRIS has just completed her PhD in American Literature at York University. Her research interests include the early American novel and African American and women's writing.

FREDRIC JAMESON is a professor of French and Comparative Literature and the Director of the Institute of Critical Theory at Duke. His works include *Marxism and Form*, *The Political Unconscious*, *Postmodernism, or, the Cultural Logic of Late Capitalism*, and *A Singular Modernity*.

ISAAC JULIEN came to prominence with *Looking for Langston* (1989). *Young Soul Rebels* (1991) won the Semaine de la Critique prize at the Cannes Film Festival. Julien was nominated for the Turner Prize in 2001. His recent film installations explore high art and popular culture, race, sexuality, and beauty.

Alphabet City Director JOHN KNECHTEL founded the company in 1991, and has lead the development of its nine volumes, as well as its conferences and exhibitions. In 2000 he was invited to curate Canada's official entry—entitled *Next Memory City*—at the 8th International Venice Biennale for Architecture.

JACK LEWIS is a Capetown video/film producer and activist whose documentaries include the award-winning *Casa de la Musica*; *A Normal Daughter: the life and times of Kewpie of District Six*; *Apostles of Civilized Vice*; *Sando to Samantha*; and *The Devil Breaks My Heart*, with Zackie Achmet. He is currently producing the fourth season of *Beat It!*, a nationally-broadcast magazine program on HIV/AIDS. *Proteus* is his first dramatic feature.

GILBERT LI's design work has been recognized by the Advertising and Design Club of Canada, the Alcuin Society, *Applied Arts*, Graphis, and *Communication Arts*. In 2003 he received a coveted 50 Books/50 Covers award from the American Institute for Graphic Artists for the design of *Alphabet City no. 8*.

BRENDA LONGFELLOW is currently the Acting Chair of the Department of Film & Video at York University where she teaches production and film theory. Her last film, *Tina in Mexico*, which follows the life of photographer Tina Modotti, has garnered numerous prizes and been broadcast internationally.

Born in Northern Ireland in 1959, STEFANA McCLURE attended art college in London, subsequently spending twelve years in Japan before moving to New York. Much of her work investigates the structure and visual properties of language. She has exhibited extensively internationally and is represented by Cristinerose|Josée Bienvenu Gallery, New York.

CALIN-ANDREI MIHAILESCU is a tetralingual writer who teaches at the University of Western Ontario in the Department of Modern Languages and in the Centre for the Study of Theory and Criticism, which he directs. His industry includes four books in the last year and the editorship of Literary Research/Recherche littéraire.

NEGAR MOTTAHEDEH is a professor of film and literature at Duke University. Her work has been published in *Camera Obscura*, *Signs*, and *Comparative Studies of South Asia, Africa, and the Middle East*. She is currently working on a monograph on national variations in cinematic language and the new Iranian cinema.

JOHN MOWITT is professor of Cultural Studies and Comparative Literature at the University of Minnesota. He has published widely on matters of cultural politics and critical theory. His most recent book, *Percussion: Drumming, Beating, Striking* appeared from Duke UP in 2002. He is also a senior editor of *Cultural Critique*.

HAMID NAFICY is Nina J. Cullinan Professor of film and media studies and chair of the department of art history at Rice University. He is the author of *An Accented Cinema: Exilic and Diasporic Filmmaking* and editor of *Home, Exile, Homeland: Film, Media, and the Politics of Place*.

ULRIKE OTTINGER has been making films for thirty years. Her work is regularly shown at festivals and exhibitions worldwide, and includes such films as *Madame X—An Absolute Ruler* (1977), *Freak Orlando* (1981), *Johanna d'Arc of Mongolia* (1989), *Exile Shanghai* (1997), and *A Journey to the New Blank Spots on the European Map* (2002).

B. RUBY RICH is a journalist (*The Guardian*, *New York Times*, *Village Voice*, *San Francisco Bay Guardian*), adjunct professor (University of California, Berkeley), and author of *Chick Flicks: Theories and Memories of the Feminist Film Movement* (Duke). She has frequently been a film festival curator, guest director, juror, and chronicler.

LAURENCE A. RICKELS is a theorist and psychotherapist who has published a series of books and many articles on occult and technical media, the genealogies of psychoanalysis, and contemporary art. His study of Ulrike Ottinger's oeuvre, titled *The Autobiography of Art Cinema*, is coming soon to a bookstore near you.

Filmmaker PATRICIA ROZEMA's credits include *Mansfield Park* (1999), *White Room* (1990), and *I've Heard the Mermaids Singing* (1987).

AMRESH SINHA teaches in the department of Culture and Communication at New York University and The School of Visual Arts. He is currently working on a book, *Memory, Mimesis, Film: Readings in Adorno, Bejamin, and Alexander Kluge.*

GARINÉ TOROSSIAN is a filmmaker and photographer. Fifteen of her films have shown internationally. Retrospectives of her work include New York's Museum of Modern Art, Stan Brakhage's First Person Cinema, Erevan's Cinematheque, Berlin Arsenal, and Telluride Film Festival. She's been awarded prizes and mentions at Berlin, Melbourne, and Houston film festivals.

TRINH T. MINH-HA is a writer, filmmaker, and composer. Her work includes two large-scale multimedia installations, seven books, and seven feature-length films that have been given thirty retrospectives around the world (including at Documenta 11 2002). She is Professor in Women's Studies and Rhetoric at the University of California Berkeley.

SLAVOJ ŽIŽEK is Senior Researcher at the Institute for Social Studies in Ljubljana. His books include T*he Sublime Object of Ideology*, *The Plague of Fantasies*, *The Fragile Absolute*, and *Welcome to the Desert of the Real.*

legal representation CASPAR SINNIGE

thank you MATTHEW ADAMSON
ANDREW BUCK
AMY CHAN
SARAH CLIFT
GUGU HLONGWANE
MICHAEL KIRSCHENBAUM
CAROL TO
SIMONE URDL
ROBERT WOOD

contact WWW.ALPHABET-CITY.ORG
MAIL@ALPHABET-CITY.ORG

ALPHABET CITY MEDIA, INC.
is a non-profit company incorporated in the province of
Ontario, Canada

Alphabet City no. 9
Subtitles: On the Foreignness of Film

designed by ATOM EGOYAN
GILBERT LI

typeset by GILBERT LI
composed in AG SCHOOLBOOK
AG BOOK
typefaces designed by GÜNTER GERHARD LANGE

images prepared by CLARITY (Toronto)

printed and bound by HUNG HING (Hong Kong)

Subtitles was funded in part by

 Canada Council **Conseil des Arts**
for the Arts **du Canada**

THE HENRY N. R. JACKMAN FOUNDATION

ONTARIO ARTS COUNCIL
CONSEIL DES ARTS DE L'ONTARIO

Canadian Film Centre

Centre canadien du film

ASSET DIGITAL

CLARITY

THE TORONTO ARTS COUNCIL